SKILL PRACTICE

GRADE 4

IncentivePublications
BY WORLD BOOK

Many thanks to Leland Graham, Frankie Long, Charlotte Poulos, Sheri Preskenis, and Diana Standing, whose adapted exercises are included in this book.

Thank you to the children who contributed pieces of original writing to this book. Additional thanks to poet David May, who inspired many of the writers during his sessions as "Poet in Residence" at Briscoe and Helman Schools in Ashland, Oregon. The pieces below are used with permission from the writers.

Page 26—Paul I. for "Magic"
Page 30—Tahli O. for "Terror of the Wind"
Page 43—Kathryn H. for "Something's Coming"; Linda N. for "Far From Civilization"
Page 123—Ramon T., Alyssa M., and Jason W. for their "Red" poems
Page 128—Kayla B. for "Losing a Friend"; Simone W. for "Poets are like..." and "Falling through space is like..."; Ariana L. for "Math is like a hurricane..."; Matthew B. for "When my little brother is angry..." and "Writing a new story is like..."; Tessah J. for "The scratching of a pencil is like..."; Laura A. for "Life is like a dark pool of water..."; Rachael W. for "Math problems are like..."; Camille M. for "Life is like a gift..." and "Life is like..."; Greg C. for "A Kid in Class"; Jamie C. for "I Am the Universe"
Page 140—Tahli O. for "Coffee"
Page 293—Ashley R. for "I Hear"; Chloe H. for "I Hear"; Tessah J. for "What I Hear"; Christopher B. for "Silence"
Page 294—Sophie D. for "What I WAS and What I AM"; Joseph Z. for "The Wind"

Written by Imogene Forte and Marjorie Frank
Illustrated by Kathleen Bullock
Cover by Brenda Tropinski

Print Edition ISBN 978-1-62950-486-5
E-book Edition ISBN 978-1-62950-487-2 (PDF)

World Book, Inc.
180 North LaSalle Street
Suite 900
Chicago, Illinois 60601
USA

For information about World Book and Incentive Publications products, call **1-800-967-5325,** or visit our websites at **www.worldbook.com** and **www.incentivepublications.com.**

Printed in the United States of America by Sheridan Books, Inc.
Chelsea, Michigan
1st printing June 2016

TABLE OF CONTENTS

Words & Vocabulary Skills Exercises

Spelling Skills Exercises

Grammar & Usage Skills Exercises

Writing Skills Exercises

SOCIAL STUDIES

Geography Skills Exercises

Map Skills Exercises

SCIENCE

Science Skills Exercises

MATH

Computation & Numbers Skills Exercises

Graphing, Statistics, & Probability Skills Exercises

INTRODUCTION

Do basic skills have to be boring? Absolutely not! Mastery of basic skills provides the foundation for exciting learning opportunities for students. Content relevant to their everyday life is fascinating stuff! Kids love learning about topics such as galaxies and glaciers, thunderstorms and timelines, continents and chemicals, tarantulas and tornadoes, poems and plateaus, elephants and encyclopedias, mixtures and mummies, antonyms and Antarctica, and more. Using these topics and carefully designed practice, they develop basic skills which enable them to ponder, process, grow, and achieve school success.

Acquiring, polishing, and using basic skills and content are a cause for celebration—not an exercise in drudgery. *Skill Practice: Grade 4* invites students to sharpen their abilities in the essentials of language arts, social studies, science, and mathematics.

As you examine *Skill Practice: Grade 4*, you will see that it is filled with attractive, age-appropriate student exercises. These pages are no ordinary worksheets! *Skill Practice: Grade 4* contains hundreds of inventive and inviting ready-to-use lessons based on a captivating theme that invites the student to join an adventure, solve a puzzle, pursue a mystery, or tackle a problem. Additionally, each illustrated exercise provides diverse tools for reinforcement and extension of basic and higher-order thinking skills.

Skill Practice: Grade 4 contains the following components:

- **A clear, sequential list of skills for nine different content areas**
  Checklists of skills begin each content section. These lists correlate with the exercises, identifying page numbers where specific skills can be practiced. Students can chart their progress by checking off each skill as it is mastered.

- **Over 300 pages of student exercises**
  Each exercise page:

      . . . addresses a specific basic skill or content area.

      . . . presents tasks that grab the attention and curiosity of students.

      . . . contains clear directions to the student.

      . . . asks students to use, remember, and practice a basic skill.

      . . . challenges students to think creatively and analytically.

      . . . requires students to apply the skill to real situations or content.

      . . . takes students on learning adventures with a variety of delightful characters!

- **A ready-to-use assessment tool**
  Four skills tests follow the skills exercises. The tests are presented in parts corresponding to the skills lists. Designed to be used as pre- or post-tests, individual parts of these tests can be given to students at separate times, if needed.

- **Complete answer keys**
  Easy-to-find-and-use answer keys for all exercises and skills tests follow each section.

HOW TO USE THIS BOOK:

The exercises contained in *Skill Practice: Grade 4* are to be used with adult assistance. The adult may serve as a guide to ensure the student understands the directions and questions.

Skill Practice: Grade 4 is designed to be used in many diverse ways. Its use will vary according to the needs of the students and the structure of the learning environment.

The skills checklists may be used as:

　　. . . record-keeping tools to track individual skills mastery;

　　. . . planning guides for instruction; and

　　. . . a place for students to proudly check off accomplishments.

Each exercise page may be used as:

　　. . . a pre-test or check to see how well a student has mastered a skill;

　　. . . one of many resources or exercises for teaching a skill;

　　. . . a way to practice or polish a skill that has been taught;

　　. . . a review of a skill taught earlier;

　　. . . reinforcement of a single basic skill, skills cluster, or content base;

　　. . . a preview to help identify instructional needs; and

　　. . . an assessment for a skill that a student has practiced.

The exercises are flexibly designed for presentation in many formats and settings. They are useful for individual instruction or independent work. They can also be used under the direction of an adult with small groups.

The skills tests may be used as:

　　. . . pre-tests to gauge instructional or placement needs;

　　. . . information sources to help adjust instruction; and

　　. . . post-tests to review student mastery of skills and content areas.

Skill Practice: Grade 4 is not intended to be a complete curriculum or textbook. It is a collection of inventive exercises to sharpen skills and provide students and parents with tools for reinforcing concepts and skills, and for identifying areas that need additional attention. This book offers a delightful assortment of tasks that give students just the practice they need—and to get that practice in a manner that is not boring.

As students take on the challenges of the enticing adventures in this book, they will increase their comfort level with the use of fundamental reading, writing, and language skills and concepts. Watching your student check off the sharpened skills is cause for celebration!

LANGUAGE ARTS

Skills Exercises
Grade Four

Reading Spelling Vocabulary Grammar Writing

SKILLS CHECKLIST
READING COMPREHENSION

✔	SKILL	PAGE(S)
	Use information gained from text to make inferences	24
	Paraphrase or summarize a written text	25, 28, 29, 49
	Choose the best title for a selection	26
	Read to find answers to questions	26, 27, 30, 31, 34–37, 40–45, 48
	Identify supporting details	26, 27, 37
	Gain information from reading titles and captions	26, 39, 46
	Identify literary techniques used to enhance written pieces	30
	Identify literal and implied main ideas	31
	Identify elements of a story (setting, plot, characters, theme)	32
	Analyze characters used in written pieces	32, 33
	Interpret charts and tables	34, 44
	Predict future actions or outcomes	35
	Draw logical conclusions from written material	35, 40
	Make generalizations based on material read	35, 40
	Explain personal responses to written material	36
	Read to find details and information	36, 38, 40, 41, 43, 48, 49
	Determine sequence of events	38
	Identify cause-effect relationships	39
	Identify the author's point of view and purpose	41, 43
	Make use of illustrations or graphics to understand a text	42, 44
	Interpret and make graphs	45
	Determine word meaning from context	47
	Recognize and use synonyms	47

SKILLS CHECKLIST
WORDS & VOCABULARY

✔	SKILL	PAGE(S)
	Use a dictionary to find word meanings	50, 54, 56–59, 61, 70, 73
	Learn new words in a variety of categories	50, 56–58
	Learn and use new words	50, 56–59, 61
	Identify words used correctly in context	51, 54
	Choose the correct word for a particular context	51, 66
	Use context clues to determine a word's meaning	51, 73
	Identify and use figurative language	52, 53
	Distinguish between words that are easily confused with one another	54, 66, 67, 76
	Distinguish between words that have similar sounds or spellings	54, 66, 67, 76
	Use correct words to complete analogies	55, 72
	Identify the meanings of common root words	60
	Recognize and use roots to determine meanings of words	60
	Recognize and use antonyms	62
	Recognize and use synonyms	63
	Identify the meanings of common prefixes	64
	Recognize and use prefixes to determine meanings of words	64
	Identify the meanings of common suffixes	65
	Recognize and use suffixes to determine meanings of words	65
	Distinguish between homophones; select correct one for a context	66, 67
	Identify and use homophones	66, 67
	Identify and define multiple meanings of a word	68
	Classify words according to meaning and use	69
	Distinguish between denotation and connotation	70
	Give the denotation and connotation of words	70
	Explore the history and origin of words	71
	Use a dictionary to find information about word history and origin	71
	Find the origin of words borrowed from foreign languages	74
	Recognize, form, and use compound words	75

SKILLS CHECKLIST
SPELLING, GRAMMAR, & USAGE

✔	SKILL	PAGE(S)
	Correctly spell words with double consonants	77
	Identify words that are spelled incorrectly	77, 80, 87, 92, 100
	Correctly spell words that use the *ie* rules	78
	Identify words that are spelled correctly	78, 79, 83, 89
	Correctly spell compound words	79
	Correctly spell words with confusing initial consonant sounds and blends	80
	Follow rules to spell plural nouns correctly	81
	Choose the correct ending for a specific word	82–86
	Distinguish among similar endings	82–86
	Use knowledge of roots to spell words correctly	87
	Spell words that contain silent letters	88
	Correctly spell words that contain special letters: *q, s, w, x, y, z*	89, 90
	Correctly spell words with special vowel combinations	91
	Correctly spell very difficult or unusual words	92
	Correctly spell words that fall into a variety of categories	93, 95, 96, 97
	Correctly spell words that break the rules	94
	Correctly spell big words	98
	Correctly spell small words	99
	Use knowledge of spelling to edit brief passages	101
	Distinguish among parts of speech	102, 103, 107–109
	Identify and use common and proper nouns	103
	Identify and use verb tenses: past, present, and future	104, 105
	Identify and use adjectives	106
	Identify and use adverbs	107
	Identify and use prepositions and prepositional phrases	108, 109
	Identify and form contractions	110
	Make corrections in improper capitalization	111–113
	Use proper capitalization for sentences, proper nouns, and adjectives	111–113
	Use proper capitalization in a variety of situations	111–113
	Make corrections in improper punctuation	114
	Properly use a variety of punctuation marks	114

SKILLS CHECKLIST
WRITING

✔	SKILL	PAGE(S)
	Recognize and use effective words (specific, unusual, colorful, active, etc.)	115, 116, 118–120, 140
	Revise writing for clarity, sequence, or effectiveness	116, 122, 127, 141
	Recognize and create strong beginnings	117, 122
	Recognize and replace overused or ordinary words and phrases	118
	Recognize and use active rather than passive words	118
	Recognize and choose precise words for accurate meaning and interest	118, 119
	Arrange words within sentences for clarity and an interesting sound	118, 141
	Recognize and include sensory appeal in writing	120, 123, 140
	Recognize and create fluent sentences and paragraphs	121, 122, 124–126, 130
	Recognize and write clear, interesting sentences	121, 141
	Identify poetry; use writing skills to write poetry	123, 140
	Recognize and choose words that produce strong visual images	123, 140
	Recognize and supply plenty of interesting, relevant details to a written idea	124
	Recognize imaginative writing; use writing skills to write an imaginative selection	124
	Recognize a clear main idea; create pieces that clearly reveal the main idea	124, 125
	Recognize and include details that are surprising, unusual, or extraordinary	124, 125
	Recognize and write selections that have a clear beginning, middle, and end	124, 125, 130, 131
	Recognize expository writing; use writing skills to write an expository selection	125
	Recognize and write good connections between ideas or parts of ideas	125
	Recognize and write clear questions	126
	Recognize and include literary techniques to make writing effective	128, 129, 134, 135
	Recognize and include metaphors, similes, and other figurative language in writing	128, 129, 135
	Identify opinions; use writing skills to write personal opinions	130, 131
	Infuse personal flavor into a selection	131
	Adapt form, style, or content for a specific purpose	132, 133
	Recognize and include dialogue in writing	136
	Recognize and choose words and phrases to create a specific mood	137
	Recognize descriptive writing; use writing skills to write a descriptive selection	138, 139
	Revise sentences for clarity	141

FOLLOW THE FLAGS

The fourth graders are excited about the new pen pal program. The pen pals live in many countries around the world. Each pen pal in the picture below is carrying the flag from his or her country. Read each description. Write the letter of the matching flag beside it. Then color the flags with the correct colors.

__B__ 1. China's flag has one big star and four small stars.

__F__ 2. Turkey's flag has a moon and a star.

__D__ 3. Canada has a maple leaf on its flag.

__A__ 4. Chile's flag has one star.

__C__ 5. United Kingdom's flag has four stripes that cross each other.

__E__ 6. Republic of the Congo's flag has a diagonal yellow stripe across the middle.

Name __Athena E Gordon__

22

FOLLOW THE FLAGS, CONT.

___J___ 7. Peru's flag has two wide red stripes and one white stripe.

___K___ 8. South Africa's flag has a big green Y lying on its side.

___H___ 9. South Korea's flag has a large red and blue circle in the center.

___I___ 10. The flag of Finland has a blue cross on a white background.

___G___ 11. Panama's flag has two stars.

___L___ 12. The flag of the United States has 50 stars and 13 stripes.

Name ___Athena E Gordon___

THE THRILL OF A BIG WAVE

Mike loves to surf. He dreams of visiting Hawaii, Australia, South Africa, and South America in search of the biggest waves in the world! His Hawaiian pen pal, who is also a surfing fan, sent him the following quiz.

Read the statements about the surfers. Then answer the questions below.

Jeri wears glasses.

Jules is from Malibu.

Jess is not from Big Sur.

Jo is not from Mexico.

Jo is not from Big Sur.

Jo wears stripes when surfing.

Jamie is not from Australia.

The surfer from Maui is male.

The oldest surfer is from Malibu.

The surfer from Mexico wears glasses.

The surfer from Australia has curly hair.

Jess always wears a life vest when surfing.

_____ 1. Which surfer lives in Big Sur?

_____ 2. Which surfer is from Australia?

_____ 3. Which surfer is from Mexico?

_____ 4. Which surfer is from Maui?

_____ 5. Which surfer wears a polka-dotted suit?

Name _____

LEAH'S VACATION LETTER

Leah writes long letters to her pen pal Jackie.
Actually, her letters are much too long.
Jackie lives in Greece and postage becomes very expensive.
Help Leah summarize her letter to cut down on the amount of postage she will need.

Dear Jackie,

I want to tell you all about my vacation trip. It was so exciting. My family of five traveled many miles in our brand new blue car. We love our car. My mother says my father drives too fast, but my brother and I love to go fast. We left home very early in the morning and stayed in fun motels every night. We went to the Great Smoky Mountains in Tennessee and North Carolina. The mountains are beautiful. When we were there, the mountain laurel bushes were covered with beautiful blossoms, some white and some purple. You should have seen them. There are many lovely flowers in the mountains.

We took some wonderful pictures of black bears. We saw a baby bear climbing into a garbage can. Just as we were about to get his picture, the cub's mother came lumbering out of the woods and looked right at us. We ran for the car and jumped in as quickly as we could!

We stayed five days in Gatlinburg. The cabin we stayed in was beside a mountain stream. The water in the stream was so clear we could see fish swimming around. One night we ate dinner in a restaurant that served apples with every meal. They had apple cake, apple sauce, apple bread, apple pie, and even apple soup! There are lots of good restaurants in Gatlinburg.

Gatlinburg is nestled at the foot of the mountains on the Tennessee side. The mountain crafts are lovely. I spent a lot of money on a wooden bowl for my grandmother. My sister bought a handmade candle for our aunt and a box of apple taffy for her best friend.

I hope we can go to the mountains again next summer. I even like a mountain vacation better than a trip to the beach! Which do you like best?

Write soon and tell me about your summer vacation.

Sincerely Yours, Leah

Write a short summary of Leah's letter to Jackie.

_____

_____

_____

_____

_____

_____

Name

CATCH A LEPRECHAUN

Cindi's pen pal in Ireland wrote to her about the legendary leprechauns. These friendly little elves are said to possess magic powers, and it has even been said that the person who catches one may find a pot of gold as well.

With magic you can soar in the clouds with the angels. You can say hello to the fairies, fly on winged unicorns` backs, or go to the Amazon jungle and play with boas and black panthers. Be a wizard, a superhero, a monster, or almost anything! You can smell the prehistoric air, create a time machine, and go to the future. Build a starship from a giant hunk of metal. Be the first boy or girl to dig to the pit of Earth. You can pull a bunny out of your hat, glide from the stars, and slide down bright, colorful rainbows. Wherever you are, whatever time it is, you can find magic in your heart and you can be anything, and do anything you may want to do!

Paul I., Gr. 4

Using the poem above, finish the sentences and questions.

With magic, you can . . .

1. Say hello to _____.

2. Slide down _____.

3. Play with_____ in the Amazon.

4. Be the first to _____.

5. Pull _____ out of your hat.

6. Glide from _____.

7. Create _____.

8. Smell _____.

9. Be _____.

10. Fly on _____.

11. Where can you find magic?
   _____.

12. What would be the best title of the poem?
   a. Flying on Unicorns
   b. Soar with Angels
   c. Magic: Do You Believe in It?
   d. The Magic Hat

13. Which of the magic things would you like to be able to do?

   _____
   _____

14. What else would you do if you could work magic?

   _____
   _____

Name _____

20,000 FEET AND STILL CLIMBING

Jodi's pen pal in Alaska invited her to participate in a most exciting adventure. "Come climb the Great Denali with me," he wrote. *Denali* means *The Great One* in the language of the Athabascan Indians of Alaska. It is the highest mountain in North America. Jodi will need lots of special equipment for this adventure because the height of "the great one" is 20,310 feet.

Get ready for climbing by shopping for equipment and supplies.

USED EQUIPMENT
picks
sleeping bags
tents
maps
camping stoves

GREAT DEALS!
Mountain Supply
552-9900

ZOOM
HEADLAMP
Best one on the market!
$39
Saturday Only
Camping, Ltd.
201 First St.

THE
ULTIMATE
TENT
See it! Try it!
100% waterproof
lightweight shelter
easy to set up in snow!
double-sewn seams
weight—4 lbs

ON SALE, NOW

Climber's Shop
1000 Broad St.

CARABINERS
you can count on
New 3-D shape
Every one tested!
Lightweight!

Stop & see them!
Mountain Store
3910 Abby Lane

VIDEO
CLIMBING DENALI
See the climb before you do it!
$20.00
Video Stop Shop
550-2980

SLEEPING BAGS
for cold places
100% fine goose down
Good to −60°
High Quality design
ALL BAGS 30% OFF

Camping, Ltd.
201 First St.

1. What is the weight of the ultimate tent?

   _____

2. Are used climbing ropes advertised?

   _____

3. What product is advertised as having a 3-D shape? _____

4. Which products are advertised as lightweight?

   _____

5. Where can you buy a product that is 100% waterproof?_____

6. What would you pay for a ZOOM headlamp and the video?_____

7. Where is the Mountain Store located?

   _____

8. What can you see on the advertised video?

   _____

9. Where can you buy maps?

   _____

10. What store is on First Street?

    _____

11. How many stores have phone numbers advertised? _____

12. What phone number would you call to ask about camping stoves? _____

13. Where can you buy carabiners? _____

14. How much money would you save on a $250 sleeping bag at Camping, Ltd?_____

15. What is the lowest temperature for the sleeping bags at Camping, Ltd? _____

Name _____

JOIN THE CIRCUS!

Nancy and her pen pal Dana have exchanged riddles, poetry, and puns. This week, Nancy is mailing 14 proverbs for Dana to paraphrase.

HASTE MAKES WASTE.

NOTHING VENTURED, NOTHING GAINED!

HE WHO HESITATES IS LOST!

A proverb is a wise saying that teaches a lesson. Paraphrase these proverbs. (Rewrite them in your own words.)

1. Haste makes waste. _____

2. He who hesitates is lost! _____

3. Strike while the iron is hot. _____

4. A stitch in time saves nine. _____

5. Every cloud has a silver lining. _____

6. A rolling stone gathers no moss. _____

7. Nothing ventured, nothing gained! _____

8. Fish and visitors smell in three days. _____

9. Fools rush in where angels fear to tread. _____

10. Three may keep a secret if two are dead. _____

11. A bird in the hand is worth two in the bush! _____

12. Don't count your chickens before they hatch. _____

13. Don't change horses in the middle of a stream. _____

14. You can lead a horse to water, but you can't make him drink. _____

Name _____

RIDE A RAGING RIVER

There's no thrill quite like a whitewater thrill! Roberto invited his pen pal Thomas to travel to Costa Rica to take on some breathtaking rapids.

An **idiom** is a kind of figurative speech. The words in an idiom mean something different from what they actually say.

Paraphrase each of the idioms below. (Rewrite each idiom in your own words to explain what it really means.)

I got through the rapids by the skin of my teeth!

1. Are you pulling my leg? _____

2. She's going bananas. _____

3. We're in the doghouse now. _____

4. Has the cat got your tongue? _____

5. Will you please get off my back? _____

6. He's an old stick in the mud. _____

7. You'd better button your lip. _____

8. You've got me over a barrel. _____

9. I have a bone to pick with you! _____

10. It's a bad idea to rat on your friends. _____

11. Last night I slept like a log. _____

12. I went out on a limb for you. _____

13. She let the cat out of the bag. _____

14. She put her foot in her mouth again. _____

15. Time flies when you're having fun. _____

16. I thought the test was a piece of cake. _____

17. Well, that accident was the last straw. _____

18. These kids are driving me up a wall. _____

19. I passed the test by the skin of my teeth. _____

20. You could have knocked me over with a feather. _____

Name _____

HIGH SEAS ADVENTURE

The Terror of the Wind
by Tahli O., Gr. 5

The sea was roaring up with thunder
Up to the angry winds,
Which tore through the air dancing to and fro.
Once again the lightning slipped another cut into
*   the dancing air,*
Which wailed and wailed from the lightning-sharp knife.
The sea kept moaning from the mountains that rose
*   higher and higher as they crawled upon its back,*
And again the thunder crashed through the air, trying
*   to hide itself from the pounding rain,*
As it poured through the air.
Then after all its strikes, the lightning's knife grew dull,
As it stabbed the sea once more.
Then the sea could no longer hold the towering mountains
*   upon its back.*
As the rain grew tired of falling,
It carefully settled down to lay,
As the thunder rolled back up to the sky to sleep for the night.
The wind's feet could not take another step,
As tired as it was,
The wind could not say another word,
As one last drop of water fell from the sky,
And landed on the top of the sea, to settle down to sleep in
The dark coldness of the night.

Kevin loves the sea. He lives in Nova Scotia and collects poems about the sea to send to his pen pal Jim. Here's your chance to share the poems with Jim.

Read the poem about the sea.
Then answer the questions.

1. Find five examples of personification. Circle them in red.

2. Which one is your favorite? _____

3. Which words suggest the lightning is alive? _____

4. What went to sleep at the very end of the poem? _____

5. How do you know the wind was tired? _____

6. Which poem line did you like best?_____

    Why?_____

7. What would you like to tell the poet about your response to her poem? _____

_____

Name _____

MYTHICAL SEA CREATURES

Heather's pen pal Hazel writes to her from Scotland, where tales of sea creatures have been passed down for centuries. Last summer, Hazel was part of a ship's crew searching for the mythical mermaids.

Read the letters Hazel wrote to Heather while aboard the ship. Write the main idea for each of her entries.

Thursday, May 18

Dear Heather,
Today I joined the crew of the submarine named *Explorer*. We are going on a hunt for mermaids. I have wanted to do this all my life. I am so excited! I hope I see one!
—Hazel

The main idea is_____

_____

_____.

Saturday, May 20

Dear Heather,
I've been learning about the history of mermaids today. Irish legends say that mermaids were women who did not follow the religion of their day in Ireland. Because of this, they were banished from the earth by St. Patrick. The only place they had to live was in the sea.
—Hazel

The main idea is_____

_____

_____

_____.

Tuesday, May 23

Dear Heather,
Along with their belief in mermaids, many people in Ireland and Scotland believe in sea serpents. There are frequent reports of people sighting them. These are huge sea snakes that are about 300 feet long. Stories of the Scottish Loch Ness monster and the kraken of Scandinavia have been told for years. I'm hoping to see a sea serpent, too!
—Hazel

The main idea is_____

_____

_____.

Friday, May 26

Dear Heather,
How thrilling! I am just sure I saw a mermaid today. She had the head and upper body of a woman. Below the waist, the creature was a fish with scales and a long tail. Really! I did see one swimming off the side of the boat!
—Hazel

The main idea is_____

_____

_____.

Name_____

THE WORLD'S LUXURY TRAIN

Marie loved the mystery story that her pen pal in Paris made up about a trip on the Orient Express. She couldn't wait to share the story with the class.

Read about the mysterious happenings on the Orient Express on the next page (page 33). Then write five to ten words that you think would describe each character.

The Porter _____

_____

Countess L'Orange _____

_____

Dr. Plumper _____

_____

The Mystery Man _____

_____

Madeline Merry _____

_____

Mrs. Mergatroid Matisse _____

_____

Oliver Snooze _____

_____

The Burglar _____

_____

Use with page 33.

Name _____

SOMETHING IS STRANGE ON THE ORIENT EXPRESS

At first it seems like an ordinary train trip, but then, no trip on the Orient Express is ever really ordinary! This train has such a history of luxury and mystery that you can almost smell strange happenings in the air!

Madeline Merry wanders around to explore the train. This is her first trip on the Orient Express. She looks like an innocent child playing in the aisles, yet she loves to play detective. She is really out snooping. As she passes Countess L'Orange, she notices that her little dog has a small packet hidden beneath his neck. Her watchful eye does not miss the countess slipping something into Doctor Plumper's open bag as she squeezes past him in the aisle. Next, she knows that Oliver Snooze, the man in the berth, is snoring, but why are his eyes peeking out from beneath mostly closed lids? He does not seem to care that a sneaky fellow is reaching out for his watch.

Madeline plays with her yo-yo, but her ears do not miss the whispering behind a closed curtain. Nor can she ignore the large lump in the pocket of the proper-looking Mrs. Mergatroid Matisse. Why is Mrs. Matisse hovering awfully close to the mysterious man who hides behind his collar? And what is in the package she is guarding so closely?

As Madeline roams along the aisle, the train suddenly jerks to a stop. Baggage and people fly everywhere, and then the lights go out. There is much squealing and screaming in the dark. When the lights are turned back on, the woman who claims to be a countess is screeching, "My doggie! My doggie! Someone has taken my doggie!" As passengers are scurrying around, Madeline sees that the doctor's bag is on the shelf and another bag is in his hand. Mrs. Mergatroid Matisse has lost her hat, and the porter is missing. Just then, Madeline's mother comes and grabs her by the hand. It is time for her family to leave the train.

Write a short explanation for each element of the story.

Story Theme	
Characters	
Setting	
Plot	
Point of View (Who is telling the story?)	

Use with page 32.

Name _____

DROP INTO THE ALPS

Louis's Swiss pen pal has invited him to go on the most extraordinary vacation imaginable. They will fly by helicopter into the Swiss Alps.

Swiss SkiDrop, Inc.
HELICOPTER SCHEDULE

DEPARTURE CITY	Destination	Departure Days	Return Days
ZURICH	**Drop 1**	Tues, Thurs	Fri, Sun
	Drop 2	Wed, Sat	Mon, Thurs
	Drop 3	Sun, Wed	Tues, Fri
BASEL	**Drop 1**	Wed, Sat	Sun, Wed
	Drop 2	Sun, Wed	Tues, Fri
	Drop 3	Thurs, Sun	Sat, Tues
BERN	**Drop 1**	Fri, Tues	Mon, Fri
	Drop 2	Wed, Tues	Sun, Fri
	Drop 3	Sat, Wed	Tues, Fri
LAUSANNE	**Drop 1**	Mon, Fri	Wed, Sun
	Drop 2	Thurs, Tues	Mon, Thurs
	Drop 3	Sun, Tues	Wed, Sat
CHUR	**Drop 1**	Thurs	Mon
	Drop 2	Mon	Fri

Use the information from the table to answer the questions.

1. Leaving from Basel, can they fly to Drop 1 and stay for only 3 days (including travel days)? _____

2. If they wanted to head for Drop 2 on a Wednesday, what cities could they depart from?

_____

3. Which drops can they use on Tuesday from Lausanne? _____

4. Can they fly to Drop 3 from Chur? _____

5. What days can they return to Bern from Drop 3? _____

6. Can they return to Zurich from Drop 2 on Tuesday? _____

7. If they want to leave Zurich on Wednesday and return the following Monday, which ski area must they choose to be dropped in? _____

8. Can they fly to Drop 1 from Chur on Monday? _____

9. How many choices for departure are there on Friday? _____

10. How many choices for returns are there on Sunday? _____

Name _____

RACE WITH THE DOGS

Nanook told his pen pal Henry to bring his warmest clothes to Alaska, because he would be driving a team of racing dogs over a snow-covered course! He said he might help Henry prepare for his trip by reading the weather reports for several days of the Iditarod, Alaska's famous sled dog race.

Read the weather reports below. Then use your judgment to make the predictions and draw the conclusions asked for below.

DAY 1: WEATHER REPORT
The skies will be clear today, with temperatures at 0°. Light, fluffy snow covers the ground.

DAY 2: WEATHER REPORT
Temperatures are warming. Expect a light rain, which will turn to freezing rain this afternoon.

DAY 3: WEATHER REPORT
Heavy fog will move in, bringing moist, wet air hovering over the snow. Winds will be harsh this evening.

DAY 4: WEATHER REPORT
Extreme blizzard conditions are reported today. Warnings are out for complete white-out conditions. Winds are blowing at 60 mph with drifts up to six feet.

DAY 5: WEATHER REPORT
Today the temperatures will climb to 20° with light snow showers and light winds.

DAY 6: WEATHER REPORT
Temperatures have taken a plunge. At noon, we recorded −25° with a −80° wind chill factor. Everyone is warned to stay indoors. It is extremely dangerous for people or animals to be outdoors in these conditions.

What do you think?

_____ 1. On what day might the racers have the best conditions?

_____ 2. If ice is a problem, what day(s) might give the racers problems?

_____ 3. What troubles might the drivers and dogs have on Day 4?

_____ 4. What troubles might they have on Day 3?

_____ 5. What kind of progress do you think they'll make on Day 5?

_____ 6. What do you think the racing teams will do on Day 6?

Name _____

HUNTING FOR NESSIE

Heather enjoyed Hazel's letters from the sea so much that she sent Hazel a poem in return. Along with the poem she sent a list of questions. **Read the poem and answer the questions for Hazel.**

TERROR IN SCOTLAND

I've seen the fierce winged dragon
With mouth of flame and smoke,
And dreamed of the elusive Sasquatch
Still chasing me when I awoke.

I've ridden the great Greek Satyr
With body part man, part beast.
Done battle with the monstrous Hydra
Who wore nine heads, at least!

I've flown on the grotesque Griffin
Eagle head, lion body and tail.
Come face to face with a Yeti,
And shuddered till I grew pale.

I've danced with a mighty Unicorn
(Now does that sound absurd?)
Escaped from a deadly Siren,
A creature half woman, half bird.

But I've never shrieked in horror,
Never trembled and shook with dread.
I have never cried like a baby,
Nor stopped breathing like the dead.
No, I never knew sheer terror,
Not awake or asleep, I confess...
Until I saw, for a moment
The Monster of Loch Ness...
The massive
rising
grasping
writhing
SERPENT
of
Loch
Ness.

1. Which creature in the poem would you least like to meet? _____

2. Which line in the poem gives the best description of a creature? _____
_____
_____

3. Tell why the title is a good one. (Or tell why it is not.) _____
_____
_____

4. What are some of the most effective words the poet used? _____
_____
_____

5. Write a one-sentence summary of the poem.
_____
_____

Name _____

ROCK INTO THE FUTURE

Alec's pen pal, Simon, is an avid music fan. He sent the challenge below to Alec and asked Alec to time himself to see how long it would take him to complete it.

Time yourself to see how long it takes you.

> **A** = alliteration
> **PN** = pun
> **I** = idiom
> **M** = metaphor
> **P** = personification
> **S** = simile
> **R** = rhyme
> **E** = exaggeration

____ 1. Rock and roll always grabs my soul.

____ 2. That song was longer than a comet's tail.

____ 3. That last singer is an old stick in the mud.

____ 4. His singing is like a brilliant laser light show.

____ 5. Oooh! That cute drummer has caught my eye.

____ 6. Haratia's hairdo is wider than an asteroid belt.

____ 7. Lagoola is crying her eyes out over that song.

____ 8. Her singing is as spectacular as a meteor shower.

____ 9. Don't you love that rollicking rock and roll rhythm?

____ 10. Don't try to worm your way out of going to the concert.

____ 11. Her voice is so sweet, it turns the clouds to sugared candy.

____ 12. The heavy drumbeats wrap their fat fingers around my ears.

____ 13. The comets in the sky shout the secrets of a thousand years.

____ 14. Music is a banquet that feeds all species, with plenty of leftovers.

____ 15. The music yanks me to my feet and makes me her dancing partner.

____ 16. Six serious singing Sagook sisters swayed slowly to smooth soft sounds.

____ 17. I hear that the guitar player has been stringing his girlfriend along for weeks.

Name _____

FIGHT THE FIERCEST BULL

Marie wrote to Eddie from Madrid about the bullfighting adventures that take place there.

These limericks about bullfighting are all mixed up. Number the lines in the right order so that each poem makes sense!

1.

____ By the creature's right horn,

____ A nervous matador named José

____ But the crowd just kept shouting, "Olé!"

____ Tried to outwit a bull yesterday.

____ His shoulder was torn

2.

____ And the people of Spain called him, "COOL!"

____ A bull had the name of Raoul

____ Anyone who would fight him was a fool.

____ His stomping was fearful,

____ And his snort was an earful.

4.

____ A man bought a bull in Madrid

____ In return for their adoring

____ So they traded him in for a squid!

____ As a pet for Alberto, his kid.

____ The bull got busy goring,

3.

____ As I did, I could hear the crowd roar.

____ And without thinking, I ran for the door!

____ And charged straight for my head,

____ Then the bull, he saw red,

____ I waved the cape, like a brave matador.

5.

____ "I can outsmart that old bull, no doubt!"

____ On a stretcher they carried her out.

____ But it sure was her worst!

____ The fight wasn't her first,

____ She said with an arrogant shout.

OLD NEWS IS GOOSE NEWS

Mother Goose lives in a house in Boston, Massachusetts, that was built in the 1700's. While visiting Mother Goose's home last summer, Bori composed the Mother Goose challenges below to mail to her pen pal in Nairobi. Pretend you are the pen pal, and circle or underline the correct sentence in each box.

Read each headline that has come straight from one of Mother Goose's rhymes. The headlines give a result or effect of something that has happened. For each newspaper, choose the sentence that you think tells the cause of each headline.

1

Paws Tribune
Morning Edition
KITTENS SUFFER FROM COLD PAWS

a. They forgot their mittens.
b. They got their mittens.
c. They hid from their mother.

2

LAMB'S GAZETTE
BAA BAA BLACK SHEEP HAS EMPTY BAGS

a. He never had any wool.
b. He hasn't bought the wool yet.
c. He gave away his three bags of wool.

3

Daily News
Spider Is Washed Out

a. Itsy Bitsy went up the waterspout.
b. The sun came out.
c. The rain came down.

4

Quickston Evening News
JACK JUMPS QUICKLY

a. He's in a hurry to get to bed.
b. He's jumping over a hot flame.
c. He's training for a hurdle race.

5

Evening News
PORRIDGE TURNS COLD

a. Porridge was never hot.
b. The porridge has been in the pot for nine days.
c. The porridge burned in the pot.

6

Country Daily News
FARMER'S WIFE CUTS TAILS OFF MICE

a. The mice ate her cheese.
b. The mice were blind.
c. The mice chased the farmer's wife.

7

Duckland Gazette, July 19
PETER PIPER IS WORN OUT

a. Peter blew his horn all night.
b. Peter went to market.
c. Peter picked a peck of pickled peppers.

8

Goose Gazette, Thursday
JACK BREAKS HEAD OPEN

a. Jack went up the hill.
b. Jack fell down the hill.
c. Jill came tumbling after.

Name _____

A LITTLE SLUGGISH

Marie received the following message from California.

Can you visit me and attend a very unusual event? It may be the only slug race in the world. Would you want to miss it? Travel into the giant redwoods of California for one of the most unusual races you'll ever see. We can get front-row tickets. We can even race a slug if we want to!

Morning Edition

Daily News

Valley Weather: Partly Cloudy

Vol. XXXIX No 14235 · Sunny Valley, California July 10 · 35¢

SLUG RACES COMING TO AREA SOON

There's more wildlife to watch and enjoy next month in the Pacific Coast redwoods of Northern California.

Visitors flock to Prairie Creek Redwoods State Park on the Pacific Ocean for many reasons. After they play in the ocean, they can watch elk, bears, bobcats, and foxes, which are plentiful in the ancient forest park. Campers can park trailers and hike the beautiful trails through the canyons to the ocean.

But next month, there will be another fascinating reason to visit the park. On August 16, the 32nd annual Banana Slug Derby will be held. A variety of races will be held and prizes will be awarded to winning slugs in several categories.

One of last year's top-winning banana slugs poses with her owner and her trophy. Over 700 spectators watched the races last year.

Two hundred trophies made by locals will be given. There will be food and fun for everyone.

Visitors are invited to attend the derby. "You can bring your own slug, or we'll loan you one from our slugarium at the visitor's center," said Park Ranger Robert Roberts. Park rangers have already started hunting for speedy slugs. Visitors need to know, however, that this is a very competitive race. Therefore, any slugs brought in from the outside will be given a slug drug test before they are eligible to take part in the races.

For information about the Banana Slug Derby, call the Prairie Creek Park Visitor's Center at 707-488-2171.

Answer the 9 questions T (True) or F (False) based on your reading of the article.

_____ 1. Visitors come to the park only for the slug races.

_____ 2. The park is a beautiful place to stay.

_____ 3. Camping is permitted in the park.

_____ 4. The Banana Slug Derby is a lot of fun.

_____ 5. No one would want to look at slugs.

_____ 6. The derby is a new idea.

_____ 7. Everyone who races a slug brings it along from home.

_____ 8. The local people support the idea of the derby.

_____ 9. Park rangers do not allow anyone to touch the slugs that live in the park.

10. What would you conclude about a slug that was disqualified from the race?

_____

_____

Name _____

YOUR NAME IN NEON!

Marta loves country music, so she chose a pen pal from Music City, U.S.A. You can imagine how happy she was to receive this note!

Dear Marta,

Come visit with us in the home of country music, Nashville, Tennessee. Live your dream of performing at the Grand Ole Opry! Maybe even become a star! Hope to see you soon.

Love, Dilly

Read these pieces of writing about Nashville and neon! Then help Marta tell the author's purpose and point of view for each one.

1. How exciting to see Talula's name in lights! She's been a'singin' her heart out since she was just an itsy, bitsy girl. I watched her make a pretend microphone from her mama's egg beater when she was just knee-high to a dinner table. She just stood there and belted out the tune "Your Cheatin' Heart" at the top of her little lungs. If anyone deserves to be a big star—it's Talula.

Who's writing? Circle one.
   a. a character in the story
   b. a narrator who is not in the story
   c. a narrator who is a character in the story

What is the author's purpose in writing this?

_____

_____

2. I headed for Nashville at age 16 with my guitar over my shoulder and a song in my head. I planned to be a star. Ten years later, without a dollar to my name and no hit songs, I headed out of town. Everyone in Nashville wants to be a star. I heard "No thanks" a thousand times. No one wanted my singin', my song writin', or my guitar playin'. This is a town that'll break your heart and your bank account.

Who's writing? Circle one.
   a. a character in the story
   b. a narrator who is not in the story
   c. a narrator who is a character in the story

What is the author's purpose in writing this?

_____

_____

NEWS FLASH!!

3. Rising Star James T. Twang has a new hit. His song "You've Broken My Phone, My Computer, and My Heart" leaped to the top of the Country Music Charts last week. This is good news for a hometown boy.

Who's writing? Circle one.
   a. a character in the story
   b. a narrator who is not in the story
   c. a narrator who is a character in the story

What is the author's purpose in writing this?

_____

_____

IT'S A GAS!

4. Every time you see those brilliant colored lights, you'll know that they are made with gas. A French scientist, Georges Claude, figured out how to take rare gases out of the atmosphere and put them into tubes. An electric spark is sent streaking through the tubes. Different gases give off different colors as the spark goes through them, so different gases are put in the tubes to create different colors. Other colors are made by using tubes that are tinted or coated with certain powders that give off a colored glow. When someone's name lights up in neon, this is how it happens!

Who's writing? Circle one.
   a. a character in the story
   b. a narrator who is not in the story
   c. a narrator who is a character in the story

What is the author's purpose in writing this?

_____

_____

Name _____

AN ANCIENT ART

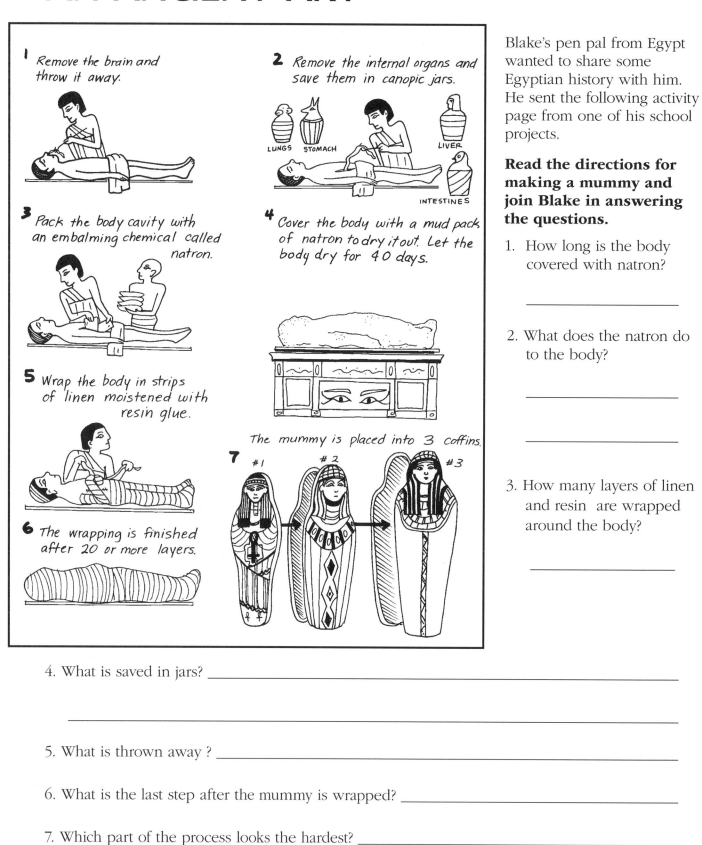

1 Remove the brain and throw it away.

2 Remove the internal organs and save them in canopic jars.

LUNGS STOMACH LIVER INTESTINES

3 Pack the body cavity with an embalming chemical called natron.

4 Cover the body with a mud pack of natron to dry it out. Let the body dry for 40 days.

5 Wrap the body in strips of linen moistened with resin glue.

6 The wrapping is finished after 20 or more layers.

The mummy is placed into 3 coffins.

7 #1 #2 #3

Blake's pen pal from Egypt wanted to share some Egyptian history with him. He sent the following activity page from one of his school projects.

Read the directions for making a mummy and join Blake in answering the questions.

1. How long is the body covered with natron?

_____

2. What does the natron do to the body?

_____

_____

3. How many layers of linen and resin are wrapped around the body?

_____

4. What is saved in jars? _____

_____

5. What is thrown away ? _____

6. What is the last step after the mummy is wrapped? _____

7. Which part of the process looks the hardest? _____

Name _____

ALONE IN THE TANGLED WOODS

Hanna's pen pal invited her to join her for a camping trip in the Black Forest of Germany. Would you like to go along? This will be the ultimate camping experience. You will pack some basic supplies and be dropped off in a deep, tangled forest. You can enjoy the solitude while you test your endurance. Who knows? Maybe you won't really be alone out there!

Something's Coming
by Kathryn H., Gr. 5

Something's coming!
Coming, coming closer!
Closer, closer still!
It walks, it talks, it stalks in the night.
Feel its breath upon your face.
Shield your eyes from its brilliant glow.
Something's coming!
Coming, coming closer!
What is it?
Who knows?

Tell what you think . . .

1. What is coming?

_____

2. What will happen next?

_____

_____

3. What was the author's purpose as she wrote this?

_____

_____

4. What line or phrase is most effective?

_____

Tell what you think . . .

5. What is the place that is far from civilization?

_____

6. What are the clues?

_____

7. What was the author's purpose as she wrote this?

_____

8. What line or phrase is most effective?

_____

_____

Far From Civilization
by Linda N., Gr. 5

I know I am far from civilization
When I hear the fish jumping
The rain hitting the tent
And
Rocks falling
When I feel the cool chill in the air
When I see the top of my west wind
Tent
And
When I smell the sweet scent of
White bark pines
And
Fresh air.
That is how I know I am
Far from civilization.

Name _____

A RIDE WITH "THE KING"

Andrea's pen pal in Memphis, Tennessee wrote to her about Elvis Presley's famous automobiles. After reading more about the life of "The King," Andrea became interested in items owned by other famous musicians.

Read Andrea's chart to learn some unusual facts that you can use to impress music fans.

Most Expensive Items of Rock Stars' Belongings Sold at Auctions

Item	Year of Sale	Price
John Lennon's 1965 Rolls-Royce Phantom V touring limousine	1985	$ 2,299,000
Jimi Hendrix's Fender Stratocaster electric guitar	1990	$ 370,260
An acoustic guitar that had been owned by George Michael, Paul McCartney, and David Bowie	1994	$ 341,000
Buddy Holly's Gibson electric guitar	1990	$ 242,000
John Lennon's 1970 Mercedes-Benz 600 limousine	1989	$ 213,125
Elvis Presley's 1942 Martin D-18 guitar	1991	$ 180,000
Elvis Presley's 1960 Rolls-Royce Phantom V touring limousine	1986	$ 162,800
Charlie Parker's Grafton saxophone	1991	$ 144,925
John Lennon's recording of his singing at a 1957 church fair	1994	$ 121,675
Buddy Holly's Fender Stratocaster electric guitar	1990	$ 110,000

Use the information from the chart to answer the questions below.

_____ 1. How many cars are listed?

_____ 2. How many guitars are listed?

_____ 3. How many musical instruments are included that are not guitars?

_____ 4. What was the highest price brought by an item in 1994?

_____ 5. What was the highest price brought by an item in 1990?

_____ 6. Which sold for more money: Elvis's guitar or his car?

_____ 7. Which sold for more money: John Lennon's car or recording?

_____ 8. How much more was paid for Buddy Holly's Gibson guitar than the Fender guitar?

_____ 9. How many items were sold from 1985 to 1990?

_____ 10. How much was spent for the items sold in 1990?

Name _____

HIGH CLIMBER

Barbara's pen pal in New York City sent her a postcard with a picture of the Empire State Building, once the world's tallest building. Barbara began to think how much fun it would be to try a building-climbing adventure at the Empire State Building. Who knows, she thought, maybe I could go on to try more of the world's tallest buildings.

Help her plan for this imaginary adventure. Use the information on the graph to answer the questions.

THE WORLD'S TALLEST BUILDINGS

height in feet	1,400	1,600	1,800	2,000	2,200	2,400	2,600	2,800	3,000
Petronas Towers *Malaysia*									
Burj Khalifa *United Arab Emirates*									
Taipei 101 *Taiwan*									
Makkah Royal Clock Tower Hotel *Saudi Arabia*									
Zifeng Center *China*									
Shanghai World Financial Center *China*									
International Commerce Centre *China*									
Shanghai Tower *China*									
One World Trade Center *New York City*									
Willis Tower *Chicago*									

1. Which building is 2,073 feet tall? _____

2. What is the tallest building shown? _____

3. What is the shortest building shown? _____

4. Which two buildings are closest in height? _____

5. Which building is almost 2,000 feet tall? _____

6. Which building is over 2,700 feet tall? _____

7. Which building is 1,450 feet tall? _____

8. Which country has the highest number of the world's tallest buildings? _____

9. In what country is the world's tallest building located? _____

10. Which building is about 50 feet taller than Taipei 101? _____

Name _____

LESSONS IN SILLINESS

Rollo wants to be a clown when he grows up. He spent a month at Clown College. Of course, he had to write his pen pal in Prague all about the silly stuff he learned. You can go to Clown College, too, and learn a lot about clowning around!

Read the titles of the books that would-be clowns must read in college. Then follow the directions below.

Write the letter of the book in which you would expect to learn each of these things:

_____ 1. how to make clown faces

_____ 2. complicated jokes

_____ 3. how to keep from injuring your back during somersaults

_____ 4. jokes, when you know none

_____ 5. how to choose your first costume

_____ 6. what to do about a bad rash on your nose

_____ 7. how to make your nose look great

_____ 8. how to fix a flat tire on your unicycle

_____ 9. tricks to do with balloons

_____ 10. funny ways to move your body

_____ 11. how to walk with big feet

_____ 12. why clowns have big feet

_____ 13. how to get nine clowns on a skateboard

_____ 14. getting makeup out of your eyes

A. CLOWN NOSES EVERYTHING YOU NEED TO KNOW

B. The Complete Collection of BEST JOKES Beginner to Advanced

C. Creative Costumes

D. the 300 WORST CLOWNING INJURIES Prevention Guide

E. a short history of BIG Feet!

F. Unicycle maintenance A 12-STEP MANUAL

G. A CLOWN'S HAND BOOK of TRICKS

H. MAKEUP GUIDE FOR UNIQUE CLOWN FACES

Name

CURES & COURAGE

Vinnie's pen pal, Yolanda, lives in the largest swamp in the world—the deep, damp Everglades. She sent Vinnie a fictional article from her local newspaper that was written on April Fool's Day to give readers silly, false advice about alligator wrestling.

Read the article and help Vinnie with the word-matching activity Yolanda sent with the article.

PREVENTING ALLIGATOR BITES

Endeavor to avoid alligator bites at all costs. **Appease** the alligator with the offer of a bag of rippled potato chips before you start the wrestling match. As a **precautionary** measure, get yourself an alligator-proof suit that is too thick for alligator teeth to **penetrate.** Of course, the **surefire** way to avoid bites is to avoid the alligator!

HOW TO HEAL ALLIGATOR BITES

If an alligator bites you, mix the juice of 12 tomatoes with cooked oatmeal. Squeeze in 7 drops of root beer. Spread this over the **affected** area right away. Then cover the area with warm banana peels and wrap **securely** with plastic wrap. After just an hour, the bite will be **substantially** on its way to healing.

CURE FOR WARTS

If you end up with warts after an **encounter** with an alligator, you'll be in need of this potion. Pick 3 fresh cabbages. Slice them and drop them in a blender with 2 cups of chocolate milk. Sprinkle in a handful of **tangy** chili powder. Add a **dollop** of mustard and a tablespoon of vinegar to the mixture and blend for 2 minutes at high speed. Drink this at bed time and sleep for 12 hours. When you awake, the warts will be gone.

CURE FOR A HEADACHE

It's not uncommon to have a **throbbing** headache after a good wrestling match. The best cure is a good old-fashioned onion wrap. Boil 20 onions in 2 quarts of water for an hour. Add $\frac{1}{2}$ cup of molasses. Soak some old rags in the liquid for several minutes. When they are **saturated,** squeeze out the juice and **envelop** your head with the rags. Sit very still in a dark room, and your headache will **vanish** for sure in 15 minutes.

Match the words from the cures with their correct meanings. Use the context to help you.

_____ 1. endeavor	a. considerably
_____ 2. appease	b. pounding
_____ 3. precautionary	c. disappear
_____ 4. penetrate	d. try
_____ 5. surefire	e. spicy
_____ 6. affected	f. soaked
_____ 7. securely	g. preventive
_____ 8. substantially	h. enter
_____ 9. encounter	i. satisfy
_____ 10. tangy	j. wrap
_____ 11. dollop	k. large drop
_____ 12. throbbing	l. tightly
_____ 13. saturated	m. foolproof
_____ 14. envelop	n. hurt
_____ 15. vanish	o. meeting

Name _____

LETTERS TO LEONARDO

Instead of writing letters to pen pals, Charlie likes to write letters to the fan clubs of famous artists whose work he admires.

Read these fan letters to artist Leonardo da Vinci over the centuries, then answer the questions below.

Venice, April 1515
Dear Leonardo,
I have been a fan of yours for years. You are a remarkable man. I am so impressed with your paintings, the *Mona Lisa*, which you painted in Florence in the early 1500s, and *The Last Supper*, which you painted earlier in Milan. Why did you never finish your early painting of *St. Jerome*? I wish I could meet you.

Georgio

Florence, May 1970
Dear Leonardo,
I am so impressed with your notebooks, where the most important information was put into your drawings. I hear there are over 30 of them. They are full of amazing drawings and notes about painting, architecture, human anatomy, mechanics, biology, and other things. When did you have time to write them all?

Alicia

Chicago, June 2016
Dear Leonardo,
I am surprised to learn that you drew plans for an airplane and a helicopter 300 years before flying machines were successfully built. I have also been amazed to see your perfect drawings of human anatomy. I always thought you were only an artist! But now I have learned that you were also a scientist, sculptor, architect, mathematician, military advisor, and engineer!

charlie

1. Which letter mentioned an unfinished painting? _____

2. What surprised Charlie? _____

3. Which two fans mentioned Leonardo's drawings? _____

4. Which painting was completed earlier, Mona Lisa or The Last Supper?_____

5. Which fan was excited about Leonardo's drawings of flying machines? _____

6. Where did Alicia live? _____

7. Which fan wrote his or her letter first? _____

8. Name three topics in Leonardo's notebooks. _____

Name _____

EXPLORE THE SUNKEN *TITANIC*

Jamie wanted to share the story of the sinking of the *Titanic* with his pen pal in Nigeria. The only problem was that he wanted to write it on a postcard with a picture of the great ship on the front. Help Jamie summarize the story so that it will fit in the space available.

THE VOYAGE OF THE TITANIC

They called it "unsinkable," but the *Titanic* was not. They called it a floating luxury hotel, and indeed it was! It was like a huge palace, with huge rooms, gold-plated light fixtures, a swimming pool, and steam baths. No ship this big or beautiful had ever been built before! Hundreds of passengers and families boarded the *Titanic* in Southampton, England, on April 10, 1912. The great new ship was bound for New York on its maiden voyage.

Twenty minutes before midnight on April 15, 1912, disaster struck the *Titanic*. Actually, the ship struck disaster—in the form of an iceberg. At first, passengers didn't realize that the accident was serious. There was a command for people to get into the lifeboats. Unfortunately, the company that built the boat was so convinced it was unsinkable that they had sent lifeboats for only about half the people on board.

The ship sent out distress signals, hoping nearby ships would come to help. The bow of the *Titanic* was sinking when a loud, roaring noise went up from the ship. The *Titanic* was breaking apart. It stood up in the air for a short while, and then disappeared beneath the waves. The next day, another ship, the *Carpathia*, came to rescue many survivors. Survivors included about 700 passengers and crew members. More than 1,500 people did not survive.

There are many theories about why the *Titanic* sank. Almost 75 years after the sinking, and after much searching, the wreckage of the *Titanic* was found. Small submarines have explored the wreckage. Maybe some of the mysteries will now be solved.

Write a one sentence summary of the story.

_____

_____

_____

_____

Name _____

WHAT WOULD YOU DO WITH IT?

Julianne has found an unusual use for a flounder!
What would you do with a flounder?

Look at each of the words below. Circle the
most reasonable thing to do with each of
the items listed. You may need some help
from your dictionary!

What would you do with a . . .

1. flounder?	use it as a bookmark	fry it for lunch	wear it on your head
2. plankton?	put it on a pizza	feed it to a fish	write a letter on it
3. snorkel?	live in it	take it swimming	fry it with bacon
4. brooch?	bury it	write to it	put it in a jewelry box
5. scoundrel?	tickle it	avoid it	water it
6. grotto?	explore it	color it red	make noise with it
7. query?	clean it with soap	plant it	find an answer to it
8. rumba?	mail it	dance it	dress it up
9. soufflé?	measure it	bake it	wear it to dinner
10. trophy?	show it off	melt it	sing to it
11. banister?	slide on it	plant it	put frosting on it
12. marimba?	feed it	dance with it	make music on it
13. foe?	wrap it up	draw with it	make friends with it
14. sophomore?	send it to school	paint it	put it on a sandwich
15. sieve?	slice it	put it in the bank	pour water through it
16. architect?	boil it	hire it	put it in an envelope

Name

SUNKEN TREASURE

A treasure chest has been sitting on the bottom of the ocean for years. How did it get there? These words sank along with the treasure, but some words are missing from the tale!

Read the 10 possible explanations, and write in the missing words. Choose a word from the chest that will make each sentence meaningful.

How Did the Treasure Get Here?

1. A crafty pirate pushed it overboard from his ship and _____ to find it later.

2. It was _____ off an island by a _____ tidal wave.

3. Someone found it in a pirate's cave and threw it off a high _____ into the ocean.

4. The chest was picked up by a whirling _____ and dropped into the ocean.

5. It fell overboard from a ship being _____ around in a wild _____ .

6. Two divers _____ the chest off a beach at midnight and _____ it here.

7. It slid into the _____ during a terrible, shaking _____ .

8. A whale's _____ knocked it off the deck of a pirate _____ .

9. A pirate ship _____ against the rocks and _____ in a hurricane.

10. No one really knows how the chest got here!

    It is a huge _____ .

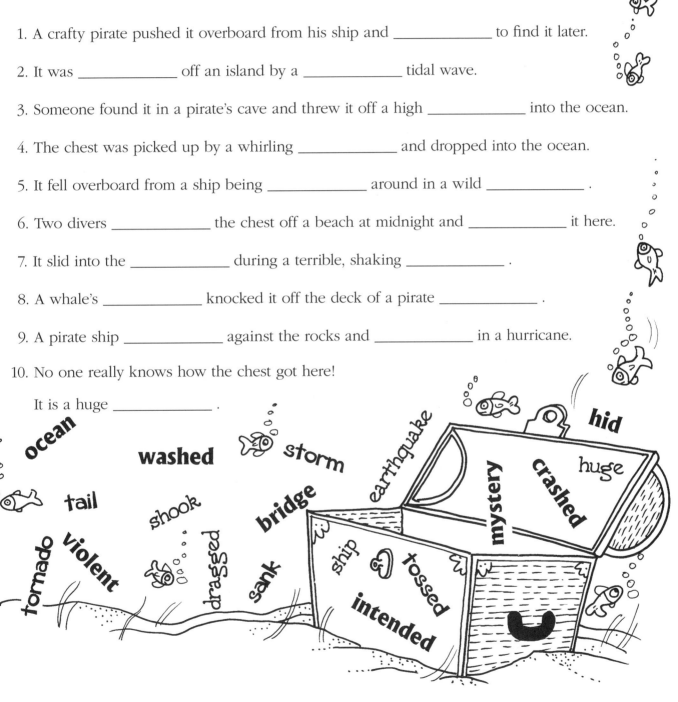

HAPPY AS A CLAM

Are clams really happy? How do you know? What does it mean when someone is "happy as a clam" or "mad as a wet hen"? These are examples of **figurative language.** They have a meaning that is a little different from what the words actually say.

At the beach picnic, all these friends and family members are using figurative language. Write what each saying really means! Then, on the back of this page, draw what each saying would look like if the words meant what they actually say!

Name

GOOD TASTE IN FRIENDS

What does it mean to have "good taste in friends"? Does it have anything to do with eating your friends? No! It's just an example of figurative language. The meaning is different from what the words actually say.

At the beach picnic, all these friends and family members are using figurative language. Write what each saying really means!

_____

_____

_____

_____

_____

_____

_____

_____

Name _____

HOW MANY WHALES?

Only 4 of the 20 whales are jumping today. Is this the majority or the *minority?*
People often get these two words confused. Do you know what each one means?
There are many words that get confused with others because the two words have similar
meanings or looks. Each of these examples has a pair of often-confused words. Circle the
correct word to answer each question.

1. Only 4 of the 20 whales are jumping today.
   Is this the **majority** or the **minority?**

2. Natalie's doctor told her that she has strep throat.
   Is this a **diagnosis** or a **prognosis?**

3. We'll cook our clam chowder over low heat for a long time.
   Will we let the soup **simmer** or **boil?**

4. Those flowers by the pier only last for one year, then they need to be replanted.
   Are they **annuals** or **perennials?**

5. Hannah won free surfing lessons for perfect attendance at school this year.
   Were the awards given by the **principle** or the **principal?**

6. Barb's mom just finished writing a children's story about manatees.
   Will she get a **copyright** or a **patent** for her book?

7. Three friends found a redwood tree. They measured it by reaching their arms around the
   trunk and holding each other's hands.
   Did they measure the **circumference** or the **diameter?**

8. A widespread storm with high winds brought huge waves crashing against the island.
   Was this a **tornado** or a **hurricane?**

9. I found some sea glass that light could pass through, but I couldn't see through it.
   Was this glass **transparent** or **translucent?**

10. The sailor offered to take our whole group to the island for free. We said, "Yes!"
    Did we **except** or **accept** his offer?

Name _____

SWIMMERS' LINE-UP

When the swimmers want to swim, you'll find them in the ocean. When they want to ride a great new roller coaster on the boardwalk, however, they have to wait in a line. There's a special way to show the relationship between words. It's called an **analogy.** It shows that two pairs of words have the same relationship.

Example: swim : ocean *as* wait : line (swim is to ocean as wait is to line)
Swim is something people do in the ocean. Wait is something they do in a line.

Circle the correct word to fit in each blank in these analogies.

1. mask : face *as* flippers : _____

    swim   feet   dive   equipment

2. sunglasses : eyes *as* _____ : skin

    water   nose   sunscreen   sunburn

3. money : _____ *as* lunch : lunchbox

    buy   pocket   change   spend

4. snorkel : _____ *as* raft : float

    mask   swim   bubbles   breathe

Complete these analogies:

5. tired : sleep *as* hungry : _____

6. swim : _____ *as* jog : road

7. library : books *as* _____ : dishes

8. glass : _____ *as* paper : tear

9. _____ : lumber *as* wheat : flour

10. years : age *as* degrees : _____

11. wet : _____ *as* gritty : sand

12. hand : fingers *as* _____ : pages

13. _____ : dog *as* fins : fish

14. row : oar *as* sweep : _____

Name _____

SHOULD YOU?…COULD YOU?…WOULD YOU?

Should you *jeer* at a *stingray?* Could you swim with a *connoisseur?* Would you wear a *garish* bathing suit? You can't answer these questions unless you know what the words mean!

Use your dictionary to find the meanings of the words in **bold** below. Then write your answer to each question. Be ready to explain your answers!

1. Should you **jeer** at a **stingray?** _____

2. Could you swim with a **connoisseur?** _____

3. Would you wear a **garish** bathing suit? _____

4. Should you get **lethargic** in big waves? _____

5. Could a floating raft be **conducive** to sleeping? _____

6. Would you rub **coarse** sand on your body? _____

7. Should you be **punctual** to your lifeguard class? _____

8. Could you **contrive** a way to fix a broken surfboard? _____

9. Would you be **valiant** or **tremulous** if you met a shark? _____

10. Should you **chide** your little sister for swimming alone? _____

11. Could you cause a **calamity** with a beach umbrella? _____

12. Would you throw out **rubbish,** or keep it? _____

13. Should a **novice** play in a championship game of beach volleyball? _____

14. Could you get along with an **obstinate** neighbor? _____

15. Would you feel comfortable around a **famished** shark? _____

Name _____

COULD YOU?...WOULD YOU?...SHOULD YOU?

Could you float on a *catamaran?* Would you swim in a *maelstrom?* Should you dive into a *maw?* You can't answer these questions unless you know what the words mean!

Use your dictionary to find the meanings of the words in **bold** below. Then write your answer to each question. Be ready to explain your answers!

1. Could you float on a **catamaran?** _____

2. Would you swim in a **maelstrom?** _____

3. Should you dive into a **maw?** _____

4. Could you catch a fish in a **coupe?** _____

5. Would you see a **manatee** at a **matinee?** _____

6. Should you bargain with a **barracuda?** _____

7. Could you sniff an **aroma** on the beach? _____

8. Would you give a **marimba** to a **mollusk?** _____

9. Should you **prevaricate** to the lifeguard? _____

10. Could you take a rest in a **bungalow?** _____

11. Would you be **cordial** to a **carnivore?** _____

12. Should you float into a **treacherous** current? _____

13. Could you float on a **foible?** _____

14. Would you enjoy listening to a **monotonous** song? _____

15. Should you **aggravate** an eel? _____

Name _____

WHERE WOULD YOU FIND THIS?

Fisherman Fred has found some very strange things in his net. Is that where they belong? Decide where each one of these things would be found. Circle the correct choice. You may need to use your dictionary!

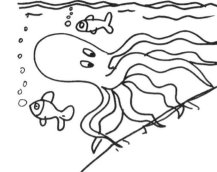

Where would you find . . .

1. . . . **a gam?**
   a. at a computer
   b. in the ocean
   c. in a candy store

2. . . . **a chauffeur?**
   a. in a shoebox
   b. in a coffee cake
   c. driving a car

3. . . . **a lexicon?**
   a. floating in a pool
   b. in a library
   c. acting on stage

4. . . . **some borscht?**
   a. in a hardware store
   b. on a menu
   c. talking on the phone

5. . . . **a molar?**
   a. making a movie
   b. in your mouth
   c. riding a motorcycle

6. . . . **a euphonium?**
   a. in a bucket
   b. growing on a tree
   c. in an orchestra

7. . . . **a vicar?**
   a. on a sundae
   b. in a church
   c. in a toolbox

8. . . . **a sternum?**
   a. in your body
   b. singing in a choir
   c. in a dresser drawer

9. . . . **a mariner?**
   a. sailing a ship
   b. growing in a garden
   c. in a salad

10. . . . **a matinee?**
    a. at a movie theater
    b. at a wedding
    c. snorkeling at a reef

11. . . . **an attorney?**
    a. in your bloodstream
    b. in your bank account
    c. in a courtroom

12. . . . **nuptials?**
    a. in a church
    b. on a sandwich
    c. on the moon

13. . . . **a subpoena?**
    a. in a shell
    b. in an envelope
    c. in a fishing boat

Name

58

WHERE WOULD YOU FIND THAT?

Fisherwoman Freeda has found some more stuff in her net. Decide where each one of these things would be found. Circle the correct choice. You may need to use your dictionary!

Where would you find . . .

1. . . . **some kelp?**
   a. in a fishing net
   b. under a bed
   c. at a wedding

2. . . . **an anemone?**
   a. at the dry cleaners
   b. in a tide pool
   c. under a desk

3. . . . **a procession?**
   a. in a parade
   b. in a science textbook
   c. on a hamburger

4. . . . **an eclipse?**
   a. in a lake
   b. on a quilt
   c. in the sky

5. . . . **a caddie?**
   a. inside a camera
   b. in your blood
   c. on a golf course

6. . . . **a garnish?**
   a. on a dinner plate
   b. in a poem
   c. riding a pony

7. . . . **a sequoia?**
   a. in some soup
   b. in a forest
   c. inside your ear

8. . . . **a patella?**
   a. under your skin
   b. on a fishing hook
   c. in a history book

9. . . . **a marionette?**
   a. in a car engine
   b. in a puppet show
   c. on a banana split

10. . . . **a bathyscaphe?**
    a. in the ocean
    b. inside a glove
    c. at a wedding

11. . . . **a manta?**
    a. on a space ship
    b. in a fishing net
    c. under a bed

12. . . . **a stethoscope?**
    a. under a ski lift
    b. around a doctor's neck
    c. on a snowplow

13. . . . **a villain?**
    a. in a movie
    b. in a flower pot
    c. under a toenail

Name _____

SUBMARINE WATCH

The submarine travels close to the bottom of the ocean. It's down there moving around among the roots! *Submarine* is a word that is formed from the root word *mar,* meaning *sea,* and the prefix *sub* and suffix *ine.* Read the roots and their meanings. Then add suffixes and/or prefixes to the roots to form some words. Try to make at least 20 words!

Root	Meaning
ann	(year)
aqua	(water)
ast	(star)
auto	(self)
bene	(good, well)
bio	(life)
cycl	(circle)
frag	(break)
geo	(earth)
graph	(write)
grav	(heavy)
labor	(work)
lib	(book)
loc	(place)
mar	(sea)
meter	(measure)
mini	(small)
mot, mov	(move)
ped	(foot)
pend	(hang)
port	(carry)
sol	(sun)
vac	(empty)
term	(end)

_____   _____

_____   _____

_____   _____

_____   _____

_____   _____

_____   _____

_____   _____

_____   _____

_____   _____

Name _____

MAKING WAVES

WORD BANK

fjord	weed
tsunami	sea
ichthyologist	mariner
habitat	archipelago
ecology	trough
grotto	abalone
flotsam	

It's a huge wave! The biggest waves in the world are caused by earthquakes. What is this kind of wave called? Find its name and the other answers in the word bank to solve the puzzle.

DOWN

1. a shell lined with mother-of-pearl
2. the study of natural environments
3. natural setting where an animal lives
4. a cave
7. a tidal wave
8. a sailor
10. kelp is a kind of sea_____

ACROSS

5. the lowest point in a wave
6. a scientist who studies fish
9. floating wreckage
11. a group of islands
12. a long, narrow inlet of the sea between tall, rocky cliffs
13. the ocean

Name _____

DON'T OBEY THE SIGNS!

An **antonym** is a word that means the opposite of another word.

Every sign and title on the beach today says the opposite of what it should!

Read each sign, label, and title. Look for one word that could be replaced with its opposite. Cross out that word and write its antonym to change the meaning of the message.

Eat at Bob's Diner
Terrible Food

Tom's Dream

S.S. Sunrise

Please
Do Not Collect Trash
On The Beach

No Waking
On The Beach

DANGER
Shallow Water!

BEACH CLOSED
9AM-9PM

Mystery
at
Straight River

The Smallest Dragon

Burglar Returns Jewelry

Earthquake
Hits
at Midnight

Name

IMPOSTORS IN THE SAND

Figure out which word in each sand castle is the impostor!

Three of the words in each castle are synonyms. Cross out the one that does not mean the same as the others. Do it quickly—before the tide comes in and washes the sand castles away!

> A **synonym** is a word that has the same meaning as another word.

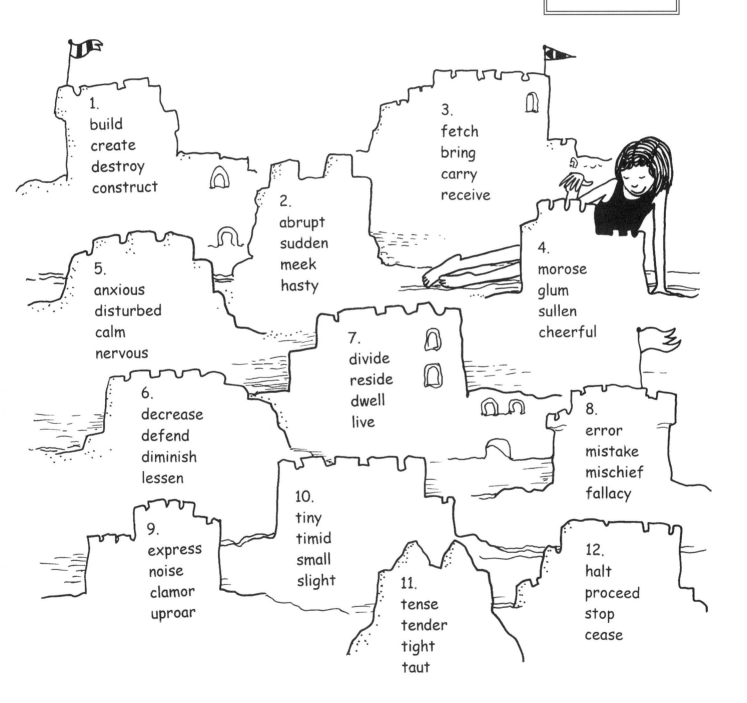

1. build
create
destroy
construct

2. abrupt
sudden
meek
hasty

3. fetch
bring
carry
receive

4. morose
glum
sullen
cheerful

5. anxious
disturbed
calm
nervous

6. decrease
defend
diminish
lessen

7. divide
reside
dwell
live

8. error
mistake
mischief
fallacy

9. express
noise
clamor
uproar

10. tiny
timid
small
slight

11. tense
tender
tight
taut

12. halt
proceed
stop
cease

Name

A BIPED ON A UNICYCLE

This *biped* on a *unicycle* is showing off his *biceps* to the camera on the *tripod!*

A **prefix** is a word part that can be added to the beginning of a word to change the word's meaning. Some prefixes come from numbers. When they are added to words, they create a word that has a number built into it! Pay close attention to the meanings of these prefixes as you follow the directions below.

Prefix Meanings

uni	(one)	hepta	(seven)
bi	(two)	octo	(eight)
tri	(three)	non	(nine)
quad	(four)	deca	(ten)
penta	(five)	centi	(hundred)
hex	(six)		

1. Draw an octopus riding a unicycle.	3. Draw some binoculars inside a pentagon.	5. Draw a decapod crawling on a hexagon.
2. Draw a tricycle inside a quadrilateral.	4. Draw a centipede sleeping in a heptagon.	6. Draw a triangle inside a nonagon.

Name _____

PERIL AT SEA!

What will happen to the storm-tossed ship? Maybe these words will give you a clue. The meanings of the suffixes will help you explain what these words mean. Write the meaning of each word on the line near the word.

A **suffix** is a word part that can be added to the end of a word to change the word's meaning.

Suffix	Meaning
en	(to make)
ful	(full of, like)
fy	(to cause to be)
ic	(like, pertaining to)
ism	(act or quality of)
less	(without)
let	(small)
ment	(act or quality of)
ness	(state or condition of)
or	one who)
ous	(full of, like)
ship	(state or quality of)
some	(full of)
ward	(toward)
y	(like, full of)

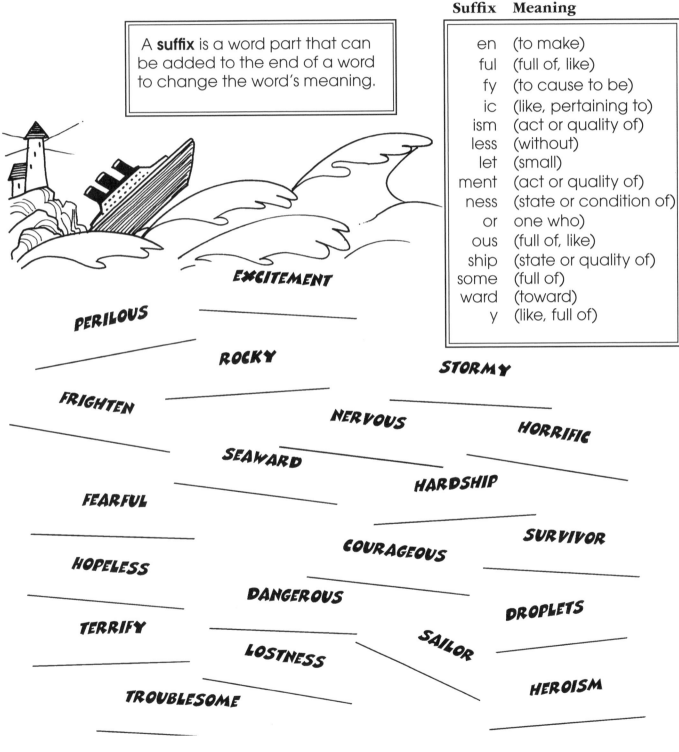

EXCITEMENT

PERILOUS

ROCKY

STORMY

FRIGHTEN

NERVOUS

HORRIFIC

SEAWARD

HARDSHIP

FEARFUL

COURAGEOUS

SURVIVOR

HOPELESS

DANGEROUS

DROPLETS

TERRIFY

SAILOR

LOSTNESS

HEROISM

TROUBLESOME

Name

THE WHOLE IN THE PALE

What's wrong with this title? It's a case of mixed-up homophones!
What should it be?

_____

Read about all the happenings on the beach today. Choose the right
homophone for each sentence.

> A **homophone** is a
> word that sounds
> like another word
> but has a different
> spelling and
> meaning.

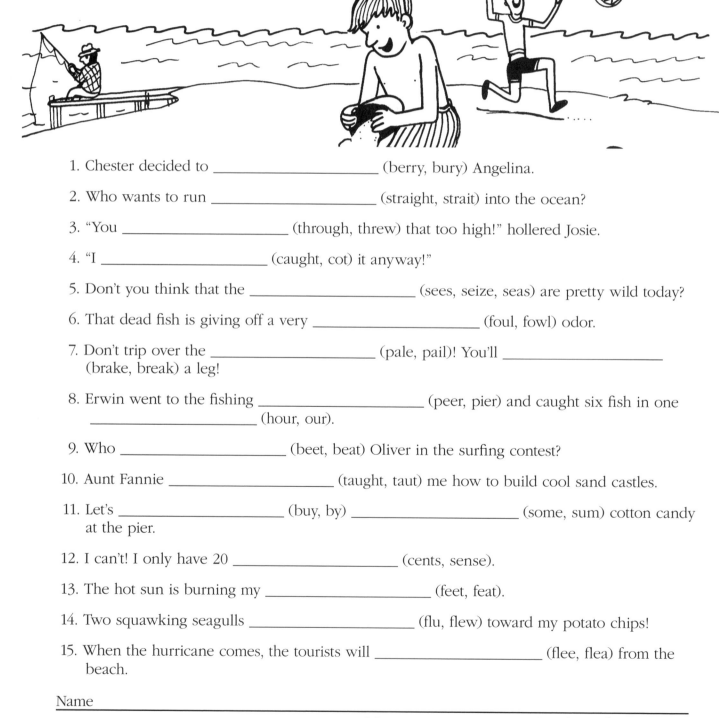

1. Chester decided to _____ (berry, bury) Angelina.

2. Who wants to run _____ (straight, strait) into the ocean?

3. "You _____ (through, threw) that too high!" hollered Josie.

4. "I _____ (caught, cot) it anyway!"

5. Don't you think that the _____ (sees, seize, seas) are pretty wild today?

6. That dead fish is giving off a very _____ (foul, fowl) odor.

7. Don't trip over the _____ (pale, pail)! You'll _____
   (brake, break) a leg!

8. Erwin went to the fishing _____ (peer, pier) and caught six fish in one
   _____ (hour, our).

9. Who _____ (beet, beat) Oliver in the surfing contest?

10. Aunt Fannie _____ (taught, taut) me how to build cool sand castles.

11. Let's _____ (buy, by) _____ (some, sum) cotton candy
    at the pier.

12. I can't! I only have 20 _____ (cents, sense).

13. The hot sun is burning my _____ (feet, feat).

14. Two squawking seagulls _____ (flu, flew) toward my potato chips!

15. When the hurricane comes, the tourists will _____ (flee, flea) from the
    beach.

Name _____

A WHALE OR A WAIL?

A **homophone** is a word that sounds like another word but has a different spelling and meaning.

What is the lifeguard hearing from the water: a whale or a wail?

Which homophone is the right word to answer this question?

_____

A pair of homophones is needed to complete each sentence about this day at the beach. Choose the correct pair from the Word Box below, and write the words in the blanks.

1. The lifeguard can _____ way out over the _____ .

2. Which _____ got badly burned by the _____ today?

3. Have you _____ about the _____ of seals on the beach?

4. Did some thief _____ the _____ bar from the lighthouse?

5. _____ you want to float in a canoe made of rotten _____?

6. He let out a _____ when he saw how big the waves had _____.

7. Lifeguard Linda was too_____ from the flu to work all_____.

8. The new lifeguard did_____ remember to tie a_____ in the boat's rope.

9. Fishermen from the pier_____ all_____ of the fish they caught today.

10. Don't forget to _____ the door of the bathhouse while you change your _____.

11. The lifeguard rescued a man who had caught his _____ on the _____ rope of his ski boat.

12. I thought the gull's leg was _____ until I saw him_____ into the sky.

Word Box

sea	see	herd	heard	not	knot
grown	groan	steal	steel	eight	ate
son	sun	wood	would	clothes	close
sore	soar	weak	week	toe	tow

BEWARE OF CRABBY CRABS!

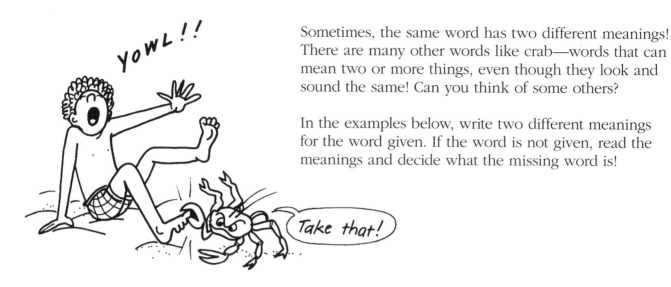

Sometimes, the same word has two different meanings! There are many other words like crab—words that can mean two or more things, even though they look and sound the same! Can you think of some others?

In the examples below, write two different meanings for the word given. If the word is not given, read the meanings and decide what the missing word is!

1. _____   crab   _____

2. the opposite of up   _____   the feathers on a duck

3. an animal footprint   _____   a place to run races

4. _____   date   _____

5. to bounce or jump up   _____   the season after winter

6. to remove from a job   _____   something that burns

7. _____   fly   _____

8. a dot on a ladybug   _____   to see something

9. _____   shower   _____

10. a home for a pig   _____   an instrument for writing

11. _____   box   _____

12. a tiny insect that digs into the skin and buries its head _____ a sound made by a clock

Name _____

THE SHIRT DOESN'T FIT

Which volleyball player's shirt just doesn't fit with the rest? All the words have something in common—except this one:

_____

In each line below, three of the four words have something in common. Decide what these three words have in common. Write the category on the line. Then cross out the word that does not belong in that category.

1. walrus	whale	dolphin	lizard	_____
2. kelp	chowder	flotsam	jetsam	_____
3. bandit	anchor	smokestack	lifeboat	_____
4. snow	sleet	rain	wind	_____
5. lobster	wren	pigeon	heron	_____
6. wail	screech	shriek	mumble	_____
7. monitor	ruler	keyboard	mouse	_____
8. wrench	wok	blender	skillet	_____
9. anemone	scorpion	coral	octopus	_____
10. cactus	bucket	sand	kite	_____
11. receiver	index	binding	title	_____
12. ligaments	liver	spaghetti	muscles	_____
13. salmon	steelhead	redwood	flounder	_____
14. vicar	attorney	priest	preacher	_____
15. stumble	leap	skip	hop	_____
16. cub	duckling	lamb	duck	_____
17. blizzard	hazard	tornado	hurricane	_____
18. frog	snake	turtle	lizard	_____

Name _____

MAROONED!

Looks like trouble, doesn't it! This poor guy is *marooned*. What does that mean?
The **denotation** (dictionary definition) of the word is pretty simple. The **connotation** (suggested meaning) can be much more complicated and may be more interesting!
Write the denotation and connotation for each word below.

MAROONED

Denotation: *Left alone on a deserted island*

Connotation: *starving, thirsty, in danger, hopeless, sunburned, ragged clothes, no escape, death*

PIRATE

Denotation: _____

_____

Connotation: _____

_____

_____

_____

SUNBURN

Denotation: _____

_____

Connotation: _____

_____

_____

_____

I'm sunburned and marooned on a deserted island surrounded by sharks and pirates and there's a storm coming!

SHARK

Denotation: _____

_____

Connotation: _____

_____

_____

_____

STORM

Denotation: _____

_____

Connotation: _____

_____

_____

_____

ISLAND

Denotation: _____

_____

Connotation: _____

_____

_____

_____

Name _____

TASTY WORDS

Macaroni Market

Graham Cracker Cafe

Frank's Frankfurters

The Doughnut Hang-Out

the Waffle Place

Banana Splits

Olive's Omelettes

TORTILLA TIME

The Fudge Shop

tangerine smoothies

How in the world did anyone ever think of *waffles*—pancakes with square patterns in them? Where did the word *omelette* come from, anyway? And how did crackers get named *graham*? Many of the foods we eat have interesting names from unusual places. See if you can find out something about the etymology of these food words.

> An **etymology** is a word history. A good dictionary contains etymologies of many words. These can be found in brackets before or after the definition.

Try to find the etymology for at least 10 of these foods.

1. macaroni _____

2. graham crackers _____

3. frankfurter _____

4. doughnut _____

5. waffle _____

6. banana _____

7. omelette _____

8. tortilla _____

9. tangerine _____

10. mushroom _____

11. cabbage _____

12. chocolate _____

13. spaghetti _____

14. tapioca _____

Name _____

BOARDWALK ANALOGIES

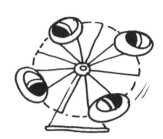

The boardwalk has great rides. The beach has great dunes.
You can use an analogy to compare the two.

> **Example:** rides : boardwalk *as* dunes : beach
> (Rides are to the boardwalk as dunes are to the beach.)

In an **analogy,** both pairs of words have the same relationship.

Fill in the blanks to complete each analogy.

1. legs : lifeguard *as* _____ : octopus

2. tidepool : anemone *as* _____ : horse

3. _____ : sailing *as* racquet : tennis

4. siren : _____ *as* cotton candy : taste

5. weight lifter : weights *as* _____ : surfboard

6. pelican : pelicans *as* mouse : _____

7. warm : _____ *as* cool : cold

8. playground monitor : playground *as* _____ : beach

9. calm : stormy *as* _____ : exciting

10. sun : light *as* stove : _____

11. _____ : bird *as* skin : person

12. rain : hurricane *as* _____ : blizzard

Can you finish these? There are several right answers.

13. ill : well *as* _____ : _____

14. _____ : _____ *as* dessert : dinner

15. student : _____ *as* athlete : _____

16. _____ : _____ *as* small : tiny

17. _____ : _____ *as* _____ : _____

18. _____ : _____ *as* _____ : _____

Name _____

HOT BEACH...COOL DRINKS

Ahhhhhh! A cool drink on a hot day! What happens when the sweaty sunbather gets a swallow of a cool, icy drink?

The sentence will tell you!

Guess what each bold word means from the way it is used in the sentence. Write your guess on the line. Then look up the word in the dictionary, and write the actual meaning.

1. A cool drink of lemonade **revived** the spirits of the sunbather.

   Guess: _____ Definition:_____

2. After the storm, the ocean was **turbid** and filled with dirt and mud.

   Guess: _____ Definition: _____

3. The weather report called for **variable** winds, so we weren't sure what to expect.

   Guess: _____ Definition: _____

4. The waves were so **tortuous** that the fishing boat had to return to the pier.

   Guess: _____ Definition: _____

5. It's easier to take a picture of a **stationary** boat than a moving one.

   Guess: _____ Definition: _____

6. Alisha was **morose** for weeks because the cast on her leg kept her from swimming.

   Guess: _____ Definition: _____

7. Stay away from Jack today! He has a **volatile** temper.

   Guess:_____ Definition: _____

8. It was an **incredible** feat of strength for Grandma to wrestle the shark!

   Guess: _____ Definition: _____

9. Sandy's **uncouth** remarks offended everyone and got her in trouble with the lifeguard.

   Guess:_____ Definition: _____

10. The crab was so **minuscule** that Kate needed a magnifying glass to identify it.

    Guess: _____ Definition:_____

Name _____

DIGGING UP WORDS

TREASURE MAP

Josiah was lucky enough to find an old treasure map belonging to Billy Bones. Instead of leading him to old, buried treasure, it led him to some words. Where did these words come from?

Many words in the English language are actually borrowed from other countries and cultures. The dictionary tells the origin (beginning place) of many words. Usually this is found at the end of the definition. The most recent place where the word was used is listed first. The earliest origin is given last. Use your dictionary to find out the earliest place each of these words was used.

1. eureka _____
2. shampoo _____
3. cul-de-sac _____
4. status quo _____
5. fiancée _____
6. hors d'oeuvre _____
7. khaki _____
8. Noel _____
9. resume _____
10. veranda _____

11. missile _____
12. diamond _____
13. sandal _____
14. onion _____
15. mosquito _____
16. kindergarten _____
17. ink _____
18. dynamite _____
19. pajama _____
20. tornado _____

Write the meaning of these words.

21. eureka _____
22. cul-de-sac _____
23. hors d'oeuvre _____
24. veranda _____
25. kindergarten _____

**property of
BILLY BONES**

SHIPWRECK!

Diver Delbert was amazed to find a shipwreck loaded with words! Oddly enough, every one of these words could be part of a compound word, like the word *shipwreck*.

Using the words on the boat as one part of the compound, make as many compound words as you can. You can make a compound word by adding another word to the beginning or the end of one of these words. Use two words from the boat, or add other words not found here! Write the words you create in the middle of the page. If you need more space, use the back of the page.

> A **compound word** is a word made up of two complete words joined together.

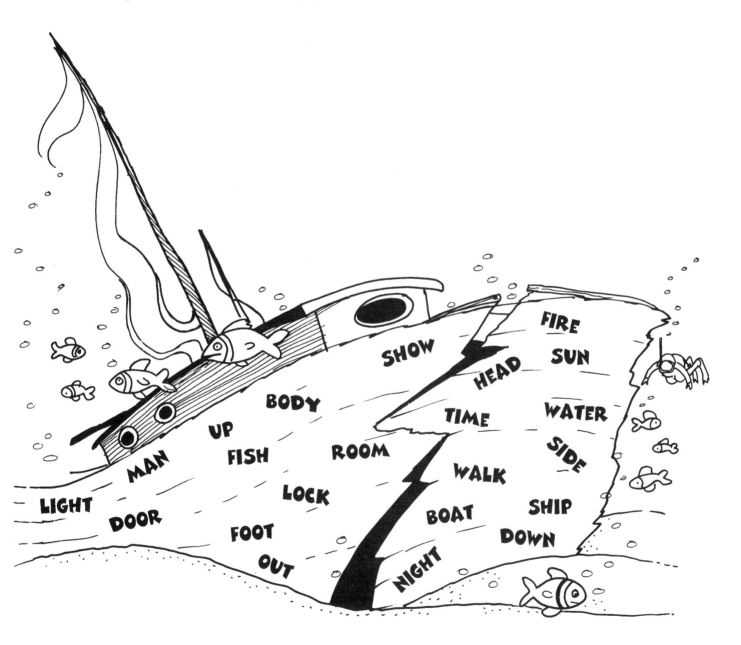

LIGHT · MAN · DOOR · UP · FISH · BODY · FOOT · LOCK · OUT · ROOM · SHOW · NIGHT · WALK · BOAT · TIME · HEAD · SIDE · NIGHT · SHIP · DOWN · FIRE · SUN · WATER

OCTOPUS OR SQUID?

People are always getting an octopus mixed up with a squid! If you want to keep from confusing these two words, you need to know the meaning of each one. There are many words that get confused with others because the two words have similar meanings or looks. Each of these examples has a pair of words that often get confused with each other. Circle the correct word to answer each question.

1. Carlos found a sea creature with 10 arms around its mouth.
   Did he find an **octopus** or a **squid?**

   Tangled up again!

2. After dinner, Jana ate her cheesecake on the beach.
   Was this her **desert** or her **dessert?**

3. The large floating object with a bell marks the channel for boats. Is this an **anchor** or a **buoy?**

4. Jay and Sheri like to sit on the beach at night and study the stars.
   Are they studying **astrology** or **astronomy?**

5. Jenna is always saying words that are the opposite of what she means!
   Does she speak in **antonyms** or **synonyms?**

6. The beach club throws a huge midnight beach party every two years.
   Is this an **annual** event or a **biennial event?**

7. Kai just bought a new boat and wants to protect it in case of damage.
   Should he buy **assurance** or **insurance?**

8. The weatherman brought an instrument to the beach to measure the wind.
   Did he bring an **anemometer** or a **barometer?**

9. When we were surfing, we saw several pieces of floating wreckage from a ship.
   Did we see **flotsam** or **jetsam?**

10. When kids drove their motorbikes in circles around our blanket, we were upset! Did we give a **compliment** or a **complaint** to the lifeguard?

11. We saw a streak of light flash through the sky, then a large rock crashed to the beach.
    Was the thing that landed a **meteor** or a **meteorite?**

Name

DOUBLE TROUBLE

Freddy Frog can never quite get his binoculars adjusted right. So, he sees everything double.
Today, he sees double consonants in all of these words. Some of them really do have double
letters. Some of them should not! Which ones are right?

Read all the words that Freddy is seeing.
Circle each word that is NOT spelled correctly.

annimal   glossary   balloon   commit

community   impress   bennefit   memmory

Tennessee   opposite   proffessor   marshmallow

necessary   flammable   scissors   tommorrow

accent   accident   address   different

catterpillar

vollunteer   suppose   horrid   struggle

misspell   accuse   baskettball   bannanna   buffalo

tellescope

attenndance   difference   illegal   irregular

terrible   immune   issue   lasso   dessert

Name _____

A TROUBLESOME TWOSOME

Freida and Fiefie are the most mischievous frogs around. Since they are cousins, everyone always gets them confused with one another. Notice that one has a name with *i* before *e*. The other has a name with *e* before *i*. Do you remember the *ie* rule?

Use the *ie* rule to clear up the trouble with these words below. Choose the correct spelling for each word.

1. a. grief
   b. greif

2. a. retreive
   b. retrieve

3. a. cheif
   b. chief

4. a. freind
   b. friend

5. a. neighbor
   b. nieghbor

6. a. receipt
   b. reciept

7. a. eighty
   b. ieghty

8. a. sleigh
   b. sliegh

9. a. ceiling
   b. cieling

10. a. riendeer
    b. reindeer

11. a. believe
    b. beleive

12. a. riegn
    b. reign

13. a. veil
    b. viel

14. a. receive
    b. recieve

15. a. freight
    b. frieght

16. a. biege
    b. beige

17. a. weight
    b. wieght

18. a. decieve
    b. deceive

Name _____

WORDS THAT STICK TOGETHER

Oops! Freddy spilled the glue all over his spelling homework. Lots of the words got stuck together. That's okay, because pairs of words have been made into compound words. The problem is, some of the compound words are spelled correctly, while others are all wrong. Use crayons or markers to color the sticky papers that have compound words spelled correctly.

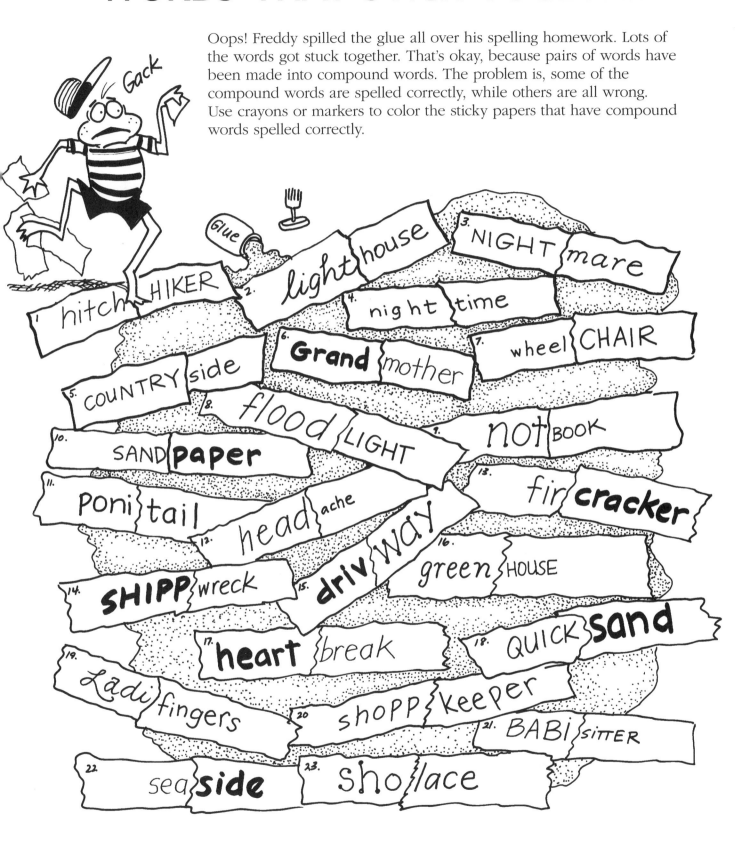

Gack

Glue

1. hitch HIKER
2. light house
3. NIGHT mare
4. night time
5. COUNTRY side
6. Grand mother
7. wheel CHAIR
8. flood LIGHT
9. not BOOK
10. SAND paper
11. Poni tail
12. head ache
13. fir cracker
14. SHIPP wreck
15. driv way
16. green HOUSE
17. heart break
18. QUICK sand
19. Ladi fingers
20. shopp keeper
21. BABI sitter
22. sea side
23. sho lace

LETTERS WITH A SECRET LIFE

Some letters are rather sneaky. The letter *c* can sound like a *k* or an *s*. And *s* sometimes sounds like *z*. Sometimes *g* sounds hard. Other times it sounds soft like a *j*. Then, there's those mysterious pairs, *gh* and *ph*. They often sound like *f*.

In her secret diary, Phoebe Phrog uses many words with these letters. See if you can find the mistakes in her diary entries! Circle any misspelled words. Then write them correctly on the lines below each entry.

Friday, June 13

What an unlucky day! At the circis, I was cheering and laffing and eating at the same time. I choked on a piece of selery, and had to be taken to the emerjensy room. Finally, I couffed up the selery. My throat is still sore.

_____

_____

_____

Saturday, June 14

Today, I got a fone call from a foney juge. He was asking me to take a sitisenship test. Isn't that ridikulous?

_____

_____

Sunday, June 15

Two gastly gosts crashed my birthday selebation today. They caused much mischeph and drank up all the sider.

_____

_____

_____

Monday, June 16

After my fizical fitness class today, I was sertainly energised. They surprized me by taking fotografs of my fifty-three pushups.

_____

_____

_____

Tuesday, June 17

I got caut in a syclone today. Afterwards, I had no patiense left to go to my skuba lesson.

_____

_____

_____

Name _____

TOO MANY FROGS

Freida never should have taken this babysitting job! There are just too many little frogs to watch at once! In fact, she's decided that more than one frog is too many!

All these words name ONE of something. How would you write them if they named MORE THAN ONE? Write the plural form of each word. Spell each one correctly!

1. child _____

2. noise _____

3. mess _____

4. wish _____

5. society _____

6. cottage _____

7. address _____

8. chef _____

9. butterfly _____

10. hero _____

11. loaf _____

12. chief _____

13. goose _____

14. echo _____

15. donkey _____

16. woman _____

17. radio _____

18. key _____

19. potato _____

20. athlete _____

21. lunch _____

22. fox _____

23. county _____

24. nest _____

25. attorney _____

THE CASE OF THE VANISHING ENDINGS

Famous Detective Sherlock Frog is searching for the endings that are missing from these words. Help him track them down. Write the correct ending for each word.

1. favor _____

2. negat _____

3. surpr _____

4. self _____

5. varn _____

6. critic _____

7. fool _____

8. prom _____

9. expens _____

10. dent _____

11. frag _____

12. apolog _____

13. van _____

14. host _____

15. coll _____

16. knowl _____

17. man _____

18. flor _____

19. garb _____

20. cour _____

It's a clue!

ise   *ish*

ize   *ite*   *ive*

ege   *age*

ile   *ist*   *edge*

Name _____

TRICKY ENDINGS

Mannifrog the Magnificent is the most respected frog magician in the land. He does the most awesome tricks and pulls the most amazing things out of his hat!

The endings coming out of Mannifrog's hat are tricky ones. They often confuse even the best spellers. For each word below, choose the tricky ending that is the right one. Circle the word with the ending that makes the correct spelling.

1. jealous
   jealus
   jealius
   jealeous

2. circous
   circus
   circeus
   circius

3. focous
   foceous
   focus
   foceus

4. tremendus
   tremendeous
   tremendous
   tremendious

11. outrageus
    outragius
    outrageous
    outragous

12. luscious
    lusceous
    luscus
    luscius

13. Venus
    Venuous
    Venous
    Veneus

5. melodus
   melodious
   melodeous
   melodius

6. generus
   generius
   generous
   generuous

7. marvelus
   marvelous
   marveleous
   marvious

8. conscious
   conscius
   consceous
   coinscius

9. cautious
   cauteous
   cautus
   cuteous

10. radeous
    radeus
    radius
    radious

14. nerveous
    nervus
    nervous
    nervious

15. cacteous
    cactus
    cactuous
    cactius

Name

83

ANTS FOR SALE

On weekends, Freddy operates the Frogville Sweet Shop, where he sells yummy chocolate-covered ants, minted flies, caramel grasshoppers, and other tasty delights. Many of the candies contain ants.

Many of these words contain ants also. Which ones end with *ant*? Which ones end with *ent, ence,* or *ance*? Choose the correct ending for each word.

WRITE THE WHOLE WORD!

1. dist (ant, ent, int) _____

2. evid (ant, ent, int) _____

3. hydr (ant, ent, int) _____

4. independ (ant, ent, int) _____

5. pleas (ant, ent, int) _____

6. eleg (ant, ent, int) _____

7. vac (ant, ent, int) _____

8. excitem (ant, ent, int) _____

9. ignor (ant, ent, int) _____

10. import (ence, ance) _____

11. appli (ence, ance) _____

12. eleph (ant, ent, int) _____

13. restaur (ant, ent, int) _____

14. sci (ence, ance) _____

15. abs (ence, ance) _____

16. insur (ence, ance) _____

17. attend (ence, ance) _____

18. evid (ence, ance) _____

Name _____

TANGLED ENDINGS

Freida is the top forecaster for Frogville's Weather Channel 10. She predicted this violent whirlwind. Now she's out there, reporting live from the scene of the storm.

Notice that the whirlwind has made a mess of these words. It has mixed up all the endings.

Untangle these endings. Find the correct ending for each word. Cross out the wrong ending and write the correct one above it to spell the word right.

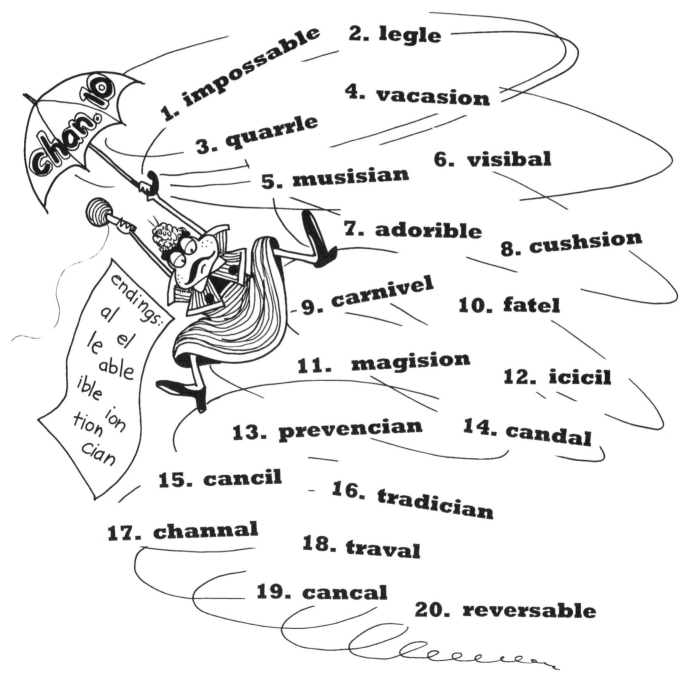

1. impossable
2. legle
3. quarrle
4. vacasion
5. musisian
6. visibal
7. adorible
8. cushsion
9. carnivel
10. fatel
11. magision
12. icicil
13. prevencian
14. candal
15. cancil
16. tradician
17. channal
18. traval
19. cancal
20. reversable

endings:
al   el
le able
ible ion
tion
cian

Name _____

YOU ATE THAT?

EAT and ATE are built right into many words. Some of them are good for eating. Some are not. Alexandria Amphibian ate them all. Now she's sorry!

Decide what the correct ending is for each of these words. Choose from these four endings.

1. chocol _____

2. accur _____

3. rot _____

4. retr _____

5. imit _____

6. loc _____

7. del _____

8. celebr _____

9. favor _____

10. gradu _____

11. educ _____

12. def _____

13. decor _____

14. hibern _____

15. compl _____

16. separ _____

17. candid _____

18. defin _____

Name _____

AT THE ROOT OF IT ALL

When you need to spell a word with a prefix or suffix, it helps to think about the root. Get the root's spelling right, and you're well on your way to the correct spelling of the whole word.

Use your knowledge of roots to help you find the errors in these words. If a word is spelled wrong, write it correctly on the lines at the bottom of the page.

1. supernatral
2. accidental
3. export
4. suspend
5. completly
6. fevorish
7. difference

8. prefer
9. frequently
10. biograffy
11. magecal
12. disapear
13. preskool

14. selfish
15. toothless
16. musacal
17. unlock
18. favorable
19. imperfect
20. advertizement

Finally! We've gotten to the ROOT of the matter!

gulp

voilà!

Name _____

LAZY LETTERS

Some letters fall asleep on the job, and make no sound at all! You stay awake and investigate these words. Look and listen to find the silent letters.

Draw a path for the sleepwalker by joining words that have silent letters. The path should only touch words with silent letters.

stalk

sleepwalker

KNOT

envy

rhyme

dough

character

resign

ghost

burglar

knife

examine

universe

bumpy

bridge

knee

quiver

COCONUT

designer

combing

automatic

reign

honest

wrote

erupt

wriggle

SWORD

Name _____

SURPRISING S

S is a wonderful letter. It sneaks and sizzles, spies and snoozes.

What is the correct way to spell these words that are homes to the letter *S*? Use a colored marker to circle the words that are spelled correctly.

1. slippery
2. squerm
3. straght
4. suspec
5. serius
6. soccer
7. spinich
8. stomach
9. saveings
10. susage
11. suspect
12. satasfy
13. sombody
14. serious
15. stereo
16. sneek
17. silance
18. smothe
19. scarcly
20. sammwich
21. secretery
22. seventh
23. strengthen
24. scissors
25. hissing
26. surely
27. successful
28. sosiety
29. special
30. seize
31. squirm
32. studio

Name

WHO'S GONE WRONG?

Sheriff Wilbur Wise Walfrog has just posted the pictures of all the scoundrels WANTED in Frogville for doing something WRONG.

He has some trouble with his spelling. Please write the names correctly under each picture.

William Waitlifter   Retched Ray   Werst   Wodepecker

Weird Wanda Werm   Wressler Rachel   Weekend Warriar

Find the mistakes in these words. Write each word correctly.

1. aweful _____

2. waistful _____

3. windowsil _____

4. wieght _____

5. wunderful _____

6. wepons _____

7. wich _____

8. wer'e _____

9. knowlege _____

10. wreeth _____

11. wispher _____

12. wraping _____

13. whiped _____

14. Wenesday _____

15. rinkled _____

16. weekness _____

Name _____

WINNING COMBINATIONS

Cousins Francine and Flossie are a winning combination on the tennis court. They always get the right score in their doubles matches.

See if you can get a perfect score by finding the winning vowel combinations for each of the words below. Vowel combinations can be used more than once.

1. app____r

2. thr____gh

3. str____ght

4. r____ned

5. f____ght

6. n____ghty

7. ag____n

8. f____ntain

9. dr____d

10. n____sy

11. cl____

12. excl____m

13. p____ple

14. aud____nce

15. ann____nce

16. c____ght

17. wr____th

18. us____l

19. t____ght

20. be____ty

ea ua eo
au oa ie ai ou ue ui oi

Name _____

Copyright © 2016 World Book, Inc./
Incentive Publications, Chicago, IL

PECULIAR WORDS

Dr. Frogenstein is very proud of the very peculiar creature he has created. He also enjoys collecting peculiar words. But he is never quite sure how to spell them!

Check out each word in Dr. Frogenstein's collection. Circle the words that are spelled correctly. If a word is not spelled correctly, cross it out, and write the correct spelling nearby.

Speak, oh monster of mine.....

RIBBIT

bizarre

kazoo

opaque

gnome

mustache

enough

ziggzagg

unique

scheme

De Moines

vacum

neumonia

vague

lama

toung

Conneticut

bronkitis

bough

karate

amnesia

WORDS THAT MAKE YOU LAUGH AND CRY

Some words make Frankie laugh. Others make him cry. Once he gets started laughing or crying, it's hard to get him to stop!

LAUGH

humor
joking
snicker
silliness
absurd
tickling
giggles
funniest
laughter
hilarious
comedy
amusement

Here are 12 words of each kind.
They are all spelled correctly.

Choose 5 or more of the laughing words.
Use them in a short paragraph telling why he is laughing.
Make sure you spell the words right!

_____

_____

_____

_____

_____

_____

_____

Choose 5 or more of the crying words.
Use them in a short paragraph telling why he is crying.
Make sure you spell the words right!

_____

_____

_____

_____

_____

_____

_____

CRY

injury
terror
insults
whine
sorrow
teasing
accident
loneliness
embarrass
dangerous
frightening
disappointment

Name _____

RULE-BREAKERS

Some words just don't follow the spelling rules.
Instead, they break the rules!

Read each rule. Then look at the group of words which
follows it. Circle every word that BREAKS the rule.

RULE # 1
When a word ends in **o,** and there is a consonant
before the **o,** make the word plural by adding **es.**

---

tomatoes   torpedoes   pianos   volcanoes   potatoes   solos

RULE # 2
i comes before **e,** except after **c** or when sounding like **a** as in *neighbor* or *weigh.*

---

weird   beige   chief   receive   ancient   neither
height   their   foreign

RULE # 3
When two words join to become a **compound** word, the spelling of each part
of the new compound word stays the same as the spelling of each word before
being joined.

---

roommate   pastime   sandpaper   homework   bookkeeper

RULE # 4
When **ly** is added to the root, the spelling of the root word does not change,
unless the root ends in **y.**

---

beautifully   wholly   lately   truly   friendly   lovely

RULE # 5
When a root ends in **e,** drop the **e** before adding a suffix that begins with a
vowel (such as *ate, ous, able, y, ate*).

---

hoping   noticeable   shiny   famous   manageable

Name _____

UNEARTHLY WORDS

When Antonia Frog blasted off in the Amphibias 11 spacecraft, she had no idea she would need her spelling dictionary. Help her get the right spellings for the words she encounters in outer space.

Finish the puzzle with words to fit the clues.

1. fragments of space matter burning in Earth's atmosphere
   __ __ __ __ E __ __ __

2. large system of stars, gases, and dust
   __ __ __ __ __ X __

3. largest planet
   __ __ __ __ __ T __ __

4. study of the stars
   __ __ __ __ R __ __ __ __ __

5. Earth does this to cause day and night
   __ __ __ __ A __ __ __

6. spacecraft that carries people and equipment
   __ __ __ __ __ T __ __ __

7. one space body circling another
   __ E __ __ __ __ __ __

8. engine that uses fuel to propel crafts into space
   R __ __ __ __ __

9. having to do with the sun
   __ __ __ __ R

10. ball of gas with long tail that orbits the sun
    __ __ __ E __

11. layer of air that surrounds Earth
    __ __ __ __ __ S __ __ __ __ __

12. planet with many colored rings
    __ __ T __ __ __

13. person that travels and explores space
    __ __ __ __ R __ __ __ __ __

14. Earth does this around the sun
    __ __ __ __ I __ __

15. space bodies that orbit the sun
    __ __ A __ __ __ __

16. to propel a craft into space
    L __ __ __ __ __

Name _____

95

WORDS YOU CAN EAT

Famous Chef Pierre LaFrog serves wonderful delights at his Chez Froggie Café. Frogs who come there to dine can choose from several menus.

Read these menus carefully. Use a crayon or marker to color the menus with all the words spelled correctly. For the other menus, count the number of words spelled wrong. Write the number next to each menu.

1
bacon quiche
vegtable stew
strawberries
anchovy dip
mollasses pie

2
shrimp appetisers
artichoke butter
cocanut ice cream
diet soda
apple crum pie

3
cranberrys
spinuch salid
cucumber slices
suger cookies
brocoli tips

4
sausage balls
mushroom salad
macaroni & cheese
mustard dip
hamburger

5
fresh pastta
lam casserole
celary sticks
pinapple
bolloney sandwich

6
coconut
noodles
salmon cakes
raddishes
onion soup

7
cabbage
lettuce
custard
cinnamon cakes
cheesecake

8
cheeze biscits
appricot jam
bean burritos
chocalate sunday
bannana cream pie

We never serve frog's legs at the Chez Froggie Café !

Kiss the Chef

Name

WORDS THAT WON'T STAND STILL

Fred and Ginger Frog never stand still. As ballroom dance champions, they are always on the move!

These words are also on the move. Find the errors in spelling. Rewrite any misspelled words correctly on the line below the word.

scrammble

excape

carttwheel

climbbing

wigle

frolick

bounceing

slinkking

somersault

acrobatics

leeping

wobbel

wanderd

revolv

dancing **stumbleing**

craul

shakeing **flieing**

bustle

twirreling

Name

GIANT, COLOSSAL WORDS

Don't run away from big words. They're not as scary as the Abominable Snow-Frog.
If you write one part at a time, they are not too hard to spell!

Find the FIVE words that are spelled wrong. Circle them.
Then, choose any TEN of these words and write a sentence that explains
what the word is or what it means. Use a separate piece of paper.

Have no trepidation. I am not a monstrosity. Honest!

gymnasium
exaggerate
xylophone
civilization
videotape
caterpillar
abominable
biodegradable
monstrosity
bummblebee
encyclapedia
delicatessen
Pensylvannia
PHOTOSYNTHESIS
multiplacation

circumference
abracadabra
brontosaurus

butterscotch
electromagnetic
hippapotamus
orthodontist
perpendicular
precipitation
veterinarian

Name _____

ITSY-BITSY WORDS

Words don't have to be big or complicated to cause spelling problems. Some of the most troublesome words are those small, short ones!

Little Miss Muffet Frog has spider trouble. She also has spelling trouble. Find all the mistakes and write those words correctly.

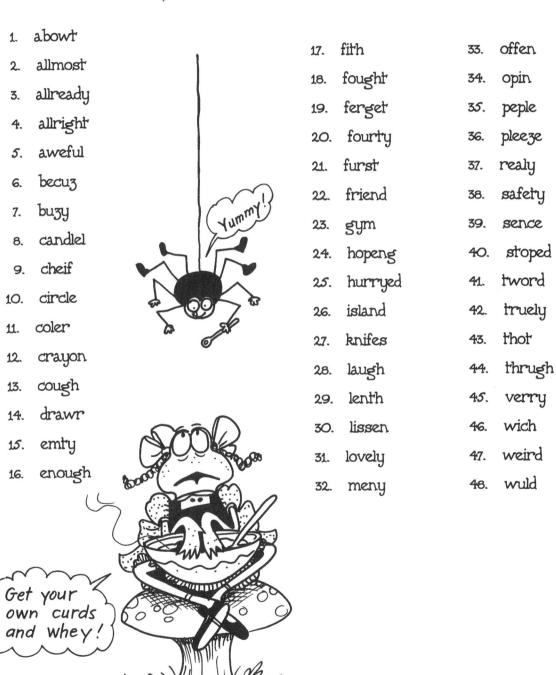

1. abowt
2. allmost
3. allready
4. allright
5. aweful
6. becuz
7. buzy
8. candlel
9. cheif
10. circle
11. coler
12. crayon
13. cough
14. drawr
15. emty
16. enough

17. fith
18. fought
19. ferget
20. fourty
21. furst
22. friend
23. gym
24. hopeng
25. hurryed
26. island
27. knifes
28. laugh
29. lenth
30. lissen
31. lovely
32. meny

33. offen
34. opin
35. peple
36. pleeze
37. realy
38. safety
39. sence
40. stoped
41. tword
42. truely
43. thot
44. thrugh
45. verry
46. wich
47. weird
48. wuld

Name

SNIFFING OUT MISTAKES

Garth, the garbage collector, follows his nose to locate the garbage cans which need emptying. He is very good at deciding which ones have leftovers and other unwanted trash.

Which cans have unwanted misspelled words in them? Use your spelling sense to figure it out. Color the cans that have one or more misspelled words. Write the number of wrong words on the lid of each can (0–5).

#1.
rinkle
tangel
shoulder
shovell
quarter

#2.
porcupine
quantity
traffick
trophie
favrite

#3.
omitt
volume
walett
trapazoid
whistle

#4.
lazyest
eastren
terkey
reconize
lemin

#5.
faucet
confuse
difference
satisfy
regular

#6.
lable
legle
benafit
physicle
explain

peee-yoo!

GARBAGE

1x3c

Name

SIGNS FOR SPELLERS

Freida is surprised by all the signs on the beach. For one thing, they are rather hard to read because of all the errors.

Fix the signs. Rewrite the message on each sign. Spell every word correctly!

1
REPORT ALL
AXIDENTS
IMMEDIATELY

2
NO HOARSES ALOUD ON BEECH

3
Marshmellow
Roasting
on
Wenesdays
Only

4
PUBLICK BEACH
NO LIFGUARD

5
Beech Closed
Until further Notise

6
NO SWIMING TO THE ILAND

7
BEWARE!
Dangrous Sea Annimals

8
Life Perservers
Rekwired
on Boats

9
Water is
Ocuppied by
Sea Monstors

Name _____

SMOOTH SAILING

Follow the directions to color the picture of campers sailing on Agate Lake at Camp Lookout. First, label the nouns (N), adjectives (ADJ), verbs (V), and adverbs (ADV) in the sentences below. Then find some of the words from each sentence in the picture. If the word is a noun, color it yellow. If the word is a verb, color it green. If the word is an adjective, color it red. If the word is an adverb, color it brown.

A **noun** is a person, place, or thing.

A **verb** tells what the noun does.

An **adjective** describes the noun.

An **adverb** describes the verb.

Example: The big raccoon ate slowly.
*   **Big** is an adjective.*
*   **Raccoon** is a noun.*
*   **Ate** is a verb.*
*   **Slowly** is an adverb.*

1. The wooden boat sailed smoothly.

2. The north wind blew hard.

3. A colorful sail flapped gracefully.

4. Often a brown squirrel chews acorns on the boat dock.

5. The deer were walking slowly along the shore.

6. Sometimes a curious raccoon rides on a sailboat.

7. The goofy camper fell awkwardly into the water.

8. Two campers swam quickly to rescue their friend.

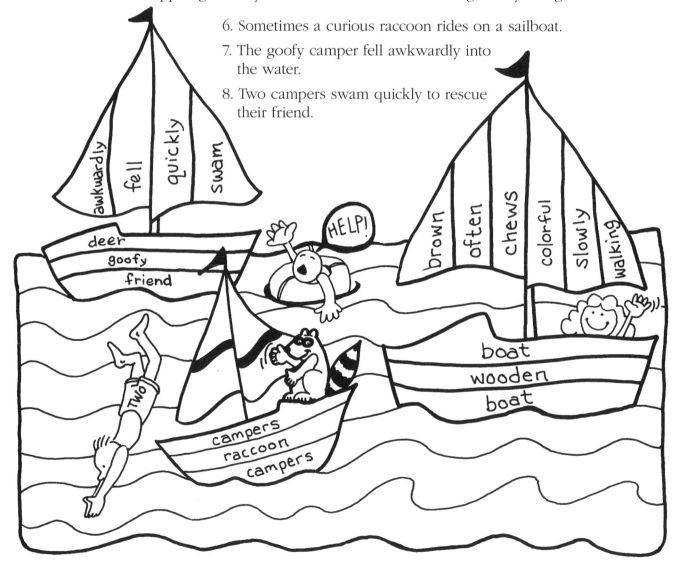

KEY CREATURES

Lisa has found herself in an uncomfortable situation. You'll soon figure out why. Try to find the route she is taking as she searches for the key to the outhouse door. Follow the directions carefully. Do one sentence at a time.

Common nouns refer to persons, places, or things in general.
Example: lake

Proper nouns refer to a specific person, place, or thing.
Example: Agate Lake

1. **Circle all the nouns. Put a C above the common nouns and a P above the proper nouns.**

2. **Find a picture of one of the nouns in the maze below.**

3. **Use the picture clues from each sentence to trace her route.**

    1. Lisa couldn't find the key to the outhouse.

    2. Last Friday, Billy had taken the key and given it to a raccoon.

    3. As Lisa walked along the trail, a snake crossed her path.

    4. Next a coyote howled.

    5. She wondered if the chipmunk she saw near a stump had the key.

    6. An old owl called, "Who, who," and she wondered who took the key.

    7. A bear was picking berries in a patch.

    8. A rabbit hopped away.

    9. She wandered close to the shore of Blue River and saw a beaver gnawing on a tree.

    10. A skunk surprised Lisa and almost made her lose her way.

    11. Huge animal tracks reminded her of the ones she'd seen last August.

    12. The tracks led to the outhouse door!

Name _____

103

AGATE LAKE

Agate Lake is a bustling center of
activities at Camp Lookout. Read
about what is going on now at the
lake. Fill in the blank in each sentence
with the present-tense form of the
verb. The first one is done for you.

1. The sun _____*shines*_____ brightly over Agate Lake. (shine)

2. Campers _____ on the lake. (sail)

3. Others _____ their boats. (row)

4. Some campers _____ in the lake. (fish)

5. Animals _____ from the lake. (drink)

6. A large fish _____ water near a boat when it jumps. (splash)

7. A deer _____ from the nearby bushes. (watch)

8. Carl and Manuel _____ a campfire. (build)

9. They _____ hot dogs and marshmallows. (roast)

10. A marshmallow _____ off the stick into the fire. (fall)

11. Ann _____ rocks on the water. (skip)

12. Maria and Lisa _____ near the boat dock. (swim)

Besides showing action,
verbs also tell when the
action happened.

A **present-tense verb** tells
what is happening right
now.

Write a short story telling about something else that might happen at Agate Lake.
Use present-tense verbs in the sentences to tell what is happening **now.**

_____

_____

_____

_____

_____

_____

Name _____

BLUE RIVER

Blue River is a popular place for the campers at Camp Lookout. Find out why in the following sentences. Read the sentences, and fill in each blank with the **past-tense form of the verb.** The first one is done for you.

> A **past-tense verb** tells what has already happened.
>
> Regular past-tense verbs are formed by adding either **ed** or **d.**

1. Carl ___*watched*___ many rafters paddle by him on the Blue River. (watch)

2. The rafters were _____ with water when they went through the rapids. (spray)

3. Justin _____ in a still, deep pool of water. (fish)

4. A beaver _____ on a tree. (chew)

5. An eagle _____ overhead. (hover)

6. Maria and Lisa _____ stories while they were rafting. (share)

7. They _____ about their classes at school. (talk)

8. Maria _____ favorite books she had read. (suggest)

9. Lisa _____ ideas for tricks to play on cabin counselors. (propose)

10. An otter _____ close to their raft. (move)

11. It _____ on its back. (float)

12. They _____ watching the otter. (enjoy)

Write a story telling about something else that might have happened on Blue River. Use **regular past-tense verbs** in the sentences to tell what **already happened.**

_____

_____

_____

_____

_____

_____

Name _____

A SCRAMBLED MENU

Campers are smelling some unusual odors, which seem to be coming from the mess hall. Check the menu below to see what's cooking. Underline the adjectives in the sentences below. The first sentence is completed for you.

> An **adjective** is a word that describes a noun.
>
> *Example: The unusual odors bothered us.*
> **Unusual** *is an adjective describing the noun.*

1. The <u>slimy, gooey</u> eggs tasted terrible.

2. The crunchy, purple ham broke a tooth.

3. Isaac complained that old, moldy bread was used to make the sandwiches.

4. One of the clumsy cooks dropped a plate of toast topped with sticky syrup.

5. The muddy, thick, cold cocoa got stuck in Maria's throat.

6. One of the counselors had a tiny, green leg sticking out of his mouth.

7. Heidi couldn't eat the strange, smelly pizza.

8. Hungry Carl chose not to eat the weird sandwiches.

Justin used three of the adjectives from above to describe Camp Lookout's food. Unscramble the letters to see what they are.

atgersn _____   ilsym _____   lmdyo _____

Write your own ideas for a menu for the camp's mess hall. Use lots of tasty adjectives!

_____

_____

_____

Name

CAMPFIRE PROCEDURES

CAMPFIRE MEETING PROCEDURES

1. Immediately bring a flashlight and your songbook.
2. Walk slowly.
3. Wait patiently until it is time to find a seat.
4. When told, sit down carefully.
5. Open your songbook and hold it firmly.
6. Do not race through the song quickly.
7. Sing loudly or softly depending on the instructions of the song leader.
8. Watch the leader closely.
9. Do not begin the songs early.
10. Now sing the theme song for Camp Lookout cheerfully and clearly.

An **adverb** is a word that describes a verb. Adverbs tell **how, when, where,** and **how often.**

Example: The camper walked cheerfully to the campfire.

Cheerfully *is the adverb that describes how she walked.*

CAMP LOOKOUT
We Love Camp Lookout
Oh yes we do......
There can't be anything
As weird as you......
When we're not here at camp
We're bluuue!
Oh, Camp Lookout we love you!

PICTURING PREPOSITIONS

Find out what is happening today at Camp Lookout. Begin practicing by underlining the prepositions in the sentences below. Check the first example.

> A **preposition** is a word that shows a relationship with other words in a sentence.
> A **prepositional phrase** includes the preposition, the object, and all the words in between.
>
> *Example: The bugs were crawling inside the sandwiches.*
> *In this sentence,* **inside** *is the preposition,*
> *and* **inside the sandwiches** *is the prepositional phrase.*

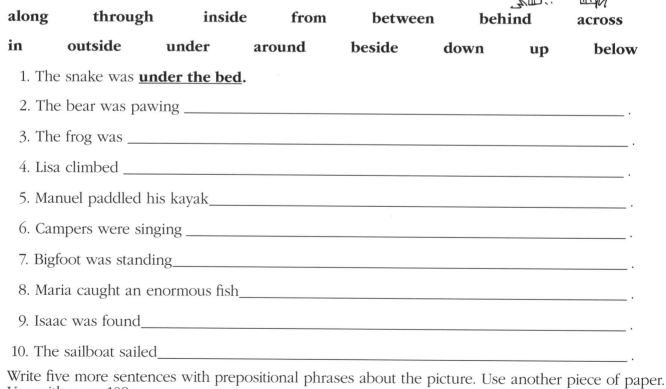

1. Ann was reading her book <u>in</u> the tree house.
2. The chipmunk was running across the boat dock.
3. Both Justin and Isaac could be found inside the mess hall.
4. She was afraid an alien was under her bed.
5. He was hiding between the pool and the cabins.
6. The horses were walking down the steep trail.

Next, use the prepositions below and the picture clues on the next page to make prepositional phrases. Write phrases that actually tell about something going on in the picture on page 109! Use these prepositions:

along   through   inside   from   between   behind   across

in   outside   under   around   beside   down   up   below

1. The snake was **<u>under the bed.</u>**

2. The bear was pawing _____.

3. The frog was _____.

4. Lisa climbed _____.

5. Manuel paddled his kayak_____.

6. Campers were singing _____.

7. Bigfoot was standing_____.

8. Maria caught an enormous fish_____.

9. Isaac was found_____.

10. The sailboat sailed_____.

Write five more sentences with prepositional phrases about the picture. Use another piece of paper. Use with page 109.

Name _____

Use with page 108.

RAPIDLY FALLING

Manuel is headed for the waterfall! Keep him from going over it by finding the contractions in these sentences. Circle all 11, and write the words that form each contraction.

YOU'D BETTER WATCH OUT!

CAMP LOOKOUT

Oh, Oh!

> A **contraction** is a shortened word formed by combining two words.
> An **apostrophe** takes the place of any letters that are left out.
> *(could + not = couldn't)*

1. It wasn't sunny, but it was hot when Manuel went rafting down the Blue River. _____

2. "I'll be fine by myself," he told the counselor when he left. _____

3. He loves to raft, but he hasn't had much experience. _____

4. When rafting, it's important to know how to paddle properly through the rapids. _____

5. There weren't as many rapids as Manuel had expected. _____

6. Because the river seemed so calm, Manuel spent lots of time watching the wild life and didn't see what was looming up ahead.

   _____

7. It was unfortunate that he wasn't paying more attention. _____

8. It wouldn't be long until he'd reach a waterfall. _____

   _____

9. He'd be in for a big surprise. _____

10. Close your eyes. Don't look! _____

Write four sentences with contractions, and write the two words that make each contraction.

1. _____

2. _____

3. _____

4. _____

Name _____

110

STORM HITS CAMP LOOKOUT

The following news article was handed to the editor of a local newspaper. There are 31 errors in capitalization. Can you find them? Circle every letter that should be capitalized.

VoL. 26 ISSUE 38 JULY 5, 1998

75¢

storm hits camp lookout

there were more than the usual fireworks on tuesday evening, the fourth of july. around midnight a big storm hit camp lookout. luckily most of the campers were asleep in their cabins. hailstones the size of golf balls pelted the wooden structures. one of the campers, maria, was quoted as saying, "the ground shook with each clap of thunder, and the sky was fully lit every few minutes. we thought it would never end."

several campers did not have the protection of a cabin. nick, isaac, and manuel had decided to spend the night camping in a tent in the nearby hills. the tent collapsed on them during the storm. a rescue crew was called, including dr. smith, who is a part of the camp lookout staff. when the crew arrived, isaac said, "i was wondering about something—what took you so long?" the boys were found in safe, wet, exhausted condition.

INSIDE ☆
INTERVIEW WITH
IMA FLOAT ☆ ☆ ☆
LIFEGUARD AT
CAMP LOOKOUT.
☆ PAGE 8

BIG WOODS
PUBLISHING
SUBSCRIPTION IS
$39.00 PER YEAR.

☐ YOUR
SUBSCRIPTION
EXPIRES THE
MONTH SHOWN
ON YOUR ADDRESS
LABEL.

Name _____

UNBELIEVABLE NEWS

The following news article needs to be checked for proper capitalization before it is sent to the local newspaper editor. Make corrections, and rewrite the article on the lines below.

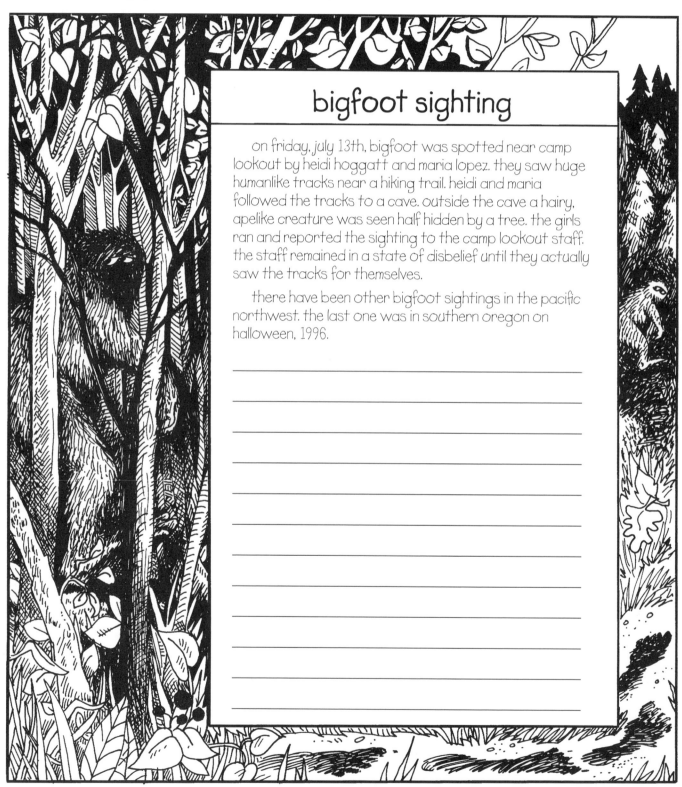

bigfoot sighting

on friday, july 13th, bigfoot was spotted near camp lookout by heidi hoggatt and maria lopez. they saw huge humanlike tracks near a hiking trail. heidi and maria followed the tracks to a cave. outside the cave a hairy, apelike creature was seen half hidden by a tree. the girls ran and reported the sighting to the camp lookout staff. the staff remained in a state of disbelief until they actually saw the tracks for themselves.

there have been other bigfoot sightings in the pacific northwest. the last one was in southern oregon on halloween, 1996.

Name

A TRULY FREAKY STORM!

The following news article needs to be checked for proper capitalization before it is sent to the newspaper editor. Make corrections and rewrite the article on the lines below.

tornado hits

a freak storm hit the camp lookout area on wednesday, june 3. tornadoes are rarely seen in this part of the united states. luckily, there were no injuries. however, there were two unusual incidents. an outhouse was lifted by the tornado and moved to another location in the campground. fortunately, no one was in it at the time. the tornado also lifted all the frogs from a nearby pond and dropped them on some campers near the horse-riding stables. justin loftus was quoted as saying, "from now on, let's say it's raining cats and frogs."

Name _____

A CAMPER'S MIDNIGHT HIKE

Isaac wrote a journal entry about his experience on a midnight hike. He forgot to include punctuation. See if you can add all the missing marks.

July 24

Dear Diary

Last night we went on a great adventure Our cabin took a midnight hike with our cabin counselor Mr O B Good He is from Boise Idaho I think he's impatient and quite old He's lucky to have us kids in his cabin Were really a good fun bunch It took a while for us to get out of camp Before we started up a mountain trail we heard Carl squeal We all got freaked out thinking maybe it was Bigfoot or something but it was only Nick He had brought a water balloon and hit Carl in the back We all thought it was funny Our counselor asked When are you going to grow up I thought this was an odd question It seems a little early to be worrying about that

The trails were hard to see so we had fun using our flashlights We'd shine them in each others faces and have laser battles They also helped us to spot deer raccoons coyotes possums and a skunk When Manuel saw the skunk he yelled Yikes We're going to get sprayed We all ran as fast as we could Justin didn't run fast enough so he had to take a bath in tomato juice

Yours truly
Isaac

A DREAM JOB

Since Lucy Ann was a little girl, she has dreamed of becoming a newspaper reporter. At last her dream is coming true. Today she begins work as a reporter for the *Tiny Town Star*.

Help her to make her very first news story more interesting. Find more interesting and sparkling words that say the same thing as each word that is crossed out. Write the new words above the ones crossed out.

Write two additional lines to give the news story an interesting ending.

A ~~big~~ fire ~~burned steadily~~ for two hours on main street yesterday. The first signs of trouble were detected at six P.M. when the fire engines ~~drove~~ down the street. People came ~~rushing~~ out of stores ~~shouting~~ and ~~gesturing.~~ Bruce's clothing store was ~~completely~~ destroyed by the ~~continuous~~ flames. Many thousands of dollars worth of clothes were ~~burned.~~ The ~~brave~~ firefighters worked ~~hard~~ to save as much of the town as possible. The fire chief said he was ~~very~~ proud of his ~~good crew.~~ Mr. Bruce said his loss was so ~~great,~~ he might not try to rebuild the business._____

_____

_____

_____

PERSONALLY SPEAKING

As a new employee, Lucy Ann was asked to fill out a special form to help her co-workers get to know her.

You can fill out the same form. Try to make each sentence as clear and interesting as you can.

Some Personal Things About Me

1. Once when I was younger _____ ,

   but if I were to do that again I would _____ .

2. Something that I am really proud of is _____

   _____ .

3. Yesterday, I saw _____ .

4. Something special about our school is _____

   _____ .

5. I get angry when I think about _____

   _____ .

6. When I am 21 years old, I would like to _____

   _____ .

7. If I could change one thing in the world, it would be _____

   _____ .

8. I wish I could _____ .

9. I really worry about _____ .

10. I would never, ever want to _____

    _____ .

11. I would really like to _____ .

12. If I had a million dollars I would _____

    _____

    _____ .

Name _____

BEGINNING THAT GRAB

The *Tiny Town Star's* publisher sent all the reporters to a seminar on imaginative writing. One of the topics they studied was good beginnings for news stories and feature articles. They learned that a beginning needs to grab the reader's attention. Lucy Ann is trying some new beginnings for her report on last night's concert where some teenagers caused quite a disturbance.

Underline the beginning that you think is the best grabber.

Unruly teenagers caused a major disturbance at last night's concert.

This was a concert that will not soon be forgotten.

Sponsors of last night's concert say the town should be ashamed of teenagers who disrupted the concert.

Attendees at last night's concert demanded their money back when the concert was interrupted by teenagers throwing eggs and shouting at the musicians.

Rewrite each of these beginnings to make them more attention-grabbing:

1. James is the outstanding player on the school soccer team.

   _____

2. The weather this summer has been hot and humid.

   _____

3. Mrs. Brown's third grade won the school's attendance award.

   _____

4. On our vacation, we saw whales, dolphins, and even a shark.

   _____

5. There were a lot of tornadoes this year.

   _____

6. Farmers in the state report an unusually good growing season.

   _____

7. Janet Jones has won the tennis trophy for the second year in a row.

   _____

8. It is 22 days until Christmas.

   _____

9. The school has purchased new science textbooks for all students in the 5th and 6th grades.

   _____

10. The last day of school is June 10th.

    _____

Name _____

CATCH THE ACTION!

Lucy Ann got to her assignment late—just as the circus parade was getting started. It was such a fun parade. The photographer did not get there in time to take photos, so Lucy Ann wrote about all the action going on. Take a close look at each sentence she has written in her notebook. Her sentences need to show more action. Rewrite the sentences to better describe the parade. Change verbs such as *came* and *went* into more active verbs. Remember, the reader wants to be able to actually picture the actions in the parade!

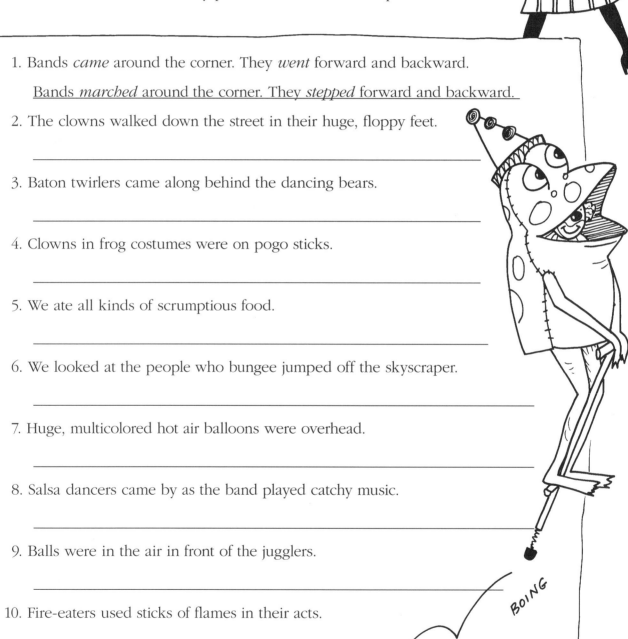

1. Bands *came* around the corner. They *went* forward and backward.

   Bands *marched* around the corner. They *stepped* forward and backward.

2. The clowns walked down the street in their huge, floppy feet.

   _____

3. Baton twirlers came along behind the dancing bears.

   _____

4. Clowns in frog costumes were on pogo sticks.

   _____

5. We ate all kinds of scrumptious food.

   _____

6. We looked at the people who bungee jumped off the skyscraper.

   _____

7. Huge, multicolored hot air balloons were overhead.

   _____

8. Salsa dancers came by as the band played catchy music.

   _____

9. Balls were in the air in front of the jugglers.

   _____

10. Fire-eaters used sticks of flames in their acts.

   _____

Name _____

PRECISELY PRECARIOUS

Lucy Ann wants to cover this story! Barnaby Bolder is going over
Precisely Precarious Falls in an old barrel! When Lucy Ann writes the story,
she needs to use words that tell precisely what happened.
Her readers will want to know!

Choose a word from this page to finish Lucy Ann's sentences
and phrases. Use a word that fits the phrase precisely.

1. the _____ roar of the falls ahead

2. a _____ smell inside the barrel

3. Barnaby's _____ ride

4. The barrel _____ over the edge.

5. What a _____ character!

6. _____ rocks waiting at the bottom

7. Would you trust this _____ barrel?

8. caught in the _____ water

9. a _____ 200-foot drop

10. a _____ adventurer

11. the _____ barrel

12. Barnaby's _____ stomach

13. the _____ space inside the barrel

14. the _____ crowd watching the fall

15. the _____ power of the water

16. Barnaby's _____ body after the fall

terrified

unbelievable

turbulent

wild

jagged

cramped

perilous

steep

foolish

damp

threatening

moldy

CRAZY

sturdy

rushing fearless

awestruck

nervous

NICE SHOT!

WOW!

swirling

battered

deafening

NAUSEOUS WHIRLING

RECKLESS

MIGHTY

threatening

treacherous

plunging

PLUMMETS

Name _____

WORDS WITH TASTE

When is a hamburger not just a plain old hamburger? When it's time to write about it in a food review for the newspaper. Lucy Ann digs up the tastiest words she can think of to write about the hamburgers at The Big Cheese Drive-in.

Try the mouthwatering burger, dripping with charbroiled flavors! It's wrapped in creamy melted cheddar and crisp fresh bacon. Then it's drenched with your choice of buttery fried onions, crisp and tangy dill pickles, plump tomato slices, or crunchy green lettuce—all nestled inside a soft, fresh-from-the-oven, home-baked bun.

Help Lucy Ann's friend with his food reviews. For each food, list several mouthwatering phrases he can use to tempt readers to rush right out to The Big Cheese!

Hot Fudge Sundae

_____

_____

_____

_____

Spaghetti with Meatballs

_____

_____

_____

_____

Deep-Dish Apple Pie

_____

_____

_____

_____

Stack of Pancakes

_____

_____

_____

_____

Fried Chicken Dinner

_____

_____

_____

_____

You choose a food!

_____

_____

_____

_____

Name _____

GOOD ADVICE

Lucy Ann writes an advice column under the name of "Aunt Lucinda." Today she is advising readers about things they should be careful never to do. She has started with a list of ideas for her column. Now she is turning some of the phrases from her list into interesting, complete sentences.

Aunt Lucinda's Advice
Don't ever...
talk back to your mother
save an ice cream bar in your pocket
forget to pay your taxes
go into a burning building
try to interview the gorilla at the zoo
wear your pajamas to work
stand on top of a bridge in the wind
eat a sandwich without mayonnaise
swallow peach pits

AUNT LUCINDA (a.k.a. Lucy Ann Green)

Dear Readers:
- *If you're asked to interview a gorilla, quickly reply, "Never!"*
- *Maude's husband, Bob, will probably never wear his pajamas to work again!*
- *My niece learned a lesson the last time she swallowed a peach pit. I don't think she will do it again.*

List some things you think people should never do. (You may need to use extra paper.) Then take eight of your ideas and expand them into interesting sentences. Be sure to include at least one declarative, one imperative, and one exclamatory sentence.

1. _____

_____

2. _____

_____

3. _____

_____

4. _____

_____

5. _____

_____

6. _____

_____

7. _____

_____

8. _____

_____

Name

SMASHING BEGINNINGS

Lucy Ann wants the beginnings of all her writing pieces to be smashing! Of course, the beginning is the first thing that "hits" the reader, so it's a good idea to make it smashing, exciting, bold, catchy, fantastic, or outrageous!

Choose eight of the topics below, or invent some of your own. Write a smashing sentence to begin each writing piece. Use a separate piece of paper.

a description of a spooky house

a friend in big trouble

a mysterious visitor

NEW RULES AT YOUR SCHOOL

a disappearing teacher

how to clean your room

an outrageous mistake

TRAVEL IN A TIME MACHINE

A MEMORY FROM LONG AGO

your most embarrassing moment

the reason for lightning

a major argument with your brother (or sister)

convincing someone to try salami cantelope bubblegum

convincing someone that you saw something unbelievable

Name _____

THE RED PAGE

In celebration of Valentine's Day, Lucy Ann and the new graphic artist are putting together a "Red Page" for the newspaper. It will have poems about *red*. Think about *red* things so that you can send something to Lucy Ann! Pay attention to all five senses. Collect ideas about things that look, smell, sound, taste, and feel *red*. Write down *red* places and experiences. Use your ideas to finish the *red* poem below.

Red burns across embarrassed cheeks.
Ramon T., Gr. 4

Cherries and berries sing of red.
Dancing and boxing are red.
Rock music is red.
Red is joy and laughter and summer.
Hot, hurting tears burn red in my eyes.
Rhubarb pie drips red on my shirt.
Mean words are red.
Alyssa M., Gr. 5

Red is a bloody nose and anger.
Red is candy hearts and roses.
Red is a cherry pie baking,
And the smell of homemade spaghetti sauce.
I feel red when someone makes fun of me.
A cold nose feels red. So does July.
Sirens scream red, and newborn babies cry red.
Red is an argument with my brother.
Hot peppers on my tongue burn red.
Jason W., Gr. 5

Red is _____, _____, and _____.

_____ is red. So is _____.

_____ and _____ sound red.

Red is the taste of _____ and _____.

_____ feels red.

My favorite red place is _____.

_____ sounds red.

Red is _____, and red is _____.

I feel red when _____.

So is _____.

Try some *green, yellow, orange, pink, black,* or *blue* writing, too!

Name _____

THE TALLEST OF TALES

FROSTBITE in MONTANA

How cold is cold? Do you think you have ever really been cold? Well, listen to this, and then you can decide. Last winter I went to Montana to visit my Uncle Fred. He told me to bring warm clothes. Was I ever glad that I did. The first morning that I was there, it was so cold that the chickens laid frozen eggs and the cows gave ice cream instead of milk. My words froze as I spoke them, and dropped right to the ground and shattered. The dog's shadow froze on the ground the minute he stepped out of the house. Uncle Fred said that shadow did not thaw until April. Well, that's the last time I'll visit Montana in the winter. Uncle Fred says to come in August. He wants me to see the chicken lay scrambled eggs from the terrible heat.

WANTED: The tallest tale in the county!

It's time for the Tall Tale Contest again. The *Tiny Town Star* is waiting for its readers to send in tall tales this year.

REQUIREMENTS: The tale **must** have facts or details that show great exaggeration. These must be things that could not possibly be true! This is one place where lies are okay! In fact, the bigger the lies, the better the tale!

Would you like to enter the contest? Choose a topic that is a good one for exaggeration. Then write a tale and polish it until it is ready to send in to the newspaper. Make sure your tale has: a good title

a smashing beginning

a solid middle

a great ending

Good luck! Maybe you'll win a tall, tall prize!

2nd prize

10 gallon hat

Start your Tall Tale here:

_____

_____

_____

_____

_____

_____

_____

_____

_____

_____

_____

_____

_____

_____

_____

_____

_____

_____

Name _____

HERE'S HOW

Once every month, the *Tiny Town Star* includes a "How To Do It" page. Readers submit written explanations of how to do something they think is important. It is Lucy Ann's job to choose the entries and polish them up for publishing. She likes this one, but it is missing all its connections! Choose some connecting words or phrases to fill in the blanks in this article.

first
second
then
at last
because
at the same time
in addition
to begin with
next
soon
later
meanwhile
after a while
finally
much later
when that is done
for example

THE WORLD'S BEST MILKSHAKE
How to Make It!

_____, you must buy the best, tastiest, creamiest, richest vanilla ice cream you can find. _____, it is necessary to have rich, whole milk.

_____, if you don't have whole milk, you could use low-fat milk.

_____, have vanilla, fresh strawberries, powdered malt, and whipped cream on hand. Start by getting the strawberries ready. Strawberries are often dirty and gritty when you buy them._____, you'll need to wash them well. _____,fill your blender ⅓ full with them. Sprinkle them with a teaspoon of sugar. _____, fill the blender up to ¾ full with ice cream. Pour in about 1 cup of milk. _____, sprinkle 2 tablespoons of malt powder on the top. Run the blender on medium speed until the shake is mixed well.

_____, get the whipped cream and one perfect whole strawberry ready. Pour the shake into a tall glass, and top it with whipped cream and the strawberry.

_____of your careful efforts, you will have a delicious shake! Enjoy!

for instance
therefore
as a result
however
much later
when that is done
for example
for instance
therefore
as a result
on the other hand
instead
because of this
also
in spite of this

Now that you have had a little practice with connections, write a how-to article of your own. Explain how do to something. Some of the ideas below might interest you, but you can also use something else! Write your explanation on a separate piece of paper.

——— HOW TO . . . ———

ride a snowboard	pass a test	catch a lizard	build a good fort	wash a dog	avoid the flu
write a poem	wrestle an alligator	get gum out of	feed a lion	climb a glacier	eat a taco
clean your room	do a somersault	hair make a pizza	make lasagna	change kitty litter	get rid of a cold

Name

ASK ME ANYTHING!

If you want to find out something, you need to ask the right questions. Lucy Ann tries to ask good questions. She plans her questions before she begins an investigation so that she will know exactly what to ask.

Think about the questions you would ask to find out interesting information about the people or events below. Get ready for some interviews by writing down the questions. Write clear, complete questions that ask exactly what you want to know! Write at least four good questions to ask each person.

1. a lion tamer

_____

_____

_____

_____

2. a basketball player

_____

_____

_____

_____

3. a high school student

_____

_____

_____

_____

Name _____

AN EDITOR'S ERROR

Rusty Ruah, the *Tiny Town Star* editor, had a bad day yesterday. He mixed up the biggest story Lucy Ann has ever written. Can you straighten it out before it goes to press?

At 8:00 P.M. the Governor declared a state of emergency.

No one could believe it had actually happened. One minute the sun was shining brightly, and the next minute thunder roared, lightning flashed, and the sky was as dark as midnight.

It was the worst storm ever recorded in the town's history.

Two buildings were completely destroyed, roofs were blown off, and many trees were downed. The wind blew furiously just before the tornado touched down.

People were going about their business as usual, unaware of the disaster that was about to strike Tiny Town.

Fortunately, since it was after 4:00 P.M., the children were not in the school building when the front wall caved in.

Several cars were overturned and many traffic signs were blown away, some even landing in trees.

Several big boats docked at pier 67 were overturned, and at press time most homes and businesses in town were still without electricity.

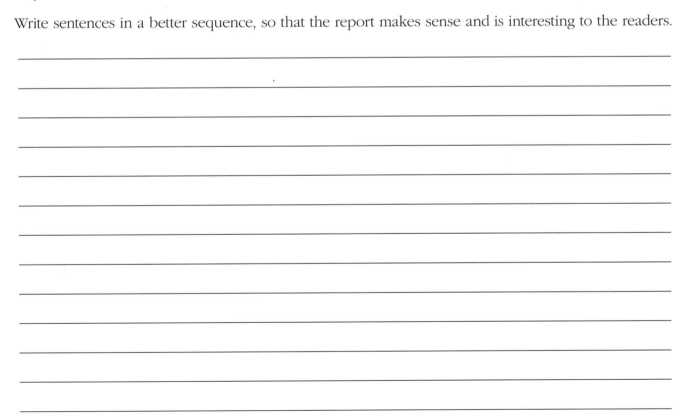

Write sentences in a better sequence, so that the report makes sense and is interesting to the readers.

_____

_____

_____

_____

_____

_____

_____

_____

_____

_____

_____

Name _____

SPEAKING IN METAPHORS

Lucy Ann likes to use metaphors in her reporting. What is a **metaphor?** It is a comparison between two things that are not alike. If a comparison uses the word like or the word as, then it is called a **simile.** It is such fun to create metaphors and similes, especially when you try to compare things that are very different!

SPARK MAGAZINE

FOR KIDS

ONLY

A kid in class looking at the clock
is like a crocodile lurking in the swamp.
Looking for his dinner,
very sneaky, very sly,
he catches every meal he spies.
Greg C.

I am the universe
The sun burning with rage
The planets dusty and lifeless
The stars hot but blue
I am the galaxy
I am.......
Jamie C.

Poets are like the wind.
Simone W.

Losing a friend is like peanut butter and jelly apart.
Kayla B.

Falling through space is like
going to school on Monday. (It never ends!)
Simone W.

MATH IS A HURRICANE OF NUMBERS.
Ariana S.

When my little brother is angry,
It's like a raging tornado
going through the house.
Matthew B.

**Writing a new story
is like creating a new world.**
Matthew B.

The scratching of a pencil
is like the scurry of a mouse.
Tessah J.

Life is like a dark pool of water—
you never know what's in it.
Laura A.

**Math problems are like
hot, boring days that never end.**
Rachael W.

Life is like a gift waiting to be opened.
Camille M.

Life is like an everlasting gobstopper.
Camille M.

Write a comparison for each thing listed on page 129.

Name

Finish the comparisons for Lucy Ann.

1. Life is like _____.

2. School is as _____ as _____.

3. The kids in my class sound like _____.

4. Writing a poem is like _____.

5. Music is _____.

6. Math problems are like _____.

7. Eating potato chips is like _____.

8. This music is as loud as _____.

9. When _____ is angry, it's like _____.

10. Morning is as _____ as _____.

11. I am like _____.

12. My temper is as _____ as _____.

13. The winter was like_____.

14. Losing a friend is like _____.

15. _____ is like _____.

16. Being in the dark is as _____ as _____.

17. Getting your feelings hurt is like_____.

18. Getting stung by a bee is like _____.

19. Moving is like_____.

20. Sisters (or brothers) are like_____.

21. _____ is like _____.

22. _____ is a _____.

Use with page 128.

Name _____

IN MY OPINION

Letters to the editor are strictly opinion. Many people write to the editor of the *Tiny Town Star*. They might comment on something that the newspaper published, or their comments might be about anything at all. Read these letters to the editor. They need some editing! Correct the spelling, punctuation, and capitalization. Cross out any unnecessary ideas. If any ideas are out of order, draw arrows to rearrange them. Make any other changes that will improve the writing.

Dear Editor:

Why are you saying negative things in yur magazine about the new city tax on food in all the restrants. What is your problem? The tax is for a good cauzze. just a small amount on each meal adds up to thousands of dollers for our parks. This is really good for kids. it gives us a wunderful swiming pool, too. This is a small price to pay for so much good stuf the cost is really pretty small And our restrants have good food. If I by a $4.00 sandwich, it only costs 20 extra for the tax. even if someone gets a very expenzave meal—say $50.00, the 5% tax stil only adds $2.50. That's not bad! It gives us nice, cleen places to play socer and softball.

Sincerely,
Whitney

Dear Editer,
In your September issue you had a great article about Pushy snowboarders. I love winter sports I think boarders should be banned from the mountain

Dear Editor,
Your article about snowboarders was terrible and untrue. Why are you picking on snow boarders? They're citizens too. There why don't you get off their backs? signed, Disgruntled

Dear Editor

No one has asked the kids! everywon in the town is talking about year-round school. All the adults keep haveing heerings and meatings to discuss this. some committee is making a plan for school to go thrugh the summer. I am really mad! I am on a dance team. if something is being planned that changes our whole lives, expecially takeing away our summers, it is unfair to go ahead without taking to the students. we have opinions, too we should be the ones to decide this, since it is all about our education.

Sincerely,
Madder Than A Wet Hen

Use with page 131.

Name

IN MY OPINION, CONT.

Write some of your opinions in letters to the editor. Write an opinion about two of the topics suggested, or choose topics of your own. Make sure your personal belief about the topic shows in your writing. Your letter should also include reasons or arguments to support your opinion.

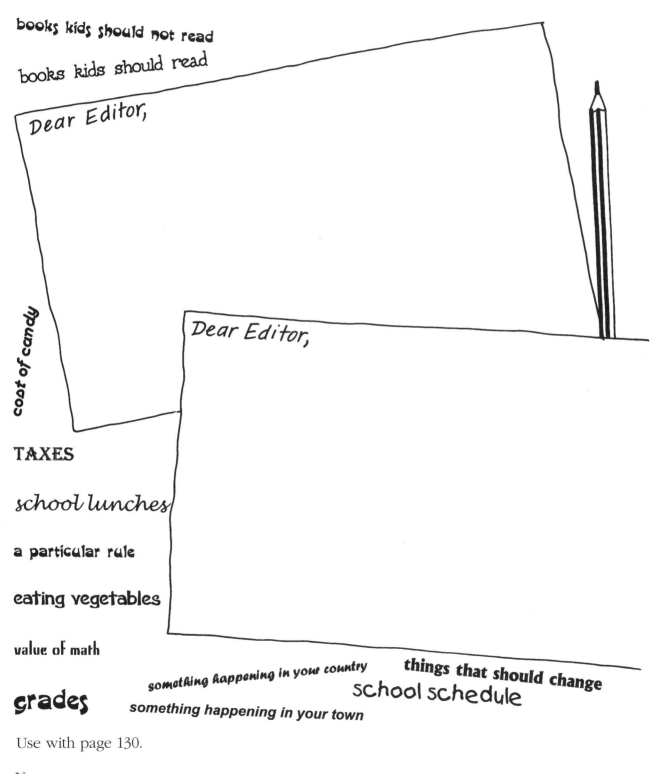

books kids should not read

books kids should read

Dear Editor,

cost of candy

TAXES

school lunches

a particular rule

eating vegetables

value of math

grades

something happening in your country

something happening in your town

Dear Editor,

things that should change

school schedule

Use with page 130.

Name

OLD NEWS IS NEW NEWS

News in Tiny Town is slow today. Lucy Ann decides to turn an old story into today's news by changing the form of writing. A Mother Goose nursery rhyme becomes a news article! She also writes the story of Jack Sprat and his wife in some other forms.

NEWS ARTICLE

COUPLE SUFFERS STRANGE DISEASE

City Center Hospital admitted a man and his wife today. Each suffers from a rare eating disorder. The man, Mr. Jack Sprat, of 1616 Hambone Lane, has a condition that makes it impossible for him to eat anything containing fat. His wife, Maryanne Sprat, of the same address, says she can eat nothing but fat. Both of them are being tested by medical experts who are looking for the cause of their ailments. Doctors are puzzled about how to treat the couple. Mr. Sprat had a positive outlook. "One good thing," he said, "no food is wasted in our household!"

WANT AD

WANTED:
Cook who can prepare both lean and fatty meals for couple.
Call Mr. Sprat
555-0001 after 3 P.M.

LIMERICK

There once was a thin man named Sprat
Whose wife could eat only fat
For dinner he found her
A nice, lean flounder
And it started a horrible spat!

LETTER

Dear Maryanne,
I cannot take it any more! Night after night I sit with my boring watercress and kale and watch while you delight with your French fries and cream puffs, fudgy ice cream, and rich gravy. I have to confess that I crave those rich, fatty foods you eat. I must try them. I beg you, please trade places with me for just one night!
Your loving, starving husband,
Jack

Jack Sprat could eat no fat.
His wife could eat no lean.
And so between the two of them,
They licked the platter clean!

ODE

Ode to a Burger
Oh, how I'd love to taste you
Once...If only I could
You know that I would!
I'd love to savor
Your charcoal flavor
To slurp those juices you've got...
But, alas, I cannot!

TONGUE TWISTER

Two twins with tricky tastes never tasted two tastes.

Use with page 133.

Name

Start with a well-known tale or story. Write it in four different forms. Choose one of the tales listed, or another one you know. Write a limerick, news article, letter, thank-you note, recipe, poem, ad, menu, announcement, song, tall tale, bumper sticker, blog post, speech, or poster based on the story.

Three Little Pigs
Red Riding Hood
Three Blind Mice
The Golden Goose
Jack & the Beanstalk
Snow White
Robin Hood
Cinderella
Little Red Hen
The Three Bears
Chicken Little
Peter Rabbit
Georgie Porgie
Jack Be Nimble
Hickory, Dickory, Dock
Simple Simon
Rapunzel

Draw a photo to go with your story.

Use with page 132.

Name

NO BONES ABOUT IT!

Dear Reader,
Don't be a couch potato!

Dr. Payne Free

The *Tiny Town Star* has just added a "Health & Fitness" page. This page features questions from readers looking for advice from Dr. Payne Free about taking care of their health!

Dr. Free's readers use lots of **figurative language** in their letters. Figurative language is the use of a word or words to mean something different from the literal or usual meaning. Circle the examples of figurative language used in the letters to and from Dr. Free.

- That's a pretty pickle!
- raining cats and dogs
- drive me up a wall
- I can see right through you.
- go out on a limb
- a bone to pick with you
- You spilled the beans.
- not worth a hill of beans
- a frog in my throat
- Don't jump the gun.
- lost her head
- gone bananas
- I'm tickled pink!
- lost her cool
- My car's a real lemon!
- ham it up
- Get out of my hair!
- a backseat driver
- She's pretty burned up.
- tongue tied
- got her nose in a book
- cook your goose
- the last straw
- Keep a lid on it!

Use with page 135.

Dear Dr. Free,
My wife says I'm making too many bones about this topic, but I must ask you about a problem. I've had a frog in my throat for two months. It began one March night when it was raining cats and dogs, and I'm pretty burned up about not being able to get rid of it. I am about to go off my rocker. Can you help me?

Sincerely,
Robert Lozenge

Dear Robert,
You are not barking up the wrong tree! I agree that you're up a creek, for sure! Take four doses of my special defrogging liquid, and you'll be in the pink before long!

Sincerely,
Dr. Free

Dear Dr. Free,
I have been tongue-tied for a long time about my problem, but I'll stick my neck out and ask you. I have been exercising my head off now for six months. Every time I go out for a jog, my ears grow longer. I am not pulling your leg! I am very down in the dumps about this. Should I quit jogging?

Sincerely,
Veronica Lobes

Dear Veronica,
Well, I'll be a monkey's uncle! This takes the cake! This blows my mind! I am stumped! This must be driving you up a wall! Get yourself to the hospital, quick as a wink, for some tests. Let me know what they find!

Sincerely,
Dr. Free

Name

Dear Dr. Free,

I need some facts straight from the horse's mouth! I am fit to be tied. My nose bleeds from sunup to sundown. My father had the same problem. I guess I'm just a chip off the old block! What do you recommend?

Sincerely,
Sam Troubled

Dear Sam,

You should be crying your eyes out, man! I'm going to pass the buck on this one and send you to a blood clinic. I also suggest that if you get near any vampires, you scream your head off and burn rubber getting out of there! Good luck!

Sincerely,
Dr. Free

Now, write a letter of your own to Dr. Free. Also write Dr. Free's answer. Use as many examples of figurative language as you can!

Dear Dr. Payne Free,

Dear _____,

- Don't let her get your goat!
- fit to be tied
- straight from the horse's mouth
- He's a bad apple.
- pass the buck
- eat humble pie
- dressed to the nines
- cat's got her tongue
- up a creek
- in hot water
- shaking in my boots
- He'll bite my head off!
- a red-letter day
- blow her top
- go off his rocker
- lost his marbles
- take the cake
- screaming bloody murder!
- quick as a wink
- Make no bones about it.
- pull the wool over your eyes
- in the doghouse
- let the cat out of the bag
- crying your eyes out
- down in the dumps
- madder than a wet hen

Use with page 134.

Name

135

HE SAID...SHE SAID

The cartoonist uses "talk balloons" to show what the characters are saying. When you write about a conversation, you must include dialogue in the paragraphs.

For each conversation in the cartoon, write a paragraph that includes the dialogue. Make sure you use quotation marks and other punctuation marks correctly. Use another sheet of paper.

Name _____

IN THE MOOD

There's screaming! There's excitement! The crowd is wild! Lucy Ann's assignment tonight is to write a story about the high school championship football game. Everyone in town will want to read about this. She needs to choose the right words and phrases to let readers know what it is like to be at the game.

Lucy Ann chose the phrases below to set the mood. Add three (or more) words or phrases to help Lucy Ann.

crashing of helmets
roaring crowd   wild cheers
screeching, screaming
wild excitement
sweet, sticky cotton candy
salty, greasy, yummy popcorn
speeding runners   crisp, fall air
inviting smell of steamy hot dogs and strong coffee
arms waving and fans jumping
cartwheels and flips of cheerleaders
nonstop celebration and backslapping
laughter, moans, groans, squeals

Your assignment is to write about the topics below. How will you set the mood? Write several words and phrases that will set a particular mood for each one. You may also write an opening line to set the mood.

A mystery	A poem about a tornado	A description of a soft snowfall

PICTURE THIS

Lucy Ann's friend Sam takes photographs to match many of her news stories. Some of the pictures for tomorrow's paper were lost. Some of the writing was lost, too! Replace the missing writing and photographs on these two pages.

If the writing is missing, write a story, article, advertisement, poem, joke, essay, opinion, letter, or other feature to match the visual story presented by the picture. If the photo is missing, draw a picture that illustrates the article.

1.

Sharks have come to our beaches! Lifeguards and swimmers have reported many sightings of sharks close to shore at the beaches south of the city. One surfer reported a very close call. A shark actually took a huge bite out of his board! Sharks rarely come into the swimming area or bother swimmers. Officials have closed the beaches to swimmers until further notice—and until the sharks move on to deeper waters!

Use with page 139.

2.

_____

_____

_____

_____

_____

_____

_____

_____

_____

Name _____

PICTURE THIS, CONT.

If the writing is missing, write a story, article, advertisement, or other feature to match the picture. If the photo is missing, draw a picture that illustrates the article.

3. Another tightrope walker attempts to cross the Grand Canyon. Tomasina M. Balance took her first steps at noon on Thursday in what was the first attempt to cross the canyon in years. She balanced for 45 minutes before breathless crowds on both sides of the canyon. Much to the relief of everyone, she successfully completed the walk!

4. The mayor gave away a key to the city today to a special guest. Tiny Town was visited by Pierre the Giant, a well-known actor who is over eight feet tall and weighs 450 pounds. Pierre was born in Tiny Town, but he has not visited the city since he was in first grade. It was quite a sight to see him stand beside Mayor Cathy Graham, who is only 5 feet 1 inch tall in her high heels!

Leonardo de Chimpa

5. _____

Use with page 138.

Name

WORDS ON THE MOVE

The words just don't seem to want to sit still on the page today! They keep winding and moving all over. Lucy Ann is preparing a page with writing that looks as if it were painted on the page instead of written in nice, neat lines. You could call this *painted* writing!

Read the page. Then choose one of the ideas from the Idea File, and try some painted writing of your own. Use another piece of paper.

Tiny Town Star —— PAINTED POEMS

COFFEE

Warm and steamy, I brew down
And swim around. I jump down,
I jump down into a big cozy mug.
I stir around with some sweet tasty
Cream. Once I settle down a little, I enjoy
Myself and start to doze, until my warm
And sweet, sweet life is stirred and
Mixed and swallowed down. Coffee.
I'm new again in rich dark
Beans. I grind and grind
And brew and stir. *

Soft dough swirls with plump raisins, and sugary cinnamon, and buttery icing.

A slithery, slinky snake sneaks under my desk, so silently and stealthily, like a whisper across my feet.

*Poem written by Tahli O., Gr. 4

IDEA FILE
a hopping bug
an octopus
sound waves
a bouncing ball
falling leaves
a secret
ocean waves
a pretzel
a juggler
a bothersome bee

angel wings
melting ice cream
music
a ski trail
a wild, winding river
swinging on a swing
a layered sandwich
footsteps
a pogo stick trail
a flock of birds

Name

140

STOMACH-FLIPPING NEWS

Today's hot news is the stomach-flipping, nerve-wracking, crowd-pleasing new *CYCLONE-LAND AMUSEMENT PARK*. It just opened yesterday, and crowds are flocking to try the thrilling rides. After Lucy Ann's friend Charlie tried a few for his report, his sentences got a bit scrambled. They don't say exactly what he means! *(For example, in #1—he seems to be saying that the stomachache was riding The Corkscrew!)* Clear up the confusion! Rewrite each sentence so that its meaning is clear.

1. While riding **The Corkscrew** for the third time, a stomachache bothered me.

_____

_____

2. As a child, my dad took me on roller coasters every weekend.

_____

_____

3. I'll write about the pirates who robbed ships in the newspaper.

_____

_____

4. While riding **The Plunge,** the wind picked up.

_____

_____

5. A clown sold cold ice cream bars to the children with sprinkles.

_____

_____

6. Some teenagers were banned from **The Train of Terror** after breaking the rules by the manager.

_____

_____

7. After fainting on the ride through **The Python's Den,** the kids worried that their mother would never recover.

_____

_____

8. Having fallen off her seat into **The Raging River,** the students tried to pull their teacher back into the raft.

_____

_____

9. To save money for a day at the amusement park, Mrs. Burton hired Tim and Tom to clean her garage.

_____

_____

10. Last, I visited the **Haunted Mansion** beside the ticket booth that was very scary.

_____

_____

Name _____

SOCIAL STUDIES

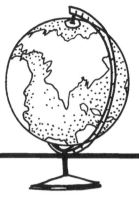

Skills Exercises
Grade Four

SKILLS CHECKLIST
Geography of the United States & Neighboring Countries

✔	SKILL	PAGE(S)
	Locate a variety of places and features on a map	146, 147, 150–155, 161–163, 166, 168–178
	Identify and locate the states of the U.S. and their capitals	146, 147, 150–159, 161
	Identify features of states	148, 149
	Locate and identify important U.S. landmarks	148, 149
	Identify and locate major bodies of water in the United States	146, 147, 155
	Identify resources, products, and features associated with specific U.S. regions	150–159
	Locate the major U.S. regional divisions and identify the states in them	150–159
	Identify some characteristics or features of the Pacific Region	151
	Identify states in the Pacific Region	151
	Identify some characteristics or features of the Mountain Region	152
	Identify states in the Mountain Region	152
	Identify some characteristics or features of the Plains Region	153
	Identify states in the Plains Region	153
	Identify some characteristics or features of the Southwest Region	154
	Identify states in the Southwest Region	154
	Identify some characteristics or features of the Great Lakes Region	155
	Identify states in the Great Lakes Region	155
	Identify some characteristics or features of the Southeast Region	156
	Identify states in the Southeast Region	156
	Identify some characteristics or features of the Middle Atlantic Region	157
	Identify states in the Middle Atlantic Region	157
	Identify some characteristics or features of the New England Region	158
	Identify states in the New England Region	158
	Identify some landmarks and institutions in Washington, D.C.	160
	Identify, locate, and describe major features of key U.S. cities	160, 165
	Identify key physical features of the United States	162, 163
	Locate, describe, and illustrate major landforms of the United States	162, 163
	Identify location of some national parks and monuments	164
	Identify and locate the world's hemispheres, continents, and oceans	166
	Locate the United States and its neighbors on a world map	166
	Identify own location in the world	167
	Make a map of own state, including major physical and political features	167
	Distinguish location of continents within hemispheres	168
	Identify key lines of latitude and longitude	169
	Use latitude and longitude lines to locate places	169–171
	Answer questions related to time zones within the U.S.; use a time zone map	172, 173
	Identify and locate U.S. neighbors in North America	174–177
	Identify political, geographic, and physical features of Canada	176, 177
	Identify political, economic, and physical features of Mexico	178, 179
	Identify political and physical features of South America	180
	Recognize city names; identify cities in own state	181
	Identify U.S. landmarks, places, and features	182, 183

SKILLS CHECKLIST
Map Skills & Geography

✔	SKILL	PAGE(S)
	Make and use map keys	184, 185
	Identify, draw, and use map symbols	184, 185, 191
	Identify many different kinds of maps	184, 185, 193, 194
	Identify different map tools and resources	184, 185, 194
	Use a variety of maps to find information	184–189, 191, 193–195, 198–201
	Use a variety of maps to answer questions	184–189, 191, 194–201
	Use maps and globes to find and compare locations	184–189, 193, 195, 198
	Identify and find directions on a map	184–189, 193, 195–199
	Recognize landforms on a map	186, 187
	Recognize continents and bodies of water on world and U.S. maps	188, 189
	Identify many countries on world or continent maps	188–190
	Become familiar with countries in North America and Central America	190
	Distinguish among cities, states, countries, and bodies of water in North America and Central America	190
	Use scales to determine distances on maps	191, 192
	Identify parts of a map: key, title, symbols, compass, scale	192
	Find information on a weather map	195
	Use a subway map to locate places	196, 197
	Locate and place objects on grids	198
	Use a floor plan to locate places	200, 201

GETTING TO KNOW THE USA

The travelers need to know their way around the great USA. This map will help them, but it has some important things missing. Finish the map, so the bikers, hikers, cyclists, fliers, and motorists can find their way around the country!

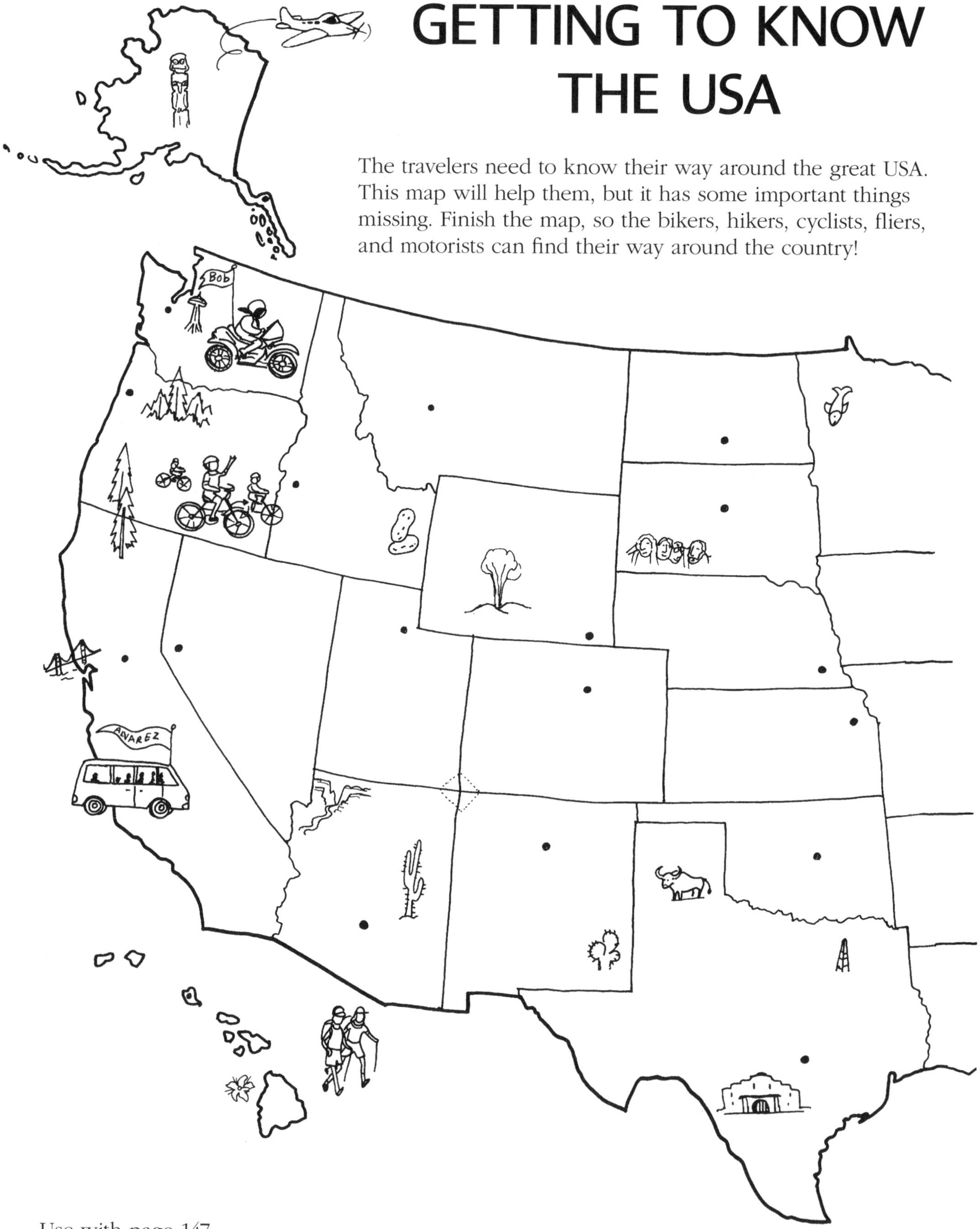

Bob

ALVAREZ

Use with page 147.

Name

146

Label the following places on the map.

1. Write the correct name on each state.

2. Write the correct capital on each state.

3. Label these: Atlantic Ocean   Lake Ontario   Pacific Ocean   Lake Erie
                 Gulf of Mexico   Lake Huron   Lake Michigan   Lake Superior

4. Find the symbols that stand for these. Write the name next to the symbol.

   Statue of Liberty   Alamo   Yellowstone National Park
   Golden Gate Bridge   Grand Canyon   Mt. Rushmore
   Sea World   Kentucky Derby   Space Needle
                          Gateway Arch

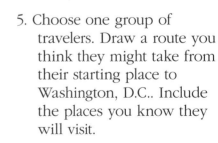

5. Choose one group of travelers. Draw a route you think they might take from their starting place to Washington, D.C.. Include the places you know they will visit.

   Color the states that they will travel through if they follow your route!

Use with page 146.

Name

WHAT A WAY . . .

Everyone wants to see the USA—and why not? It's full of awesome sights—high spots and low spots, hidden rivers, high bridges, deep caves, mysterious caverns, volcanoes, geysers, rocket launch pads, and diamond mines!

Follow these five groups of travelers as they discover the beauties and thrills of the USA and neighboring countries.

The Fairbanks Frequent Fliers leave their state of _____ (the coldest state with the highest mountain in the USA) and head east across the country. Below are clues about a few of the states they will visit. Name each state.

1. _____ Tulsa and the Cowboy Hall of Fame

2. _____ ghost towns, Sun Valley, and potatoes

3. _____ Baltimore Orioles and the U.S. Naval Academy

4. _____ Rocky Mountains, Boulder, and Mesa Verde

5. _____ Abe Lincoln's home and the Art Institute of Chicago

6. _____ site of the first gold rush and the 1996 Summer Olympics

The Honolulu Hiking Club has been planning their trip for two years. They start from their home state of _____ (the state made up of 123 islands) and fly across the Pacific to begin their hike. Below are clues about the states they will visit. Name each state.

7. _____ Country Music Capital of the World

8. _____ Bryce Canyon and the Great Salt Lake

9. _____ Yellowstone National Park and geysers

10. _____ site of Wounded Knee and Mt. Rushmore

11. _____ "Land of 10,000 Lakes" and home of U.S. Hockey Hall of Fame

12. _____ home of 8 U.S. presidents and the Arlington National Cemetery

Use with page 149

Name _____

. . . TO SEE THE USA

The Falls City Folks & Spokes Club starts its trip from the state of
_____ (site of the deepest lake and the deepest
canyon in the United States). Name the states they plan to visit.

13. _____ Mardi Gras and the U.S.'s busiest seaport

14. _____ a two-part state, makes cars, largest lake entirely in USA

15. _____ Grand Canyon, Painted Desert, and the Petrified Forest

16. _____ Mammoth Cave, Kentucky Derby, "Bluegrass State"

17. _____ Niagara Falls, U.S.'s largest city, and the Statue of Liberty

The Alvarez family is heading off to see relatives all over the
country. They start from their home state, _____
(the Golden State—home of Hollywood, the Golden Gate Bridge, and
Sequoia National Park). Name the states they plan to visit.

18. _____ the smallest state in the USA

19. _____ the "Lone Star State," home of the Alamo

20. _____ the "Buckeye State" and the Rock and Roll Hall of Fame and Museum

21. _____ home of Walt Disney World and the Everglades Swamp

22. _____ maple sugar, the Green Mountains, and the first ski tow

They're all named Bob (or some form of Bob), and they all have
motorbikes. Their club is called "Bobs on Bikes!" Their home state of
_____ has great apples, the Space Needle, and
Mt. St. Helens. Name the states they plan to visit.

23. _____ state song: "Yankee Doodle"

24. _____ home of the Liberty Bell and Valley Forge

25. _____ Civil War began here, home of Ft. Sumter

26. _____ Boston Tea Party, Cape Cod, and Plymouth Rock

27. _____ first place sun hits USA in the morning, great lobsters

Use with page 148.

Name _____

THE REASONS FOR REGIONS

The Alvarez family has so many relatives! They will visit some in every one of the eight regions of the United States. Juanita is going to mail maps to all the relatives, so they can join the trip if they wish!

The country is divided into regions according to some common features. You can learn about the regions by organizing and color-coding the states. This trick will help you remember these regions better!

First, put a star to show the location of each state's capital. Then color the states according to the color key. Use a U.S. map or an atlas to help you!

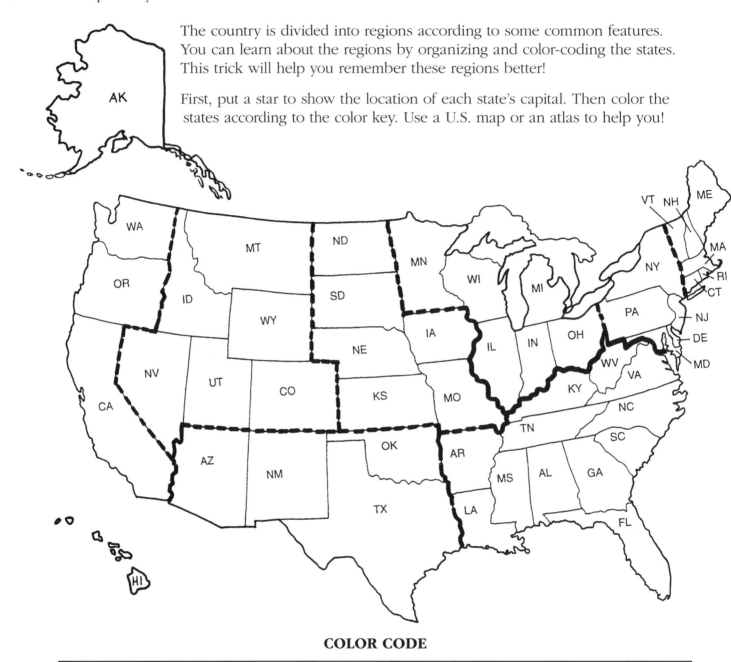

COLOR CODE

Pacific States	Blue	Plains States	Purple
Great Lakes States	Yellow	Middle Atlantic States	Red
Mountain States	Brown	Southwest States	Orange
Southeast States	Green	New England States	Gray

Name _____

BIG TREES & WILD SURF

The Pacific Region is home to all these groups who are exploring the USA! It is the western-most region in the country. The five states that make up the region have at least one thing in common—they all touch the Pacific Ocean. They each have many unique features, also. Use an atlas to learn about these states.

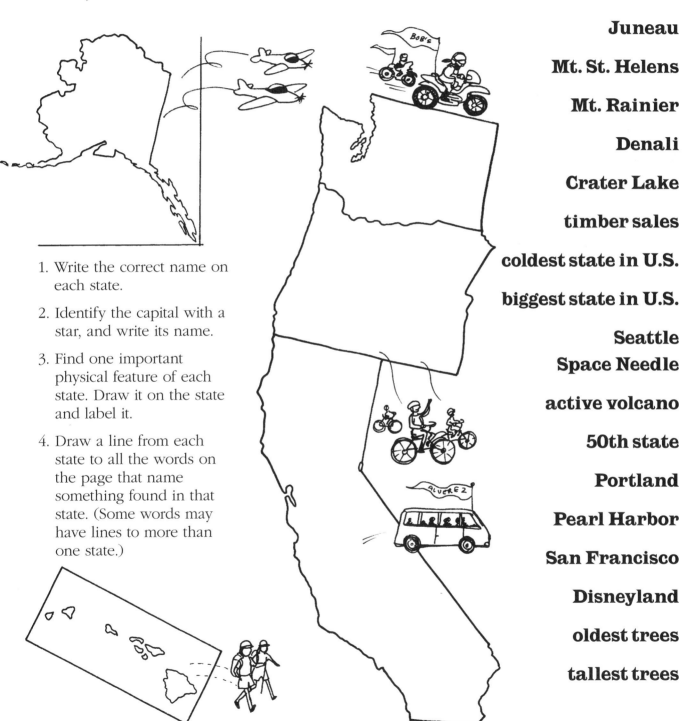

1. Write the correct name on each state.

2. Identify the capital with a star, and write its name.

3. Find one important physical feature of each state. Draw it on the state and label it.

4. Draw a line from each state to all the words on the page that name something found in that state. (Some words may have lines to more than one state.)

Juneau

Mt. St. Helens

Mt. Rainier

Denali

Crater Lake

timber sales

coldest state in U.S.

biggest state in U.S.

Seattle

Space Needle

active volcano

50th state

Portland

Pearl Harbor

San Francisco

Disneyland

oldest trees

tallest trees

Name

HIGH PEAKS & DEEP CANYONS

What a thrill to fly over the Rocky Mountains! The Fairbanks Frequent Fliers have seen plenty of mountains in their home state of Alaska, but visiting the peaks and high plains of the Mountain Region is a new adventure. The Continental Divide, Yellowstone National Park, Zion National Park, and Glacier National Park are some of the important geographic landmarks of this region. Many major rivers that flow through the western United States have their source in the Mountain Region.

Follow these directions to sharpen your knowledge about this region.

1. Label each state.

2. Locate and label each capital.

3. In addition, label one or more major cities in each state.

4. With a purple pencil, draw and label the major mountains.

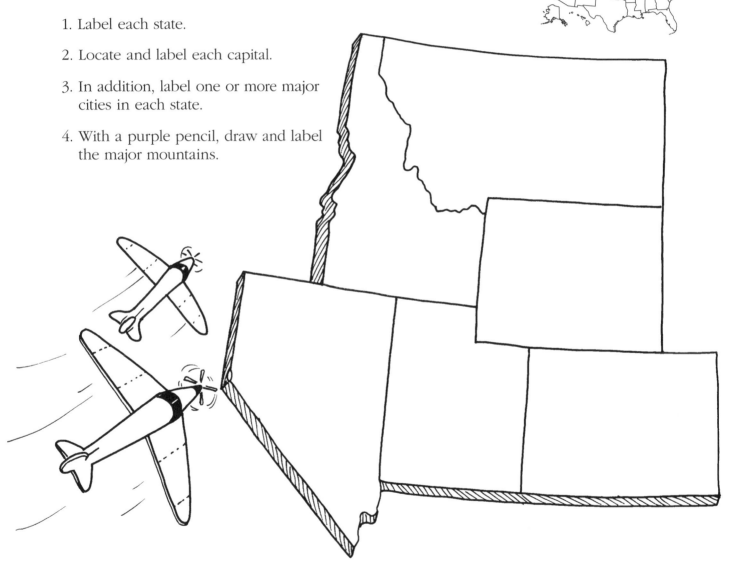

5. With a blue pencil, draw and label four major rivers and the Great Salt Lake.

6. Color the area of the Great Basin yellow.

Extra Challenge: Find all the features named in the introduction (above) and label them.

Name

TALL GRASSES & TWISTERS

The Honolulu Hikers find easy hiking on the wide, flat plains of the middle United States. They plan to hike through all six of the Plains States, a region of waist-high grasses and over-your-head corn, tornadoes, and fierce thunderstorms. They can escape this twister if you can label each state and finish the tasks. Use the back of the page or a separate piece of paper.

1. North Dakota has the largest percentage of people working in agriculture. Name at least four crops that they produce.

2. Make a sketch of what the hikers will see when they visit Mount Rushmore in South Dakota.

3. "Buffalo Bill" Cody and his Wild West shows started in the state of Nebraska. Find out three other interesting facts about Nebraska.

4. Draw a map of Iowa. Sioux City has the nation's largest popcorn plant. Cedar Rapids has the largest cereal manufacturing mill. Place both cities on the map.

5. Four important landmarks in Missouri are the Gateway Arch, Mark Twain's home and museum, the Harry S. Truman Historic Site, and the Pony Express Stables. Tell the location where the hikers can find each of these landmarks.

6. "There's no place like home," says Dorothy in *The Wizard of Oz*. Home for Dorothy and Toto was the state of Kansas. Create a poster or travel brochure telling about six things the hikers and other tourists should visit in Kansas.

Label each state with its name.

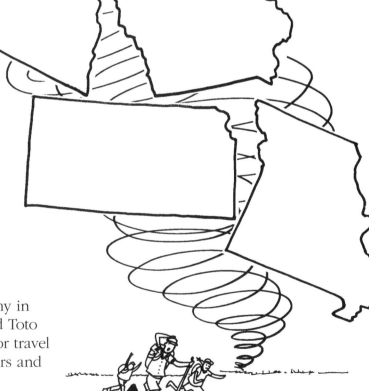

Name _____

COWS, COWBOYS, & CACTI

What comes to your mind when you think of the Southwest United States? The Alvarez kids think about cowboys, cows, and cacti. Is this what they'll find in the Southwestern states? Get some reference books, and find out about these states for yourself!

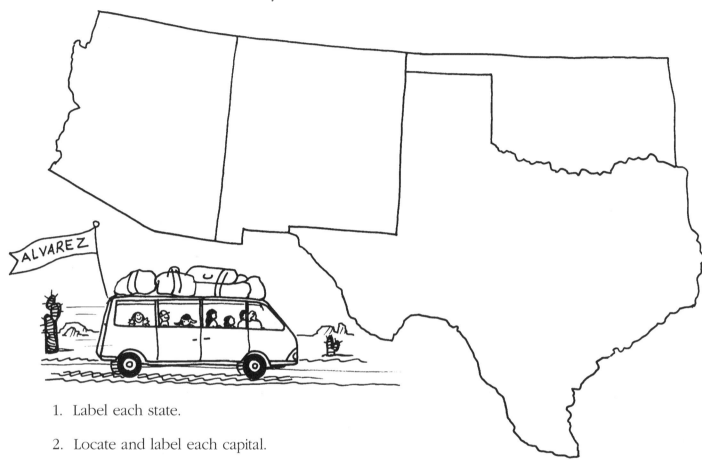

1. Label each state.

2. Locate and label each capital.

3. The Alvarez family will visit each of these cities: Yuma, Houston, Albuquerque, Amarillo, Enid, Roswell, Dallas, Flagstaff, El Paso, and Tulsa. Locate and label each city on the map, and draw a route the family might follow to these cities.

4. Draw a symbol for a major landmark in each state. Label it.

5. Write the state nickname on each state.

6. Draw a symbol for one important product from each state.

7. These four states have a rich Native American heritage. See if you can find out the names of some of the tribal groups that live or have lived in these states. List them here:

_____

_____

Name _____

154

LAKES & MORE LAKES

The bikers are racing through every state that touches one of the Great Lakes. These lakes are the largest freshwater lakes in the world. Even oceangoing ships can travel on them. The contain enough water to cover the whole United States with a flood ten feet deep. You can always remember the names of the lakes if you know that the first letters of the lakes spell **homes** (Huron, Ontario, Michigan, Erie, and Superior).

1. Label each of the Great Lakes.

2. Label each state and its capital.

3. The Bobs will learn many things as they travel the Great Lakes Region. Finish the words to show some facts about the Great Lakes states.

A. An important field crop of this region   1. ___ **o** ___ ___

B. Detroit is famous for manufacturing   2. ___ ___ ___ **o** ___ **o** ___ ___ ___ ___

C. Wisconsin is famous for producing   3. ___ ___ **e** ___ ___ ___

D. The Indianapolis 500 Raceway is located in   4. ___ ___ ___ **i** ___ ___ ___ ___ ___ ___ ___ ___

E. Source of the Mississippi River is in   5. ___ ___ ___ ___ ___ ___ ___ ___ **a**

F. Home of seven U.S. presidents   6. ___ ___ **i** ___

G. More than half of the people in Illinois live in   7. ___ ___ ___ ___ **a** ___ ___

H. Most valuable rock mined in Indiana   8. ___ ___ **a** ___

I. The only Great Lake not bordering Michigan   9. **O** ___ ___ ___ ___ ___ ___

J. State with the most water area   10. ___ ___ ___ ___ **e** ___ ___ ___ ___

Name _____

BAYOUS, BEACHES, & HOSPITALITY

The Falls City cyclists have twelve states to cover in the Southeast Region of the United States. This is an area that is proud of its culture and heritage. It ranges from the "South" to the "Deep South"! Many people get these states confused! Can you get them straight?

Directions:

1. Label each state.

2. Find the name of each capital in the word search and circle it. (Words may be written across, up, down, backwards, or diagonally.)

3. Then locate and label the capital on the state.

```
C H A R L E S T O N L T M
F R A N K F O R T M I T O
C B R I C H M O N D A T N
O D A Q O N Q S W L R N T
L N K T H J W D L X A S G
U O N Z O M H A X V L H O
M S X H S N H R D E E V M
B K M F A A R C D V I I E
I C O B S A T O W H G L R
A A V S N W P B U K H L Y
C J E D F P J R Q G D E V
S E D A T N A L T A E X H
L I T T L E R O C K B F G
```

BIG CITIES & CAPITALS

Three different cities have been capitals of the United States: New York City, Philadelphia, and Washington, D.C. The Bobs will bike through all of them on their tour of the Middle Atlantic Region. All five of the states in this region were original colonies that became the United States. Many of the country's largest cities are in this region. Solve this puzzle about the Middle Atlantic Region. If you need help, use an almanac, an atlas, or a map.

1. Label the states and their capitals.

2. Locate and label the U.S. capital.

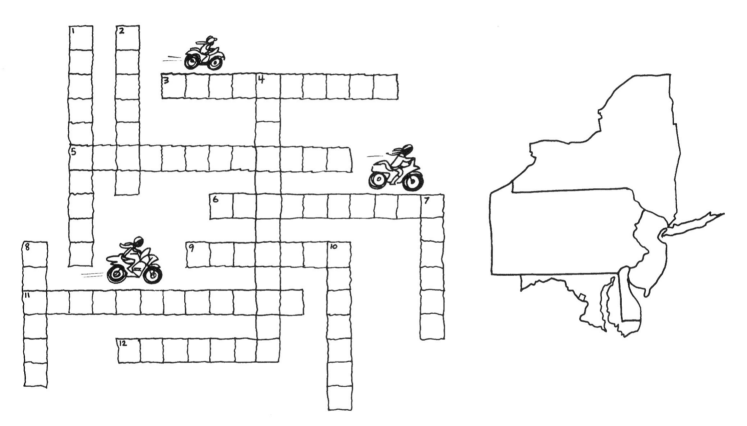

Down:

1. Delaware city known as chemical capital of the world

2. River on which Washington, D.C., is located

4. New Jersey town that was used as a model for the game of Monopoly®

7. River separating New York from New Jersey, named for Dutch explorer

8. Delaware's largest chemical company

10. Largest city in the United States

Across:

3. Bay that divides the state of Maryland

5. New York state's natural wonder

6. Pennsylvania city located at the joining of two rivers

9. Tunnel connecting New Jersey and New York City, named after a U.S. president

11. City where Declaration of Independence was signed

12. Chocolate-themed amusement park located in _____, PA

Name _____

HISTORY & HIGH TIDES

Plymouth Rock, pilgrims, cold, snow, patriots, politics, fishing, mountains, beautiful fall colors, rugged seashores—these are all things the Alvarez family will find in New England.

Locate and label each state and its capital. Use your atlas, encyclopedia, textbook, or the Internet to find information to complete the chart.

Comparing New England States

STATE	Capital	A Major River	Industry or Products	Natural Resources
Connecticut				
Maine				
Massachusetts				
New Hampshire				
Rhode Island				
Vermont				

Name

WHICH REGION?

These travel brochures have been collected from all the U.S. regions. They list several places and things to see in each region. Review the eight U.S. regions by giving the correct region name to each brochure.

America the Beautiful

1
Honolulu
tallest volcano
Disneyland
Mt. McKinley
Oregon
Puget Sound
redwood forests

2
Minnesota
dairy farming
Chicago
Indianapolis 500
Wisconsin
Lake Superior
10,000 lakes

3
Great Salt Lake
Rocky Mountains
Glacier Park
Las Vegas
Denver
Sun Valley
Montana
Yellowstone Park

for spacious skies and purple mountains majesty...America.....

4
Baltimore
Lincoln Tunnel
Atlantic City
Hershey Factories
Philadelphia
Liberty Bell
New York City

5
Dallas & Oklahoma City
New Mexico
cattle ranches
Rio Grande River
"Lone Star" State
Grand Canyon

SEE AMERICA 6
12 states
Alabama
South Carolina
Little Rock
coal mines
The Everglades
Kentucky Derby

7
North Dakota
tall grass
corn and wheat
Des Moines
Mt. Rushmore

see the U.S.A in a brand new way...from the stream waters to the great lakes

8
Hartford
Revolutionary War
smallest state
lobsters
maple syrup
Boston
Maine
pilgrims

Name

WHICH WAY IN WASHINGTON, D.C.?

Every member of the motorbike club is headed for a different attraction in Washington, D.C. Which Bob will go which way? Read the description of the monument, building, park, or other attraction in the nation's capital. Then match it up with the right Bob by writing its letter next to his or her name.

Where they went . . .

_____ 1. Bobby Joe—Lincoln Memorial

_____ 2. Bob Roberts—Vietnam Veterans Memorial

_____ 3. Bobbi Jean—Smithsonian Institute

_____ 4. Bobbo Bones—Capitol Building

_____ 5. Bob Jones—White House

_____ 6. Old Bob—National Archives

_____ 7. Bobbi Lou Laws—Supreme Court Building

_____ 8. Bob Books—Library of Congress

_____ 9. Bobby Sneak—FBI Headquarters

_____ 10. Roberto B. Curious—Washington Monument

_____ 11. Rob Ray—U.S. Holocaust Memorial

_____ 12. Bobbie Berggler—Bureau of Engraving & Printing

What they found . . .

A. place where U.S. paper money is made

B. home of highest crime agency in the U.S.

C. tall, white, marble pillar; dedicated to first U.S. president

D. white sandstone residence of the president

E. serves as national library with more than 160 million items in 470 languages

F. museum and memorial to victims killed by Hitler's regime

G. collection of 14 museums

H. large building with columns and a statue of a seated president inside

I. home of Department of Justice and Supreme Court

J. place to see the Constitution, Declaration of Independence, and Bill of Rights

K. black granite wall with 58,000 names of those who died in a war

L. home of the U.S. Congress

Name _____

160

STATE HOPPING

The Alvarez children have a great game to occupy their time while they travel. It's called "State Hopping." In the game, they draw cards that tell them how to find states by starting at other states. Use a U.S. map (or your memory) to find the states where they will land with each of these cards. Write the answer on the card. There may be more than one possible answer to some problems.

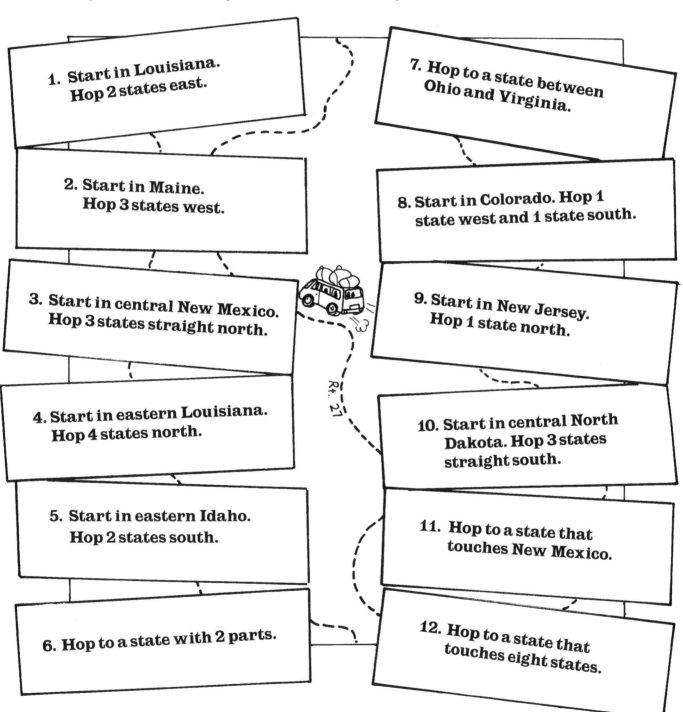

1. Start in Louisiana. Hop 2 states east.

2. Start in Maine. Hop 3 states west.

3. Start in central New Mexico. Hop 3 states straight north.

4. Start in eastern Louisiana. Hop 4 states north.

5. Start in eastern Idaho. Hop 2 states south.

6. Hop to a state with 2 parts.

7. Hop to a state between Ohio and Virginia.

8. Start in Colorado. Hop 1 state west and 1 state south.

9. Start in New Jersey. Hop 1 state north.

10. Start in central North Dakota. Hop 3 states straight south.

11. Hop to a state that touches New Mexico.

12. Hop to a state that touches eight states.

Rt. 27

Name

UP, DOWN, OVER, & AROUND

U.S. travelers need a map of the physical features of the United States. This is the only way they will know when they are going to travel over peaks, into valleys, across rivers, or around lakes.

Use with page 163.

Name _____

162

Use the map on pages 162 and 163 to locate some of the most important physical features of the United States. Write each number from the map next to the matching name in the list.

Color the bodies of water blue, the mountains purple, the plains dark green, and the deserts yellow. Color the rest of the areas light green. Outline the borders of your state in red.

_____ A. Rocky Mts.   _____ D. Coastal Range
_____ B. Lake Ontario   _____ E. Lake Erie
_____ C. Alaska Range

_____ F. Grand Canyon
_____ G. Mississippi River
_____ H. Rio Grande River
_____ I. Great Basin
_____ J. Great Plains
_____ K. Lake Huron
_____ L. Sierra Nevada Mts.
_____ M. Columbia River
_____ N. Great Salt Lake
_____ O. Green Mts.
_____ P. Denali
_____ Q. Mississippi Delta
_____ R. Missouri River
_____ S. Lake Superior
_____ T. Mojave Desert
_____ U. Appalachian Mts.
_____ V. Central Plains
_____ W. Gulf Coastal Plain
_____ X. St. Lawrence River
_____ Y. Atlantic Coastal Plain
_____ Z. Lake Michigan
_____ XX. Mt. Mauna Kea
_____ YY. Everglades Swamp
_____ ZZ. Cascade Mts.

Use with page 162.

Name

NATIONAL TREASURES

Some of the most awesome sights around the USA are protected in national parks or marked as national monuments. Millions of people visit them every year. Below are a few of them. On each stamp, write the abbreviation of the state or states where that park or monument can be found. Some states will match more than one place.

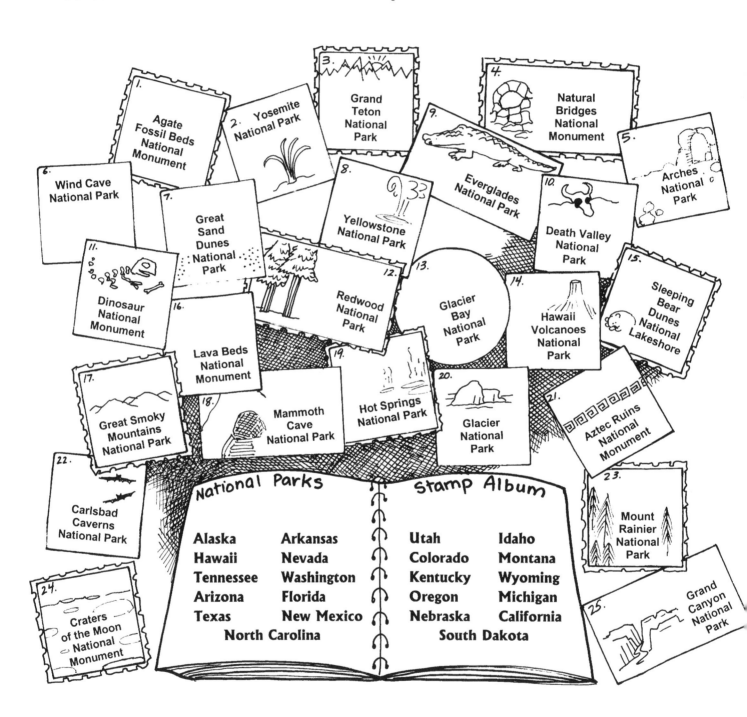

1. Agate Fossil Beds National Monument
2. Yosemite National Park
3. Grand Teton National Park
4. Natural Bridges National Monument
5. Arches National Park
6. Wind Cave National Park
7. Great Sand Dunes National Park
8. Yellowstone National Park
9. Everglades National Park
10. Death Valley National Park
11. Dinosaur National Monument
12. Redwood National Park
13. Glacier Bay National Park
14. Hawaii Volcanoes National Park
15. Sleeping Bear Dunes National Lakeshore
16. Lava Beds National Monument
17. Great Smoky Mountains National Park
18. Mammoth Cave National Park
19. Hot Springs National Park
20. Glacier National Park
21. Aztec Ruins National Monument
22. Carlsbad Caverns National Park
23. Mount Rainier National Park
24. Craters of the Moon National Monument
25. Grand Canyon National Park

National Parks **Stamp Album**

Alaska	Arkansas	Utah	Idaho
Hawaii	Nevada	Colorado	Montana
Tennessee	Washington	Kentucky	Wyoming
Arizona	Florida	Oregon	Michigan
Texas	New Mexico	Nebraska	California
North Carolina		South Dakota	

Name _____

NOT THE CAPITAL!

The Fairbanks Frequent Fliers have landed their planes in many large cities that are not capital cities. Twenty-five of these cities are hidden in this puzzle. They may be written across, up, down, backwards, or diagonally. Find a city for each of these states and circle it! (Some states have two.) The first letter of each city is given.

North Dakota (F)
Texas (E and H)
California (L)
Florida (M)
Wisconsin (M)
Alabama (M)
New Jersey (N)
Louisiana (N)
Oregon (P)
Nevada (R)
Georgia (S)
Washington (S)
Oklahoma (T)
New Mexico (A)
Maryland (B)
New York (B)
Vermont (B)
South Carolina (C)
Illinois (C)
Pennsylvania (P and P)
Ohio (C)
Michigan (D)
Alaska (F)

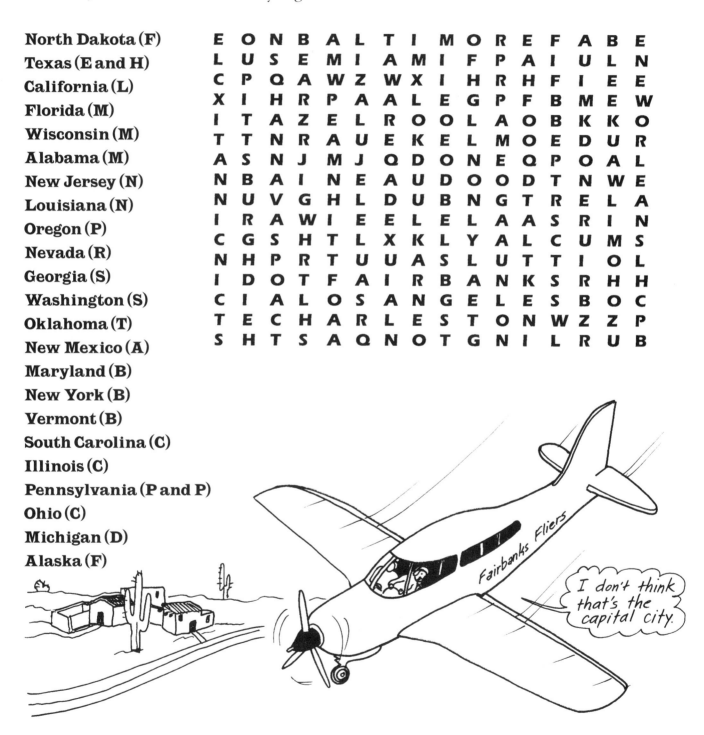

```
E O N B A L T I M O R E F A B E
L U S E M I A M I F P A I U L N
C P Q A W Z W X I H R H F I E E
X I H R P A A L E G P F B M E W
I T A Z E L R O O L A O B K K O
T T N R A U E K E L M O E D U R
A S N J M J Q D O N E Q P O A L
N B A I N E A U D O O D T N W E
N U V G H L D U B N G T R E L A
I R A W I E E L E L A A S R I N
C G S H T L X K L Y A L C U M S
N H P R T U U A S L U T T I O L
I D O T F A I R B A N K S R H H
C I A L O S A N G E L E S B O C
T E C H A R L E S T O N W Z Z P
S H T S A Q N O T G N I L R U B
```

OH, SAY CAN YOU SEE THE USA?

Where in the world is the United States of America? Help the Fairbanks Frequent Fliers zero in on the USA on this world map while you sharpen your knowledge about world geography.

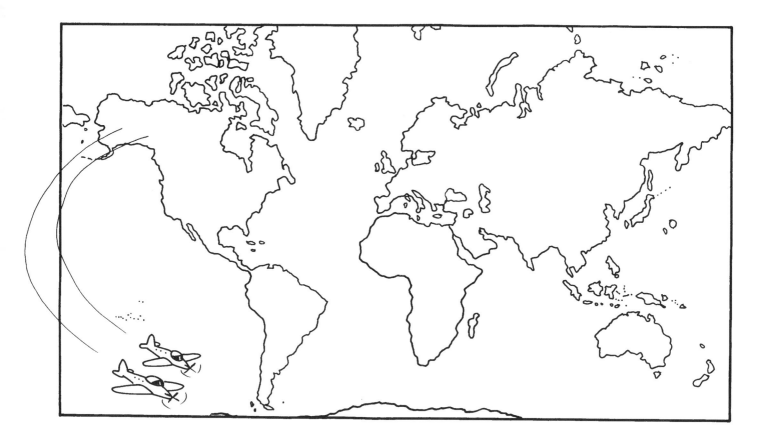

1. Using a green pencil or marker, label each of the continents pictured.

2. Label each of the world's oceans with a blue pencil or marker.

3. Next, use a blue pencil or marker to label the Gulf of Mexico, Bering Strait, and Hudson Bay.

4. With a red pencil or marker, outline the borders of the United States. Label the United States, Canada, and Mexico.

5. Place a star to locate the capitals of the United States, Canada, and Mexico. Then label each capital.

Name

WHERE ARE YOU?

Where in the world are **you?** How would any world travelers (or space travelers) find you? These visitors are trying to find you. Write your complete address to help them. Include your name, street, state, country, continent, planet, and galaxy!

Now, show the visitors some things about your home. Draw an outline of your state or province. Do not trace the map! Then put all the things on it that you see on the list. Label everything you put on the map, give it a title, and add a key.

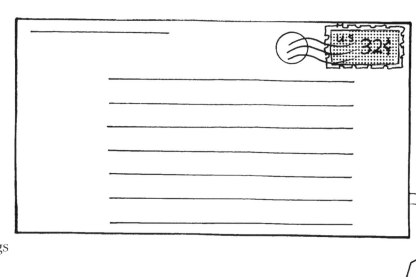

Put on Map
Your town
Capital
Major Cities
Rivers & Lakes
Historic Sites
Other features
of interest

My State

Name _____

WHAT'S IN WHICH HALF?

EASTERN HEMISPHERE

WESTERN HEMISPHERE

NORTHERN HEMISPHERE

SOUTHERN HEMISPHERE

The world is divided into four imaginary halves called hemispheres. Which half has the USA? Is the USA in more than one? Use the four maps of the hemispheres to find out what is in which half!

1. Locate and trace the equator in red on each of the hemispheric maps.

2. Mark the North and/or South Pole on each map with a green N or a purple S.

3. Where is the USA? Write the hemispheres:

   _____

   _____

4. In how many hemispheres is each continent located?

   Africa _____, Antarctica _____, Asia _____,

   Australia _____, Europe _____,

   North America _____, South America _____

5. In which hemisphere(s) are each of the oceans located?

   Arctic _____

   Atlantic _____

   Indian _____

   Pacific _____

6. Name the continents that are located partly or totally in each hemisphere.

   Northern _____

   Southern _____

   Eastern _____

   Western _____

Name _____

THE LONG & SHORT OF IT

Hannah, Henry, and all their hiking buddies can figure out where they are on the Earth's surface any time by using a great location system made of imaginary lines. Learn about these lines and use them to find places around the USA. (Use pages 169, 170, and 171 together.)

Lines running north-south (from pole to pole) are called **longitude** lines (or meridians). They mark distances in degrees east and west of the **prime meridian,** which is 0° longitude.

Lines running east-west around the globe are called **latitude** lines (or parallels). They measure distances north or south of the **equator,** which is 0° latitude. Other important parallels are the following: North Pole 90°N, South Pole 90°S, Arctic Circle $66\frac{1}{2}$°N, Antarctic Circle $66\frac{1}{2}$°S, Tropic of Cancer $23\frac{1}{2}$°N, and Tropic of Capricorn $23\frac{1}{2}$°S.

Using two sets of lines to form a grid, you can find any place on the globe. The circle below represents a globe. Label the poles, parallels, and meridian listed above. Give their names and their locations with degrees.

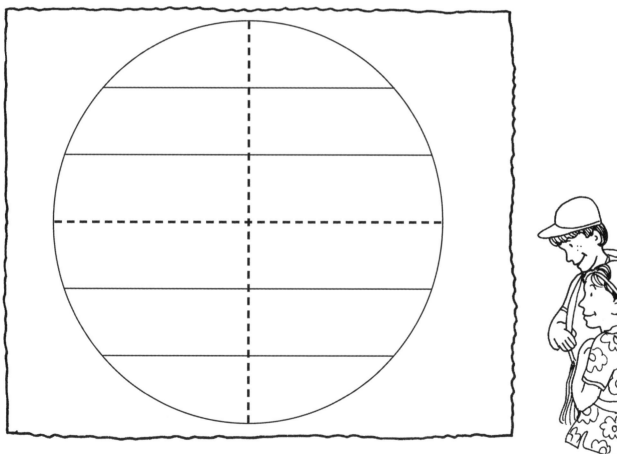

Name

LOCATING PLACES & SPACES

As they continue their hike around the USA, the Honolulu Hikers are paying attention to their U.S. map to learn about latitude and longitude locations. Can you answer the questions they are asking? Use the map on page 171. Make sure you add E, W, N, or S to your answers when giving latitude or longitude. Locations given are approximate.

1. If the hikers are in Alabama, what lines of latitude are they between? _____ & _____

2. What states will they find at 160°W longitude? _____

3. When they get to 27°N, 99°W, in what state will they be? _____

4. Longitude line 100°W passes through how many states? _____

5. Which city will they visit at (about) 40°N, 105°W? _____

   A. Kansas City, MO   B. Dayton, OH   C. Denver, CO   D. Albuquerque, NM

6. Which lines of latitude and longitude run through the state of North Carolina? _____

   A. 35°N and 90°W   B. 40°N and 75°W   C. 35°N and 85°W   D. 35°N and 80°W

7. When they reach (about) 35°N, 115°W, in what city will they be? _____

   A. Las Vegas, NV   B. El Paso, TX   C. Jefferson City, MO   D. Fresno, CA

8. 30°N latitude runs through how many states? _____

9. Name a state that spreads across more than 20° longitude. _____

10. How many states fall partly or totally between 70° and 75°W longitude? _____

11. Name a body of water that lies totally between 75° and 80°W longitude. _____

12. What body of water touches 25°N and 90°W?

    _____

13. Name a state that is at the same latitude as yours.

    _____

14. Name a state that is at the same longitude as yours.

    _____

15. How many other states are on the same latitude as yours?

    _____

I need some latitude!

Use with page 171.

Name _____

LATITUDE & LONGITUDE OF THE UNITED STATES

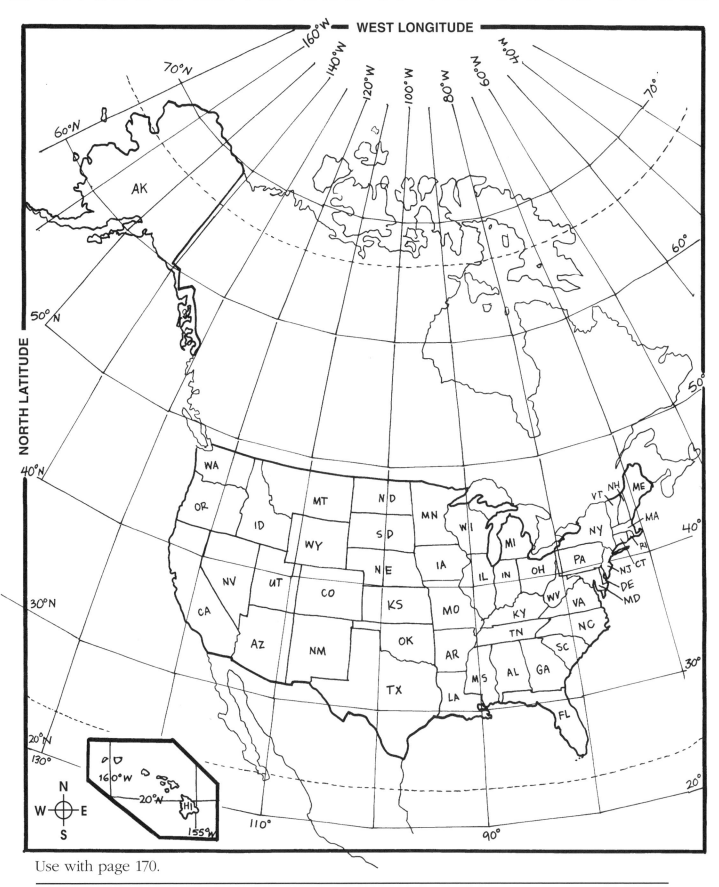

WEST LONGITUDE

NORTH LATITUDE

160°W

140°W

120°W

100°W

80°W

60°W

40°W

70°N

60°N

50°N

40°N

30°N

20°N

70°

60°

50°

40°

30°

20°

AK

WA
OR
ID
MT
ND
MN
WI
MI
NY
VT NH ME
MA
RI
CT

NV
UT
WY
SD
IA
IL
IN
OH
PA
NJ
DE
MD

CA
AZ
CO
NE
KS
MO
WV
VA
KY
NC
TN
SC

NM
OK
AR
MS
AL
GA
FL
TX
LA

130°
110°
90°
70°

N
W   E
S

160°W
20°N
155°W
HI

Use with page 170.

171

TIME FLIES

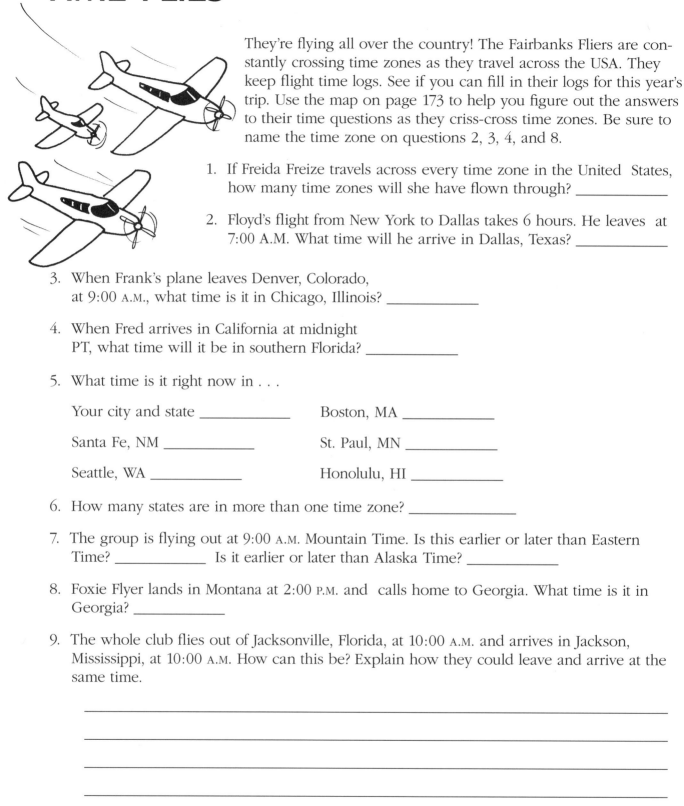

They're flying all over the country! The Fairbanks Fliers are constantly crossing time zones as they travel across the USA. They keep flight time logs. See if you can fill in their logs for this year's trip. Use the map on page 173 to help you figure out the answers to their time questions as they criss-cross time zones. Be sure to name the time zone on questions 2, 3, 4, and 8.

1. If Freida Freize travels across every time zone in the United States, how many time zones will she have flown through? _____

2. Floyd's flight from New York to Dallas takes 6 hours. He leaves at 7:00 A.M. What time will he arrive in Dallas, Texas? _____

3. When Frank's plane leaves Denver, Colorado, at 9:00 A.M., what time is it in Chicago, Illinois? _____

4. When Fred arrives in California at midnight PT, what time will it be in southern Florida? _____

5. What time is it right now in . . .

   Your city and state _____   Boston, MA _____

   Santa Fe, NM _____   St. Paul, MN _____

   Seattle, WA _____   Honolulu, HI _____

6. How many states are in more than one time zone? _____

7. The group is flying out at 9:00 A.M. Mountain Time. Is this earlier or later than Eastern Time? _____ Is it earlier or later than Alaska Time? _____

8. Foxie Flyer lands in Montana at 2:00 P.M. and calls home to Georgia. What time is it in Georgia? _____

9. The whole club flies out of Jacksonville, Florida, at 10:00 A.M. and arrives in Jackson, Mississippi, at 10:00 A.M. How can this be? Explain how they could leave and arrive at the same time.

_____

_____

_____

_____

_____

Use with page 173.

Name _____

TIME ZONES OF THE UNITED STATES

Use this map to answer the questions on page 172.

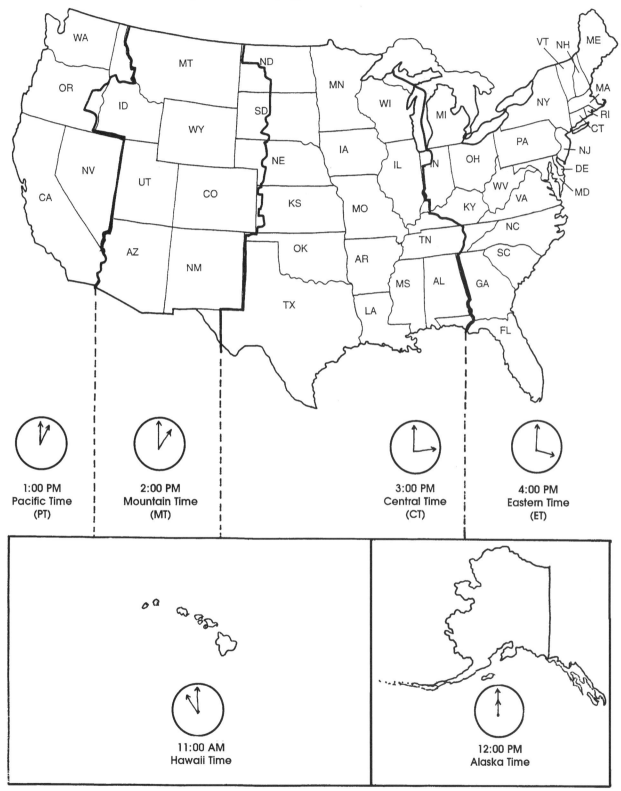

Use with page 172.

HEY, NEIGHBOR!

All five groups of travelers have planned a side trip to visit some of the neighboring countries of the United States. They will travel through North America. See the map on page 175. How well do you know your neighbors? Follow the directions to finish the map. Then answer the questions. You will need an atlas or a globe!

1. Label these countries and territories: USA, Canada, Greenland, Mexico, Belize, Guatemala, El Salvador, Honduras, Nicaragua, Costa Rica, Panama, Jamaica, Cuba, Haiti, Dominican Republic, and Puerto Rico.

2. Label these major bodies of water in and around North America: the Great Lakes, Pacific Ocean, Atlantic Ocean, Arctic Ocean, Bering Strait, Hudson Bay, Baffin Bay, Gulf of Mexico, Gulf of California, and the Caribbean Sea.

3. Use a red marker to trace the borders between the United States and its neighbors.

4. Locate and label the capital cities of the United States, Canada, and Mexico.

5. Is the Hudson Bay mostly north or south of the Arctic Circle? _____

6. Mexico is crossed by the
   A. Equator
   B. Tropic of Capricorn
   C. Tropic of Cancer

7. The bay west of Greenland is _____ .

8. Most of Canada and the United States are between what two major

   lines of latitude? _____ and _____

9. The largest island in North America is _____ .

10. Name the countries that border El Salvador. _____

11. Name the bodies of water that border Honduras. _____

12. Name the countries in the Caribbean Sea that share an island.

   _____ and _____

Use with page 175.

Name _____

EXPLORING NORTH AMERICA

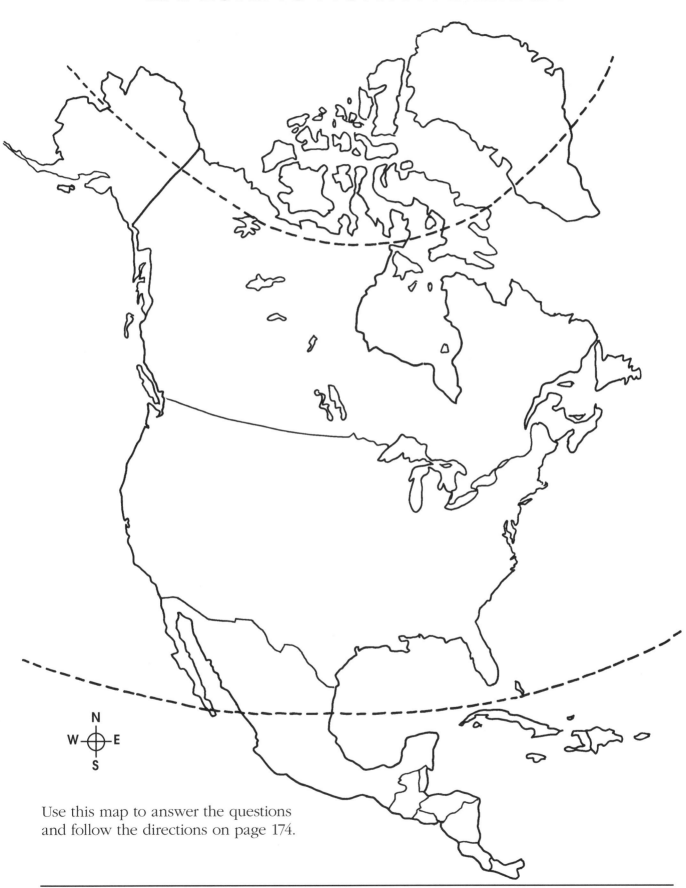

Use this map to answer the questions and follow the directions on page 174.

THE LARGEST NEIGHBOR

The Fairbanks Frequent Fliers are going to stop in every province and territory of Canada. This trip will take quite a while, because Canada is a huge country. In fact, it is the second largest country in the world. Take a good look at the map on page 177 to get familiar with the provinces, territories, cities, rivers, and geographical regions of Canada. Use the map on page 177 to help you solve the puzzle.

ACROSS

3. Canadian province extending farthest south
4. Territory that borders Alaska
5. Largest province touching the Atlantic
6. Province just west of Saskatchewan
9. Capital city of Northwest Territories
11. Capital of Ontario
12. Number of territories in Canada
13. Ocean bordering Canada on north

DOWN

1. Major river in northern Canada
2. Major city in the province of Quebec
7. Name of major city and island in British Columbia
8. Large bay bordering three provinces
10. Canada's national capital

Use with page 177.

Name

FEATURES OF CANADA

Use this map to solve the puzzle on page 176.

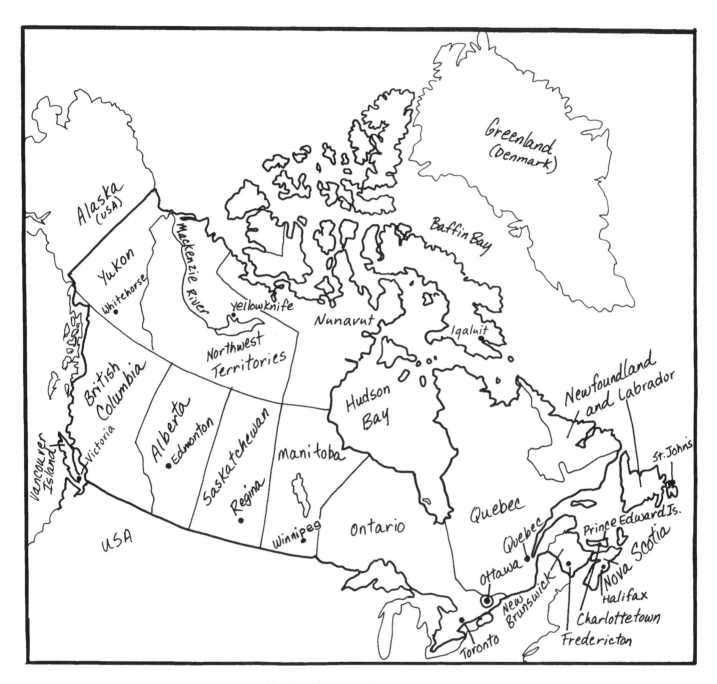

● = capital of province or territory

◉ = Canadian Capital

Use with page 176.

177

VIVIENDO EN MEXICO

The Alvarez family is taking a side trip to visit relatives in Mexico, a U.S. neighbor that is almost three times the size of Texas. They will find regions where thousands of tourists come to see the ancient ruins and enjoy beautiful beaches. They'll also travel through southern Mexico, a poor, mostly Indian region, and the growing urban and suburban area around Mexico City.

Use the map to help you decide if the following statements are correct.
Write T next to true statements; correct false sentences to make them true.

_____ 1. Baja California is over 800 miles long. _____

_____ 2. Mexico has two large peninsulas. _____

_____ 3. The Central Plateau goes northeast and southwest. _____

_____ 4. The Western Sierra Madre is Mexico's longest mountain range. _____

_____ 5. Mexico has a large lake at about 20°N Latitude. _____

_____ 6. Nearly all of Mexico is north of the Tropic of Cancer. _____

_____ 7. Mexico City is the capital. _____

_____ 8. The Yucatan Peninsula is on the Pacific Ocean. _____

_____ 9. The Colorado River makes part of the border between Mexico and Texas.

_____

_____ 10. Mexico's border touches Guatemala. _____

Can you find out what "VIVIENDO EN MEXICO" means? _____

Name _____

VALUABLES FROM MEXICO

What will the travelers find in Mexico? Some of the most valuable things are in the ground or growing in the field. Mexico's economy is mainly agricultural. Coffee, corn, rice, potatoes, sugarcane, cotton, beans, wheat, cacao, and bananas are among Mexico's chief cash crops. Manufacturing, mining, and tourism are also important. Mexico's major mineral resources include silver, gold, oil, copper, lead, and zinc.

Use the clues to circle some of these products and minerals in the word search below. The words may be written up, down, backwards, or diagonally.

CLUES

1. Another name for maize

2. Plant used to make clothing

3. Mexico is world's leading producer of this metal

4. Spanish explorers wanted this

5. A crop more often associated with Asia

6. A bean used to make chocolate

7. A mineral that begins with the last letter of the alphabet

8. Mexico's most valuable export

9. Available in many sizes and varieties, usually yellow

10. Beans that make a dark drink

11. Plant that is a source of sugar

12. A mineral that usually turns green when exposed to air

13. Starchy vegetables that grow below the ground

14. A poisonous mineral

15. Plant used to make bread

16. Prepared boiled, fried, mashed, and refried

Tia Maria!

```
C P W R I C E U B S N C
F O O H G A Q R H U A A
D C F T E Z S A O G U C
M O J F A A I C A A Z A
K R Q V E T T O A R I O
N N Q H E E O R M C N R
O D L O K R C E M A C E
T A I G E A V B S N L V
T E O P N W W X E E D L
O L P E R S J O G A R I
C O G O L D P H H P N S
C V I U S A N A N A B S
```

THE FOURTH LARGEST CONTINENT

South America is a continent of many wonders. It has crocodiles and llamas, mysterious islands and high mountains, deserts and rainforests, wild rivers and great grasslands, steep waterfalls, ancient ruins, and beautiful beaches. *Equator 0°*
It also has the longest river in the world. The Bobs on Bikes Club members are exploring the continent for a month. Follow the directions below to learn of the places and sights they will see.

1. Label the countries.
2. Label each capital city.
3. Label three oceans or seas.

Tropic of Capricorn

Correctly fill in the blanks below using the given clues.

4. Countries on the equator

_____

_____

_____

5. Countries that are entirely north of the equator

_____

_____

_____

6. Country just south of Ecuador

_____

7. The countries containing the Andes Mountains

_____

_____

8. Islands west of Ecuador

_____

9. A country close to Antarctica

_____

10. Two countries without coastlines

_____

11. Country at the south end of Brazil

_____

12. Two countries bordering Colombia on the east

_____

_____

13. Islands east of Argentina

_____

14. The mouth of the Amazon River is in this country.

_____

Name _____

EVER BEEN TO CHICKEN?

Have you ever been to Tomato, Cocoa, Volcano, Gnaw Bone, Boring, Frostproof, or Chilly? There really are towns in the United States with these names! There are also Chicken, Egg, Baconton, and Coffee! The hiking, biking, cycling, driving, and flying clubs all got together at the end of their trips and shared the crazy names of cities and towns they had visited. Read each list of cities, towns, and counties. Name the correct state for each list.

1. _____
   Early
   Coffee
   Baconton
   Chickamauga
   Bibb
   Twiggs
   Savannah

2. _____
   King Salmon
   Chicken
   Nome
   Fishhook
   North Pole

3. _____
   Bee Ridge
   Citrus
   Cocoa
   Niceville
   Treasure Island
   Frostproof
   Boca Raton

4. _____
   Bath
   Quicksand
   Dwarf
   Mousie
   Sassafras
   Louisville

5. _____
   Gem
   Salmon
   Chilly
   Santa
   Boise

6. _____
   Bald Knob
   Hoxie
   Smackover
   Tomato
   Magazine
   Little Rock

7. _____
   Chase
   Cloud
   Gas
   Agenda
   Pottawatomie
   Wichita

8. _____
   Big Tree
   Deposit
   Great Neck
   Chili
   Syracuse

9. _____
   Truth or
      Consequences
   Radium Springs
   Wagon Mound
   Pojoaque
   Albuquerque

10. _____
    Reno
    Jackpot
    Gold Acres
    Blue Diamond

11. _____
    Boring
    Crook
    Zigzag
    Portland

12. _____
    Needles
    Happy Camp
    Hayfork
    Rough and Ready
    Yolo
    San Jose

13. _____
    Bird-in-Hand
    Eighty Four
    Sinking Spring
    Black Lick
    Bethlehem

14. _____
    Dinosaur
    Eagle
    Brush
    Boulder
    Silt

15. _____
    Hackensack
    Egg Harbor
    Forked River
    Piscataway
    White Horse
    Newark

16. _____
    Frost
    Trophy Club
    Bee
    Wink
    Corpus Christi

17. _____
    Deadwood
    Porcupine
    Potato Creek
    Pierre

18. _____
    Red Cloud
    Weeping Water
    Valentine
    Broken Bow
    Omaha

19. _____
    Ninety-Six
    McBee
    Goose Creek
    Sans Souci
    Charleston

20. _____
    Rolling Fork
    Tie Plant
    Yazoo City
    D'Lo
    Biloxi
    Pascagoula

Name _____

RECORD SETTERS

The travelers have seen all the record-setting sights of the USA—the oldest, the biggest, the widest, the deepest, the highest, the first, the last, the driest, and the coldest. See if you can match up these record setters with the states where they can be found. Write the abbreviation of the correct state next to each one. A state might be used more than once.

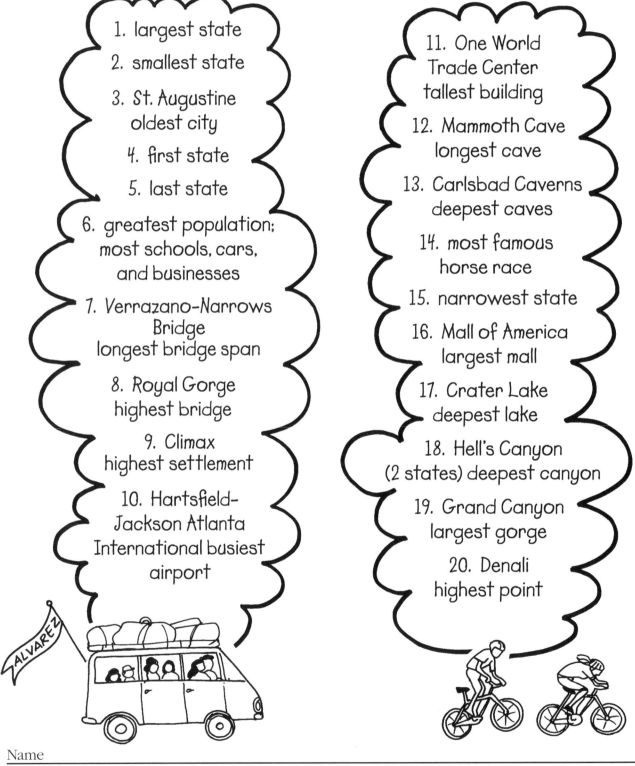

1. largest state

2. smallest state

3. St. Augustine oldest city

4. first state

5. last state

6. greatest population; most schools, cars, and businesses

7. Verrazano-Narrows Bridge longest bridge span

8. Royal Gorge highest bridge

9. Climax highest settlement

10. Hartsfield-Jackson Atlanta International busiest airport

11. One World Trade Center tallest building

12. Mammoth Cave longest cave

13. Carlsbad Caverns deepest caves

14. most famous horse race

15. narrowest state

16. Mall of America largest mall

17. Crater Lake deepest lake

18. Hell's Canyon (2 states) deepest canyon

19. Grand Canyon largest gorge

20. Denali highest point

Name

MORE RECORD SETTERS

The travelers have seen all the record-setting sights of the USA—the largest, the smallest, the windiest, the longest, the highest, the widest, the most famous, the least, and the most. See if you can match up these record setters with the states where they can be found. Write the abbreviation of the state next to each one. A state might be used more than once.

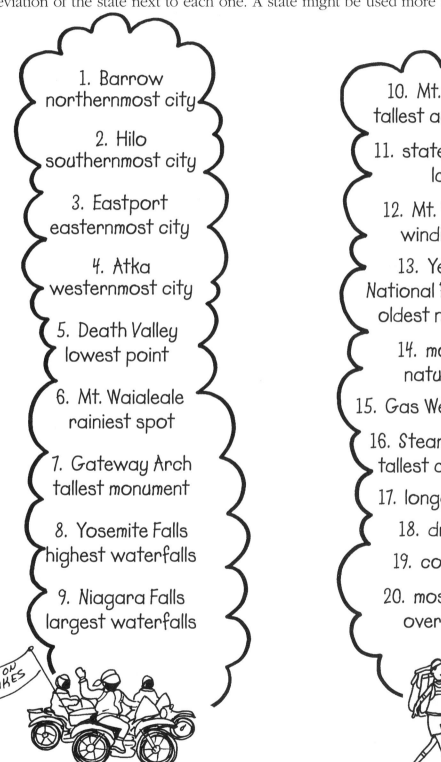

1. Barrow
northernmost city

2. Hilo
southernmost city

3. Eastport
easternmost city

4. Atka
westernmost city

5. Death Valley
lowest point

6. Mt. Waialeale
rainiest spot

7. Gateway Arch
tallest monument

8. Yosemite Falls
highest waterfalls

9. Niagara Falls
largest waterfalls

10. Mt. Mauna Loa
tallest active volcano

11. state with most
lakes

12. Mt. Washington
windiest point

13. Yellowstone
National Park (3 states)
oldest national park

14. most oil &
natural gas

15. Gas Well—deepest well

16. Steamboat Geyser
tallest active geyser

17. longest coastline

18. driest state

19. coldest state

20. most mountains
over 14,000 ft.

BOBS ON BIKES

Name

UNDERGROUND DELIVERY

Grubstake Gus insisted that his supplies be delivered to him deep down inside the Lost Moon Mine. Gus is positive that one of his ancestors buried a treasure there, and he won't come out of the mine until he finds it!

Follow Oliver's trail as he descends through the twisted maze of tunnels into the dark mine. (See page 185.) Draw a symbol on the map for each object or place he describes. Then use your symbols to create a key for the map.

1. As soon as I entered the mine, I stumbled across a big, old rattlesnake sunning himself right in the doorway!

2. I headed southwest 5 paces into the mine until some fallen boulders blocked my way and forced me to turn south.

3. I counted 6 paces south before I crossed an underground stream, and then 5 more paces south until I came to an odd set of old bones laid out like an arrow. They pointed northeast. I decided to go that way.

4. I continued northeast for 8 paces. On the west side of the room, I saw a stalactite hanging in front of the opening. I crawled around it into a narrow tunnel. I decided to follow this.

5. I had traveled west for 7 paces when something whooshed past my face. I shined my light in its direction and saw hundreds of bats hanging from the ceiling!

6. I had walked 9 paces northwest when I tripped and fell flat on my face! I had tripped over an old, broken miner's pick in my path!

7. I continued 6 paces south on the path, until I stumbled across a lump in the path. I dug into the dirt with my pick. To my surprise, I uncovered an old shoe!

8. I moved 5 more paces southwest down the corridor and found a lantern lying in the path.

9. I went on for 11 more paces southeast until I heard a low moan coming from the direction of a large, round room. I saw a white, ghostly shape moving toward me!

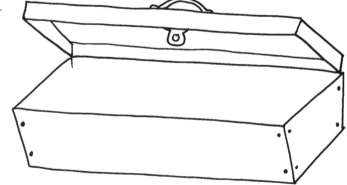

10. I screamed! It echoed all up and down the corridor! I ran west about 7 paces and stumbled smack into the old miner, Gus. I was too late! Gus had already uncovered an old treasure box.

Draw the treasure you think Gus found!

Use with page 185.

Name _____

KEY

Use with page 184.

Name

WHERE IN THE WORLD?

Ivanna Gough has an urgent overnight letter to deliver to Houseboat Harry. She must get it to him by 10 o'clock tomorrow morning, but she's having a hard time finding him. She must search every landform and body of water until she finds Harry. Use the map on the next page (page 187) and the landform list below to help you answer the questions about Ivanna's search.

1. Harry's empty houseboat is docked in the _____.

2. The lounge chair on the _____ is still warm.

3. What does Ivanna find on top of the mountain peak?_____

4. Someone set up a tent in the _____.

5. Where is Ivanna when she's on the steamship? _____

6. She hitches a ride across the plain on a _____.

7. Ivanna searches the abandoned lighthouse. Where is it? _____

8. What special feature is on the end of the landform in number 7? _____

9. Ivanna doesn't find Harry on the iceberg, but she does find a _____.

10. She finds a half-eaten plate of pasta in the tower on the _____.

11. How is she traveling through the strait? _____

12. Harry left a clue on the isthmus. What is it? _____

13. If Harry were in the delta, he'd have a _____ for company.

14. There's an empty raft on the _____ and an empty boat on the _____.

15. Why does Ivanna hurry through the swamp at top speed? _____

16. Ivanna searches Harry's favorite fishing hole at the source of the river. Draw a fish in the river's source.

17. Exhausted, Ivanna rests beneath a palm tree. Where is she? _____
    She looks up, and guess who she sees? _____

(She should have remembered that Harry is nuts about coconuts!)

Landforms

cape	isthmus	plateau	swamp
river mouth	foothills	peninsula	butte
river source	source	harbor	iceberg
lake	delta	river	mountain peak
island	strait	plain	ocean

Use with page 187.

Name

LANDFORMS

Use with page 186.

OVER LAND & WATER

When Ivanna and Oliver say "We deliver anywhere!"
they mean it! Deliveries are made on every continent.
Read the description of Ivanna's trip to find out what
she is picking up, what she is dropping off, and
where she is going. Then help her find her way!

**1. Find a world atlas or a
   good world map.**

**2. Use the map to help you
   label all the continents
   and oceans.**

**3. Draw a red line to follow
   Ivanna's path.**

**4. Color each continent
   as she stops there.**

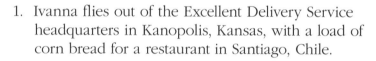

1. Ivanna flies out of the Excellent Delivery Service
   headquarters in Kanopolis, Kansas, with a load of
   corn bread for a restaurant in Santiago, Chile.

2. She picks up a case of chili sauce and takes it to scientists on
   the remote Antarctica.

3. She carries an orphaned baby penguin from Antarctica to a zoo
   in Zurich, Switzerland.

4. She flies 200 pounds of Swiss chocolate to a candy store in
   Nanchang, China.

5. In China, she picks up a huge dragon kite for delivery to a desert
   Bedouin in Libya, North Africa.

6. In North Africa, she picks up a beautiful rug and some dates. She eats
   the dates for lunch. But where in the world is she taking the rug?
   Name the continent where she'll be taking the rug. *(Remember, she has
   deliveries on every continent!)*

_____

Use with page 189.

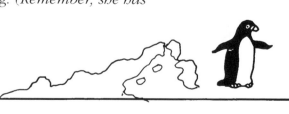

Name _____

THE WORLD

Find these countries that Ivanna will be visiting next week. Write the number of each country on the map to show where it is.

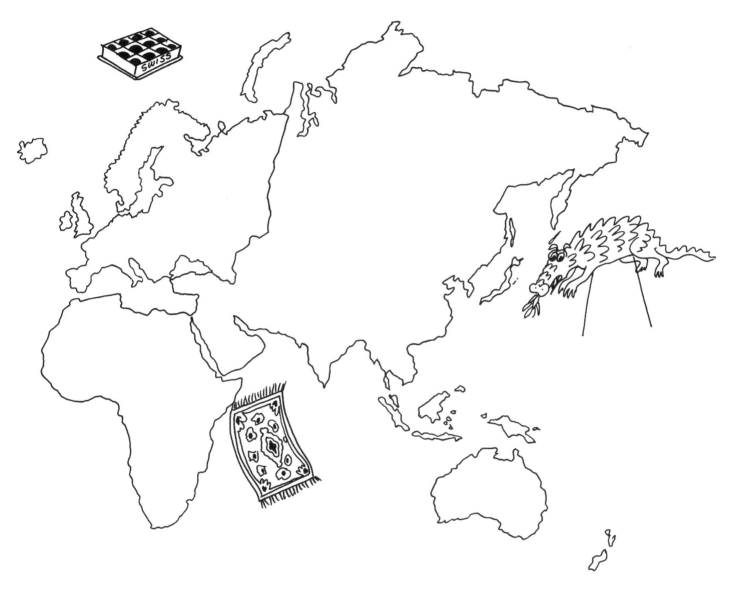

1. Denmark

2. Mexico

3. Nigeria

4. Indonesia

5. Bhutan

6. Norway

7. Poland

8. Japan

9. Bolivia

10. India

11. Iran

12. Russia

13. Italy

14. New Zealand

15. Venezuela

16. South Africa

Use with page 188.

Name

THE MISFIT PACKAGES

There are so many packages and letters to be delivered to North America that they have been organized into several stacks. One package in each stack is a misfit. Put an X on the package in each stack that does not belong, and tell why it doesn't fit with the others. Use a map to find the information you need.

1. _____

COSTA RICA
MEXICO
Guatamala
NEW YORK
NICARAGUA

2. _____

Bogota   Lima
Buenos Aires
El Paso
Santiago

3. _____

QUEBEC
ONTARIO
ATLANTA
SASKATCHEWAN
ALBERTA

4. _____

Huron
Superior
Pacific
Michigan
Erie

5. _____

BOSTON
MEXICO CITY
DALLAS
MONTREAL   ALASKA

6. _____

Seattle   Washington D.C.   Portland   Atlantic   Dallas

PIZZA
Mississippi
Amazon
Gulf of Mexico
Rio Grande
St. Lawrence

7. _____

CANADA   MEXICO
EL SALVADOR   UNITED STATES
Chicago

8. _____

Name _____

190

THE REST OF THE PARADE

Many more supplies for the big Thanksgiving Day parade were delivered to Kanopolis by the Excellent Delivery Service. Use the map scale to answer these questions about the sizes of these deliveries and other attractions in the parade. Round your answers to the nearest meter.

1. How long is the parade from beginning to end? _____

2. How tall is the cupcake (not including the legs)? _____

3. How much of the parade is on Ruby Street? _____

4. How tall are the caterpillar's antennae? _____

5. How long is the worm float? _____

6. How long is the giant ladybug? _____

7. How long is the caterpillar? _____

8. How high is the sundae? _____

9. How wide is Pearl Street? _____

10. How long is the giant ant? _____

11. How long is the car?

   _____

12. Which is taller, the cheese balloon or the sundae?

   _____

13. How wide is the cheese balloon (at its widest point)?

   _____

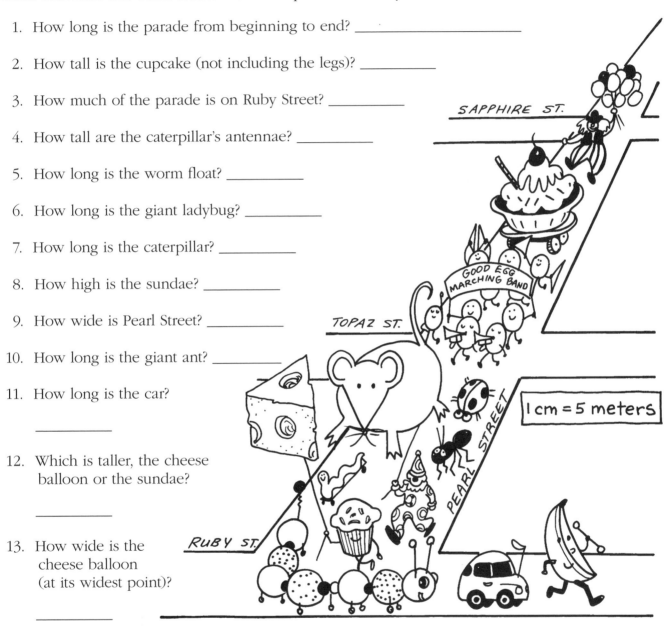

1 cm = 5 meters

14. The Good Egg Marching Band stretches over a distance of _____ .

15. Which distance is longer: Sapphire Street to Topaz Street or Topaz Street to Ruby Street?

_____

Name _____

A MOUSE ON PARADE

In September, the Excellent Delivery Service delivered a picture of a cute little mouse to the BIG, BIG BALLOON COMPANY. The picture was the pattern for a giant mouse balloon that the company wanted to make for the Thanksgiving Day parade. How will they turn it into a balloon? They will use a grid to make a larger scale drawing of the mouse. Use this grid to make your own larger scale drawing. Draw the same thing you see in each square of the small grid onto the squares of the large grid.

1 SQUARE = 1 INCH = 5 FEET

In November, Oliver will return with a truck to deliver the balloon to the parade. The scale on your grid drawing shows how big the actual balloon will be.

1. Will the finished balloon fit inside an 8-foot x 12-foot truck? _____

2. Will the finished balloon be able to move down a 50-foot wide street? _____

3. How tall would a door have to be for the balloon to get through it standing up? _____

4. How tall is the ear of the inflated mouse balloon? _____

5. How long is the tail of the finished balloon? _____

6. How long is the longest whisker? _____

7. Would the mouse balloon be taller than your house? _____

8. Compare yourself to the mouse by drawing a stick figure of yourself on the grid.

Name _____

DELIVERY ON THE SLOPES

The delivery skier needs to know directions well in order to deliver splints and hot chocolate to all the members of the ski patrol on Mount Maniac. Fill in the directions on the compass for her. Then, write which direction she will go on each part of her route. Use a red marker or crayon to trace her route on the map.

Summit Lodge

Broken Bone Run

Disaster Jump

Ski Patrol Hut

Big Curve Shelter

Halfway Hut

She starts at Recovery Lodge.
From there she goes . . .

1. _____ to Halfway Hut.
2. _____ to Disaster Jump.
3. _____ to Summit Lodge.
4. _____ to the Ski Patrol Hut.
5. _____ over to Big Curve Shelter.
6. _____ to Bunny Hill.
7. _____ to Super Slick Sledding Hill.
8. _____ up through Treacherous Woods.
9. _____ to the parking lot.
10. _____ back to town.

Treacherous Woods

Super Slick Sledding Hill

Bunny Hill

Whiplash Ski Lift

Parking Lot

To Town

Recovery Lodge

A MESSY MAP MESS-UP

Someone left the window open over the weekend. A wild wind came through and blew everything all over the EDS (Excellent Delivery Service) office! The workers are trying to reorganize the maps. Choose the drawer where each map should be filed. Write the number of the correct drawer next to each map.

1 Street and Road Maps
2 Population Maps
3 Political Maps
4 Product Maps
5 Floor Maps
6 Elevation Maps
7 Weather Maps
8 Landform Maps

Fruit County Exports

U. S. S. STAR SHIP

MOUNT TIPPY

The Western Hemisphere

Rainfall in Hat County (Annual)

CIVIC CENTER

Giggle Land

= 1 million

Boot Island

Name _____

194

¿QUÉ TIEMPO HACE?

Once more, the Excellent Delivery Service is on the road! Ivanna is going to Mexico to pick up a large order of piñatas. Should she take the company pick-up truck, or should she rent a covered van? Her decision will depend on what she learns about the weather in Mexico. Study the rainfall map of Mexico to help her decide what the weather might be like!

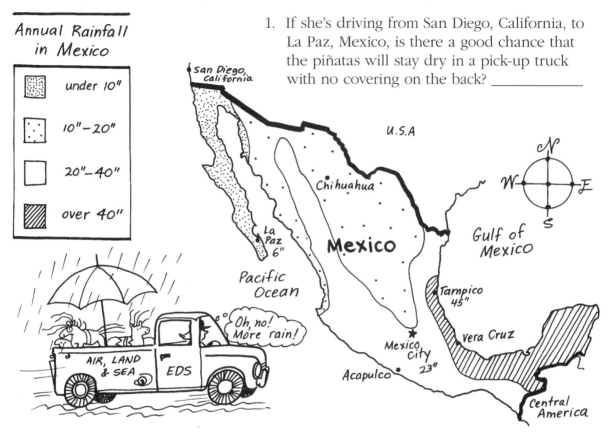

Annual Rainfall in Mexico

- under 10"
- 10"–20"
- 20"–40"
- over 40"

1. If she's driving from San Diego, California, to La Paz, Mexico, is there a good chance that the piñatas will stay dry in a pick-up truck with no covering on the back? _____

2. When she gets near Vera Cruz, will the piñatas she picked up in Mexico City probably stay dry in the back of the pick-up? _____

3. She has some more piñatas to pick up near the beach in Tampico. Will she need sunscreen or an umbrella if she plans to stay awhile in Tampico? _____

4. Should she be worried about rain in Chihuahua? _____

5. What is the average yearly rainfall in Mexico City? _____

6. Which two cities have between 20 and 40 inches of rain a year?

_____

7. Color the map as follows: under 10"—orange; from 10" to 20"—red;
from 20" to 40"—blue; over 40"—green

8. What does "¿Qué tiempo hace?" mean? _____

Name _____

DELIVERY BY SUBWAY

Oliver has a heavy job tonight. The delivery service has to get some important equipment to the weight lifters at the Muscleman Arena in time for the big match tonight. In Mega City, subways are the fastest way to make deliveries and avoid traffic jams. Answer the questions to help Oliver find the arena in time.

1. The Muscleman Arena is closest to which subway line? _____

2. If Oliver begins his trip at Station 1, how many lines will he need to ride to get the supplies to the Muscleman Arena? _____

3. Name the lines Oliver will need to ride.

   _____

4. How many times will Oliver need to change subway trains? _____

5. How many stations will Oliver go through on his whole trip? _____

6. Will Oliver cross the river on his trip? _____

7. At what station will Oliver end his trip? _____

8. How many subway lines does this map show? _____

9. Name the subway lines. _____

10. Which station is farthest north? _____

11. Which stations are closest to the river? _____

12. Which lines cross the river? _____

13. Are there any stations across the river from the city? _____

14. How many stations are outside the city boundary? _____

15. Which line or lines cross the East-West Line? _____

16. How many stations are there for changing from one line to another? _____

17. What symbol shows an interchange station? _____

18. Which lines have more than one station outside the city limits? _____

19. Could Oliver change from the River Line to any other subway line? _____

20. Where could Oliver change from the Northern Loop Line to the South Line? _____

Name _____

DELIVERY BY SUBWAY, CONT.

I am so bushed!

Use the subway map to answer the questions on page 196.

MEGA CITY SUBWAY MAP

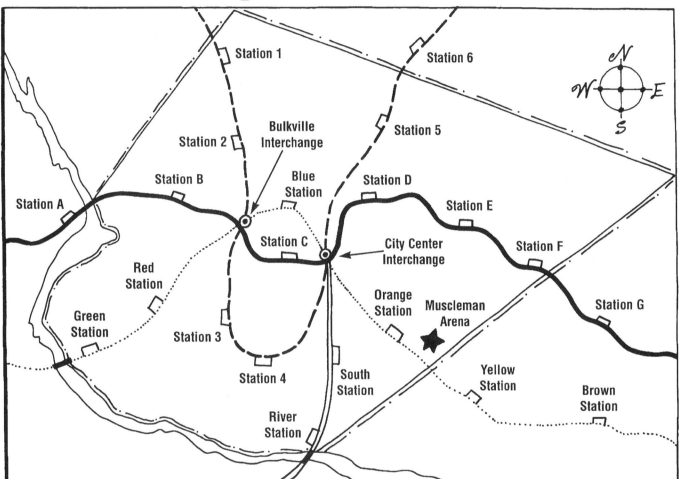

Northern Loop Line
River Line
East–West Line
South Line
⊙ Interchange Station
▭ Subway Station
Ten Ton River
Mega City Boundary

21. Which line has stations named for colors?

_____

22. Which line has stations named with letters?

_____

23. Which line has stations named with numbers?

_____

24. Which line has only two stations?

_____

Use with page 196.

Name

FRIDAY NIGHT DELIVERIES

D.J. is a new employee for the Excellent Delivery Service. It is his job to deliver videos to customers every Friday night. He has three lists of videos to find at the video store. Write the location for each in the blanks provided. First, write the letter of the column and then the number of the row (C 4).

LIST 1
Deliver to:
Sadie's Slumber Party
345 Upallnight Lane

1. Lost in the Mall_____
2. Ghastly Ghost Stories_____
3. Babysitting School_____
4. Safari Secrets_____

LIST 2
Deliver to:
Ricky's 5th birthday party
543 Noisy Street

1. Volcanoes!_____
2. Gert's Goofy Vacation_____
3. Favorite Snake Stories_____
4. Food Fight Part I_____

LIST 3
Deliver to:
Teachers' Retirement Home
Recess Road

1. 170 Ways to Cook Squash_____
2. Algebra for Fun_____
3. Exciting Verbs to Use Often_____
4. Eyes in the Back of My Head_____

Name _____

A LOAD OF OLD BONES

Professor Muddle hired the Excellent Delivery Service to bring back a carton of old bones from Bone Island to his museum in T-Rex City. He absentmindedly scribbled the directions to the island on several little scraps of paper. Now Ivanna is totally confused!

Use the map to help Ivanna get to Bone Island and back. Number the scraps of paper in the correct order from 1–9 for her to follow. She will start at the museum, go to the island, and then return to the museum.

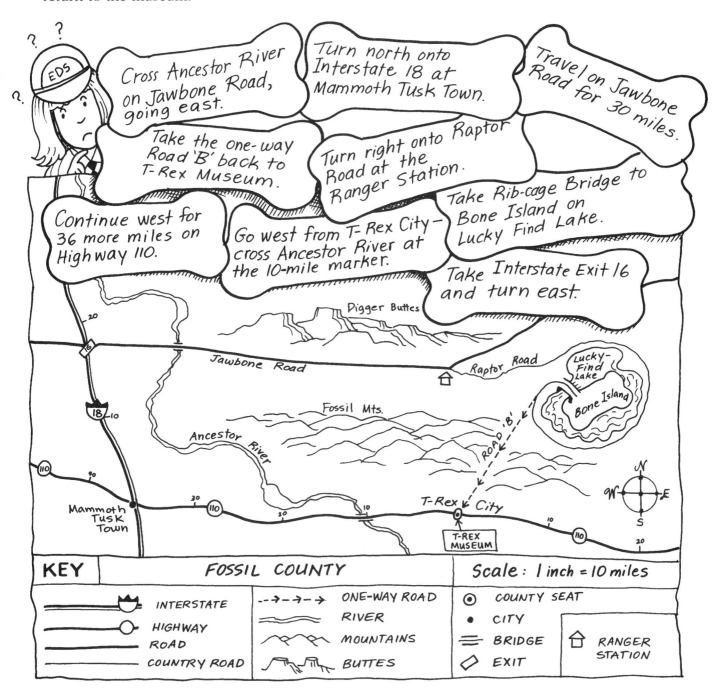

Cross Ancestor River on Jawbone Road, going east.

Turn north onto Interstate 18 at Mammoth Tusk Town.

Travel on Jawbone Road for 30 miles.

Take the one-way Road 'B' back to T-Rex Museum.

Turn right onto Raptor Road at the Ranger Station.

Continue west for 36 more miles on Highway 110.

Go west from T-Rex City— cross Ancestor River at the 10-mile marker.

Take Rib-cage Bridge to Bone Island on Lucky Find Lake.

Take Interstate Exit 16 and turn east.

Digger Buttes

Jawbone Road

Raptor Road

Lucky-Find Lake

Fossil Mts.

Bone Island

Ancestor River

ROAD 'B'

Mammoth Tusk Town

T-Rex City

T-REX MUSEUM

KEY **FOSSIL COUNTY** **Scale: 1 inch = 10 miles**

INTERSTATE	ONE-WAY ROAD	COUNTY SEAT
HIGHWAY	RIVER	CITY
ROAD	MOUNTAINS	BRIDGE
COUNTRY ROAD	BUTTES	EXIT / RANGER STATION

Name _____

SCHOOL SUPPLIES

The Excellent Delivery Service brings some of the most interesting things to West Kanopolis High School. Let's see what Oliver D. World is delivering today!

Oliver arrives at the school at 10:15 A.M. Read the list of deliveries he has for today. (See page 201.) Then use the school floor plan to figure out the speediest way for him to make them all. Keep in mind that some deliveries are urgent. (These are the ones that might melt or bite, or the ones that are needed for emergencies or deadlines.)

Number the deliveries in the order you think is best.

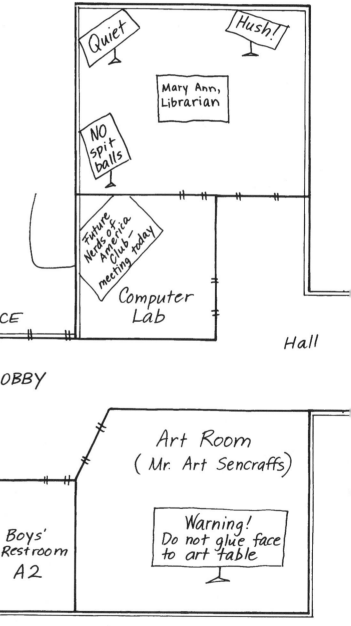

Use with page 201.

Name _____

OLIVER'S DELIVERY LIST

_____ gumball ice cream for the cafeteria

_____ mice for the science lab

_____ deodorant for the boys' locker room

_____ ice sculpture for the teachers' lounge (for Mrs. Quill's retirement party at 10:30 A.M.)

_____ glue remover for the art room

_____ air pump for the flat basketballs in the gym

_____ birthday balloons for a girl in the 11 A.M. French class

_____ aspirin for the Algebra I teacher

_____ antacid for the Algebra II teacher

_____ homework paper to boy in English class (by 10:32 A.M.)

_____ deodorant for the girls' locker room

_____ plunger for the boys' restroom

_____ lunch for the principal

_____ giant garbage bags for the courtyard after lunch break

_____ glass trophy case for the main lobby

_____ fly swatters for the geography class

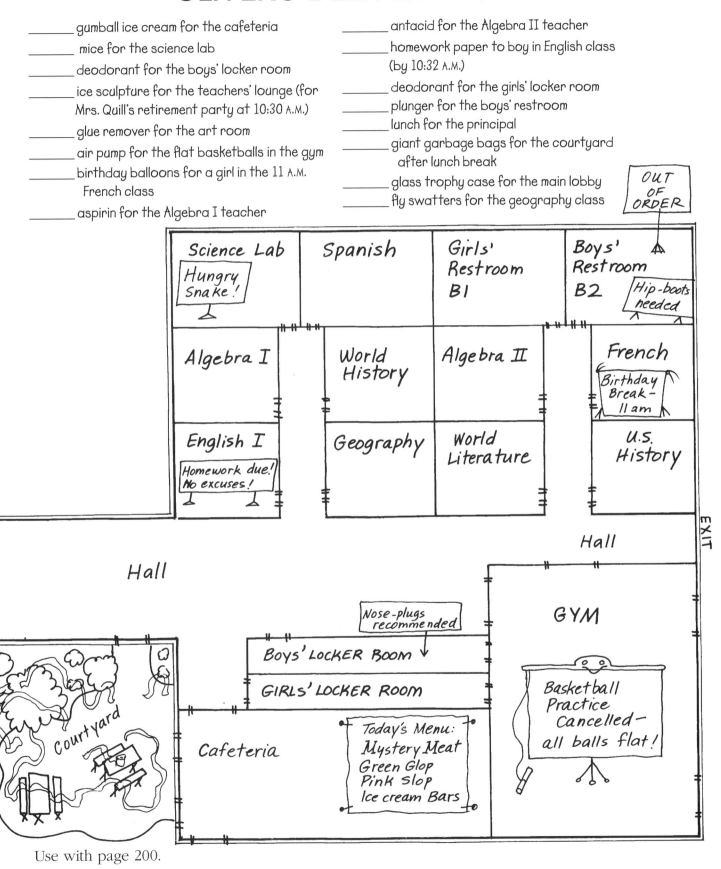

SCIENCE

Skills Exercises
Grade Four

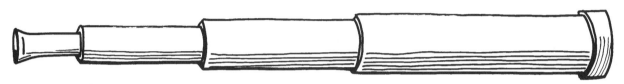

SKILLS CHECKLIST
SCIENCE

✔	SKILL	PAGE(S)
	Identify and describe concepts and laws related to motion	205
	Describe properties of sound and explain how sound travels	206, 207
	Describe and identify fields of science	208, 209
	Define vocabulary terms related to plants, animals, and ecology	208–217
	Identify classification of plants	210
	Identify plant and flower parts	211
	Identify and describe some plant processes	212
	Describe the system of classification of animals	213–215
	Identify some simple and complex invertebrates	214
	Identify characteristics and classes of vertebrates	215
	Identify and describe concepts and relationships related to ecosystems	216, 217
	Describe organs and functions of the circulatory and respiratory systems	218
	Describe organs and functions of the digestive system	218
	Define vocabulary terms related to the human body and health	218, 219
	Describe organs and functions of the skeletal-muscular system	218, 219
	Identify organs and functions related to human body systems	218, 219
	Define work; identify and explain the six types of machines	220
	Define and give examples of forces	220–227
	Define weathering and erosion and explain agents and examples of each	221
	Describe earthquakes, volcanoes, and other internal Earth processes	222
	Identify and describe features of Earth's surface	222, 223
	Identify characteristics of rocks	223
	Define and describe properties of air and Earth's atmosphere	224, 225
	Identify weather patterns and forms of precipitation	224, 225
	Define terms related to earth, space, physical, and life sciences	226
	Review facts related to earth, space, physical, and life sciences	226
	Describe and define properties of magnets and magnetic fields	227

WHAT MADE ME DO THAT?

While Thermo and his friends are enjoying some winter activities, they get some lessons about motion. A scientist named Newton wrote down some things that were learned a long time ago about motion. These are called Newton's Laws of Motion. Read the comments of each person in the picture. Next to each statement, write the number of the law that explains why they're doing what they're doing!

LAW #1   Any moving object will keep moving in the same direction at the same speed unless some force changes its direction or speed.

LAW #2   Any object speeds up or slows down in proportion to the size of the force acting on it.

LAW #3   For any action, there is an equal and opposite reaction.

1. The harder I throw this snowball, the farther and faster it will go!

2. I can move the small snowball for the snowman's head, but I'll need someone bigger to move his tummy.

3. When I push back with my poles – I move forward!

4. The harder I pull, the faster my sister moves.

5. When I slammed into this wall, a force pushed me backwards and away again!

6. The hockey puck slides across the rink at the same speed – until it hits my stick!

Name _____

SOME SOUND SCIENCE

Sound waves travel through the air. Some of the sounds begin very far away from the listener. Robo hears some strange sounds coming through the air tonight. What is making these sounds? Where are they coming from? Is there a message being sent? Read all the statements about sound on pages 206 and 207 to find out. If a statement is true, use red to color the speaker section(s) with the same number. If the statement is false, color the section(s) with silver.

1. Sounds are caused by vibrations.

2. Volume is the loudness or softness of sound.

3. Sound travels fastest in liquids.

4. Strong vibrations produce loud sounds.

5. Sound travels at the same speed as light.

6. People can hear sounds of things vibrating 20-20,000 times per second.

7. Dogs can hear sounds made by vibrations of more than 20,000 per second.

8. Pitch is highness or lowness of a sound.

9. An echo is a sound that is faster than light.

10. The faster an object vibrates, the higher the pitch of its sound.

11. Sound travels by air vibrating.

12. Sound waves cannot travel through solids.

13. Noise is unpleasant sound.

14. Sound waves travel fastest through solids.

15. Sound waves cannot travel in a vacuum.

16. The slower an object vibrates, the lower the pitch of its sound.

17. High-pitched sounds are made by objects that vibrate in a vacuum.

18. Frequency is the number of times an object vibrates per second.

19. The middle ear contains bones called the handle, the saddle, and the stirrup.

20. When a jet flies faster than the speed of sound, it causes a sonic boom.

21. Weak vibrations produce soft sounds.

22. You can speak and sing because your vocal chords vibrate.

23. It is dangerous for the eardrum to vibrate.

24. Sound causes the eardrum to vibrate.

25. Sound waves travel slowest through gases.

26. Strong vibrations produce soft sounds.

Those sound waves can hurt a robot's ears.

Use with page 207.

Name

27. An echo is reflected sound.

29. The outer ear catches sounds.

28. Soft or rough surfaces absorb sound.

31. Some loud sounds can damage the eardrum.

30. Sound waves cannot pass through liquids.

32. Sound waves are absorbed by hard surfaces.

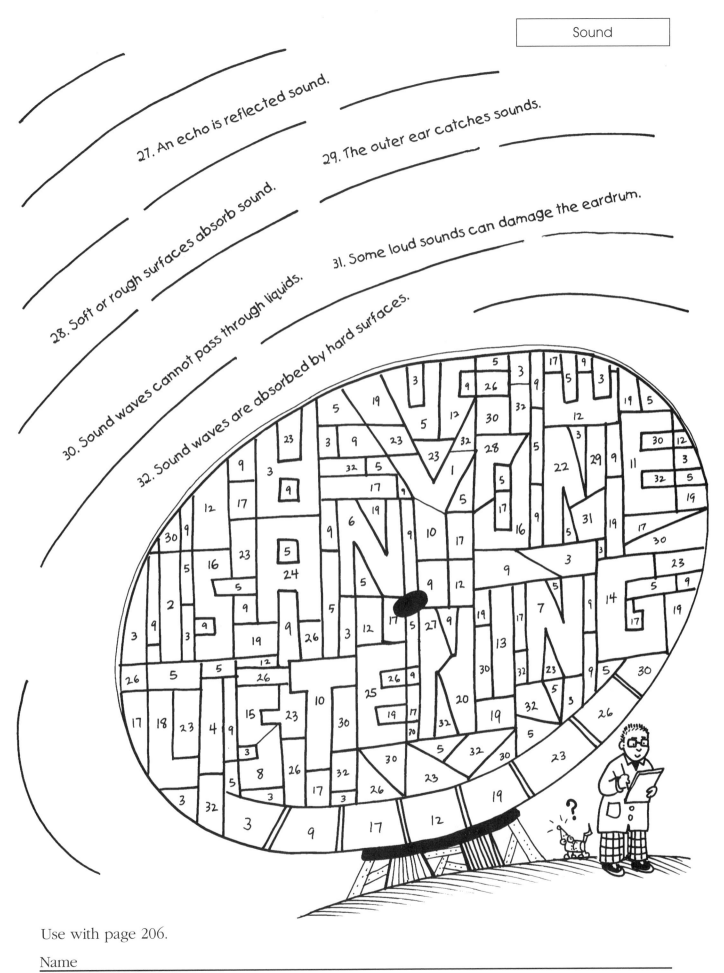

Use with page 206.

Name

SCIENCE TO BRAG ABOUT

Iris, Thermo, and Cosmo have been competing with each other most of their lives. As children, the three cousins argued about who was the fastest, toughest, or smartest. Now they are all grown-up scientists, but they are still trying to out-do each other! Today they are arguing about whose branch of science is the most important.

> I investigate all of life! I know about plants, animals, and cells; the human body, diseases, and cures; and life, growth, and death. I know about how all life is related to other life and to the whole planet! How can you think for a minute that anything is as noble as the study of LIFE SCIENCE?

> Oh, come on, Iris! Even your precious plants and animals are made up of atoms, the basic structure of matter. Everything is based on PHYSICAL SCIENCE! It's the only way to know about basic atoms, molecules, elements, and compounds; about energy, motion, forces, and work; and heat, light, sound, and electricity. It's about all the things that make the world work!

> Well! Without EARTH AND SPACE SCIENCE, you two would have nothing to study at all! I study the origins of the entire universe. If it weren't for scientists like me who understand the makeup of the Earth and other objects in space, you'd have no setting for your studies of the plants, animals, and elements that live there!

Dr. Iris de Plant   Dr. Thermo Sparks   DR. COSMO QUAKE

Read all the branches of science listed on this page and the next (page 209). Choose the answer that tells what is studied by that science.

_____ 1. **cosmology?**
a. hairdos and makeup
b. Earth's oceans
c. structure of the universe

_____ 2. **biology?**
a. plant and animal life
b. electric currents
c. nuclear energy

_____ 3. **meteorology?**
a. meteors and meteorites
b. metric measurements
c. weather patterns

Use with page 209.

Name

SCIENCE TO BRAG ABOUT, cont.

Choose the answer that tells what is studied by that science.

Meet... ...Liverwort, the flower-loving pet of Dr. Iris de Plant.

...Robo Rat, the robot pet of Dr. Thermo-Sparks.
squeap squeap

...Asteroid, the astronaut pet of Dr. Cosmo Quake.

____ 4. **ornithology?**
    a. braces on teeth
    b. birds
    c. ocean currents

____ 5. **chemistry?**
    a. tracking satellites
    b. interactions of matter
    c. flying airplanes

____ 6. **genetics?**
    a. generators and electricity
    b. diamonds and other gems
    c. genes and heredity

____ 7. **geology?**
    a. crustaceans
    b. Earth's crust
    c. pizza crusts

____ 8. **archeology?**
    a. ancient cultures
    b. arches
    c. feet

____ 9. **physics?**
    a. moraines and mountains
    b. octopi and eels
    c. matter, energy, and forces

____ 10. **ecology?**
    a. habitats and environments
    b. E. coli bacteria
    c. echoes and sounds

____ 11. **anatomy?**
    a. insides of bodies
    b. black holes and galaxies
    c. echoes and sounds

____ 12. **botany?**
    a. bottom of rivers
    b. plants
    c. amphibians and fish

____ 13. **seismology?**
    a. faults
    b. earthquakes
    c. both of above

____ 14. **hydrology?**
    a. water tables
    b. measurement tables
    c. hydras

____ 15. **microbiology?**
    a. life too small to see
    b. insides of computers
    c. clouds and weather

____ 16. **zoology?**
    a. zoo employees
    b. animals
    c. old ruins

____ 17. **cytology?**
    a. vision
    b. cells
    c. mixtures

____ 18. **physiology?**
    a. ocean currents
    b. processes in body
    c. fizzy things

____ 19. **entomology?**
    a. planets and their orbits
    b. clouds and rain
    c. insects

____ 20. **pathology?**
    a. forest trails
    b. diseases
    c. space creatures

____ 21. **astronomy?**
    a. heavenly bodies
    b. human bodies
    c. bodies of water

____ 22. **ichthyology?**
    a. animal diseases
    b. fish
    c. aquariums

____ 23. **paleontology?**
    a. fossils
    b. protozoans
    c. planets

____ 24. **thermodynamics?**
    a. flight
    b. heat
    c. light

____ 25. **astronautics?**
    a. stars and planets
    b. fortunes
    c. space travel

____ 26. **marine biology?**
    a. Army, Navy, and Marines
    b. sea life
    c. butterflies

Use with page 208.
Name

FOR BUDDING SCIENTISTS

Dr. de Plant knows that plants can be divided into two groups: those that make seeds and those that do not! Both groups are further divided into smaller groups. She plans to put both kinds of plants in her little gardens.

Look at the pictures of the plants and decide which ones are seed plants and which ones have no seeds. Then draw each plant in the correct garden.

SEED PLANTS

NONSEED PLANTS

Pine

Cactus

Fern

Daisy

Bean Plant

Liverwort

Orchid

Oak

Wheat

Moss

Horsetail

Name

PILFERED PLANTS

Oh, no! Liverwort has done it again! She's gone into the neighbor's garden and yanked up some plants. Before Dr. de Plant drags Liverwort next door to apologize, review the parts of these plants. Draw a line from each word to the flower part or plant part it names. Then color the plants.

Flower Parts

pollen grains

ovary

pistil

petal

sepal

anther

stamen

Plant Parts

leaves

root

stems

taproot

root hairs

stomata

What does pilfered mean? _____

Name _____

VITAL PROCESSES

Without plants, there could be no human life on Earth. Plants help give us good air, and they provide us with food. Liverwort is fascinated by the work of plants. What processes are being shown by each pictured plant?

Write **transpiration, respiration,** or **photosynthesis** above the correct picture. Then fill in the blanks below to describe each process.

1. _____   2. _____   3. _____

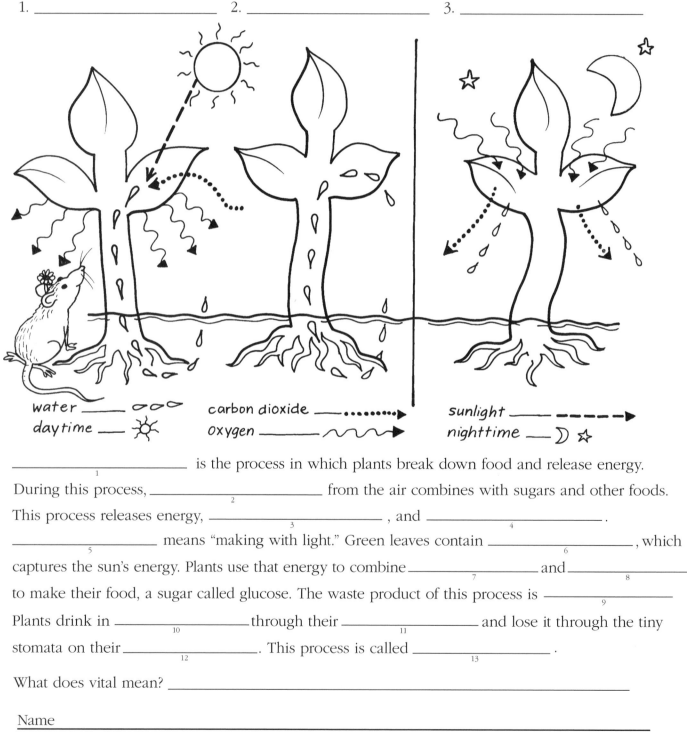

water _____ ⌀⌀⌀   carbon dioxide ___ •••••••▶   sunlight _____ ------▶
daytime _____ ☀   oxygen _____ ∿∿▶   nighttime ___ ☽ ☆

_____ is the process in which plants break down food and release energy.
_1_

During this process, _____ from the air combines with sugars and other foods.
_2_

This process releases energy, _____ , and _____ .
_3_   _4_

_____ means "making with light." Green leaves contain _____ , which
_5_   _6_

captures the sun's energy. Plants use that energy to combine _____ and _____
_7_   _8_

to make their food, a sugar called glucose. The waste product of this process is _____
_9_

Plants drink in _____ through their _____ and lose it through the tiny
_10_   _11_

stomata on their _____. This process is called _____ .
_12_   _13_

What does vital mean? _____

Name _____

"FILE 'EM" OR "PHYLUM"?

The animal kingdom is classified into nine major groups called phyla. Each group is a phylum. Help Dr. de Plant identify the animals pictured on the cards so that she can get them in the right spots in her file.

Write the correct file number on each animal card to show its phylum.

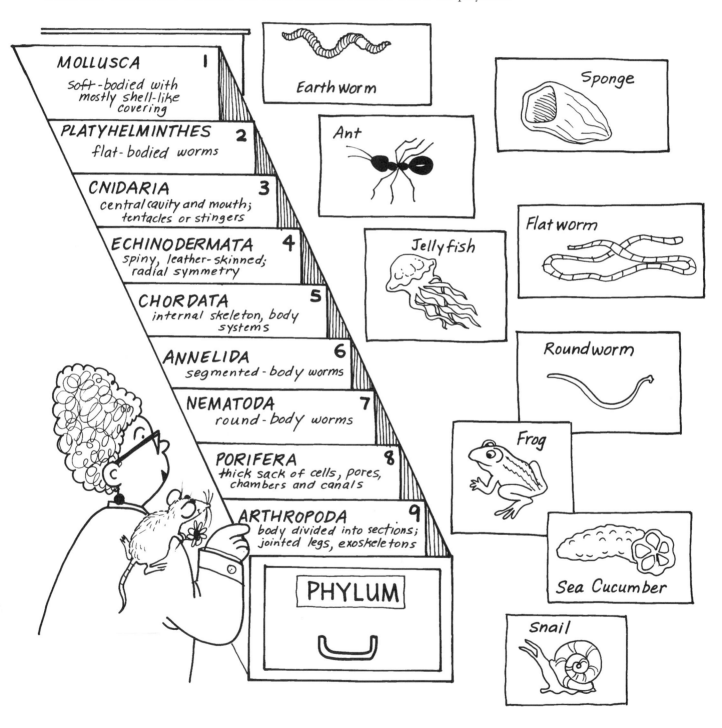

MOLLUSCA 1
soft-bodied with mostly shell-like covering

PLATYHELMINTHES 2
flat-bodied worms

CNIDARIA 3
central cavity and mouth; tentacles or stingers

ECHINODERMATA 4
spiny, leather-skinned; radial symmetry

CHORDATA 5
internal skeleton, body systems

ANNELIDA 6
segmented-body worms

NEMATODA 7
round-body worms

PORIFERA 8
thick sack of cells, pores, chambers and canals

ARTHROPODA 9
body divided into sections; jointed legs, exoskeletons

PHYLUM

Earth worm

Ant

Jellyfish

Sponge

Flat worm

Roundworm

Frog

Sea Cucumber

Snail

Name

NO BONES ABOUT IT

Not one of the animals Iris sees on her vacation at the beach has bones! They are all invertebrates ("having no backbone"). Most phyla (groups) of animals are invertebrates. Write the letter of each animal on the line next to the description of its phylum.

_____ 1. SPONGES: thick sack of cells with pores or chambers; live in water

_____ 2. CNIDARIA: mouth, central cavity and stinging tentacles; live in water

_____ 3. FLATWORMS: flat body; live in water or as parasites

_____ 4. ROUNDWORMS: round body; live in water, on land, or as parasites

_____ 5. SEGMENTED WORMS: body divided into segments; bristles on body

_____ 6. MOLLUSKS: soft bodies; some have hard shell or tough coverings

_____ 7. ARTHROPODS: segmented bodies; jointed legs; exoskeletons

_____ 8. ECHINODERMS: spiny skin; live in salt water

Name

THE MISSING CHORDATES

When Liverwort sneaks into the mini-zoo for a visit, she will be surprised to find that the animals are missing. This zoo is supposed to have animals from five classes of vertebrates (animals with backbones).

Read the description of the classes below. Label each one. Then draw one or more examples of each class in the places you think they would be in this zoo. Draw Liverwort in the picture, too. By the way, what class does she belong to?

1. _____ cold-blooded, live in water, breathe with gills, hatch from eggs

2. _____ live part of lives on land and part in water, cold-blooded, have moist skin

3. _____ warm-blooded, covered with feathers, have wings and beaks, hatch from eggs, breathe with lungs, have hollow bones

4. _____ covered with fur or hair, warm-blooded, breathe with lungs, most babies develop inside mother, mother produces milk for babies

5. _____ cold-blooded, live mostly on land, covered with scales, hatch from eggs, breathe with lungs

Liverwort is a _____.

Name

ECO-TREE

The watchful owl is a bit disturbing to Liverwort. She knows that owls are natural predators for rats, mice, and other small animals. So Liverwort is keeping her distance! The predator–prey relationship is one of many relationships in the ecosystem. Solve the puzzle to name some more ecology terms and relationships. Use the clues at the bottom of the page.

CLUES

1. organisms that eat living things
2. an area with a particular climate, plants, and animals
3. an organism that breaks down dead organisms
4. all the organisms that live together in an area
5. an animal that captures other animals for food
6. an animal that eats dead animals
7. the study of interactions between organisms and the environment
8. place where groups of organisms live and grow
9. A pathway of food and energy through an ecosystem is a food _____.
10. organism that makes food by photosynthesis
11. the animal eaten by a predator
12. A complex network of food chains is a food _____.

Name _____

A VERY "GNAW"-TY PET

Oh, oh! Liverwort is in trouble again! This time she has been munching on Dr. de Plant's notebook where she keeps facts about ecology. Fill in the missing words that Liverwort has eaten. Use words from the box below.

A. When an owl eats a rat, the rat is the

B. When an owl eats a rat, the owl is the

C. A specific area where plants and animals live is a

D. All the organisms that live in an area are called a

E. Plants are _____ and plant-eating animals are _____.

F. This is an example of a _____ : a fish eats sea plants, then a gull eats the fish.

G. Many food chains together make up a

H. A _____ lives off another living thing and is harmful to it.

I. _____ and _____ both eat dead animals.

J. Termites and beetles might _____ for the same food on a dead tree.

K. Camouflage is an _____ that lets animals blend in with the environment to hide from their prey.

When a frog catches a fly on its sticky tongue, the _____ is the prey.

frog	consumers	prey	parasite	food web	compete	scavengers	decomposers
fly	predator	producers	habitat	food chain	adaptation	community	ecology

Name

BODY TALK

_____ 1. ligaments
_____ 2. trachea
_____ 3. valve
_____ 4. intestines
_____ 5. spinal cord
_____ 6. platelets
_____ 7. ribs
_____ 8. bronchus
_____ 9. teeth
_____ 10. aorta
_____ 11. joint
_____ 12. stomach
_____ 13. cerebellum
_____ 14. cartilage
_____ 15. tongue
_____ 16. cornea
_____ 17. tendon
_____ 18. atrium
_____ 19. diaphragm
_____ 20. sternum
_____ 21. saliva
_____ 22. lungs
_____ 23. taste buds
_____ 24. white cells
_____ 25. stirrup
_____ 26. femur
_____ 27. hamstring
_____ 28. esophagus
_____ 29. neuron
_____ 30. drum
_____ 31. pupil
_____ 32. biceps
_____ 33. lens

There are certain words that get used when bodies are the subject of the conversation. Which body system does each of these words talk about?

Look at the names of the systems shown on the chart. Each body part listed is part of one or more of these systems. Write the code for the correct system next to each body part.

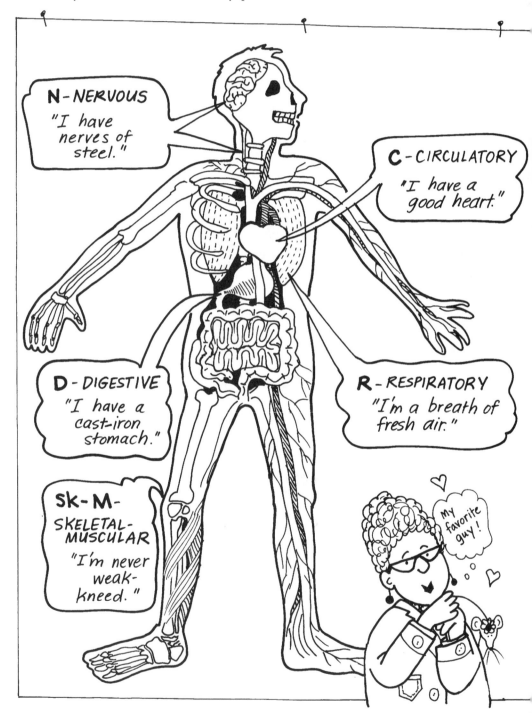

Name _____

VIEW FROM THE INSIDE

Iris knows that her body has over 600 muscles and exactly 206 bones. Together these make up about half of her entire body weight. As a biologist, she knows the names of most of those 800 body parts. Here are a few for you to review! Draw a line from each name to the matching muscle or bone.

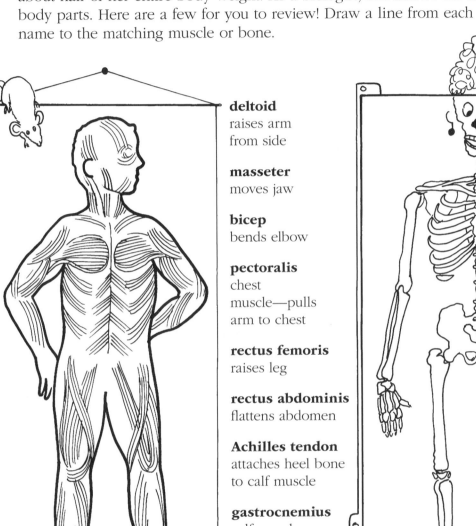

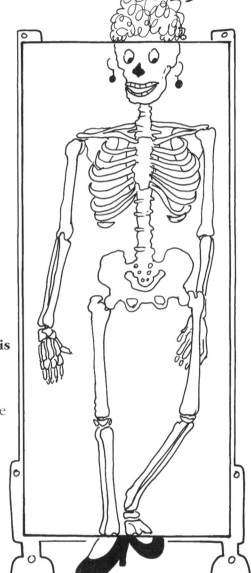

Look at me!

deltoid
raises arm from side

masseter
moves jaw

bicep
bends elbow

pectoralis
chest muscle—pulls arm to chest

rectus femoris
raises leg

rectus abdominis
flattens abdomen

Achilles tendon
attaches heel bone to calf muscle

gastrocnemius
calf muscle— raises heel

clavicle

scapula

cranium

radius

ulna

sternum

patella

phalanges

humerus

vertebra

femur

ribs

fibula

pelvis

tarsals

tibia

1. A muscle you can control is a(n) _____ muscle.

2. A muscle that you do not have to control is a(n) _____ muscle.

3. _____ attach muscles to bones.

Name _____

MARVELOUSLY SIMPLE

Machines are marvelous for helping with work. They increase or decrease a force, or they change the amount of force needed to do work. That way, they help do work that is tougher than you could do without them! (By the way, the amount that a machine increases a force is called **mechanical advantage.**) And amazingly, all machines are made from one or more of the six simple machines.

Dr. Sparks knows the value of machines. His lab is full of them! See how many you can find. Color them this way:

lever—red
inclined plane—blue
screw—yellow
pulley—green
wedge—orange
wheel & axle—purple

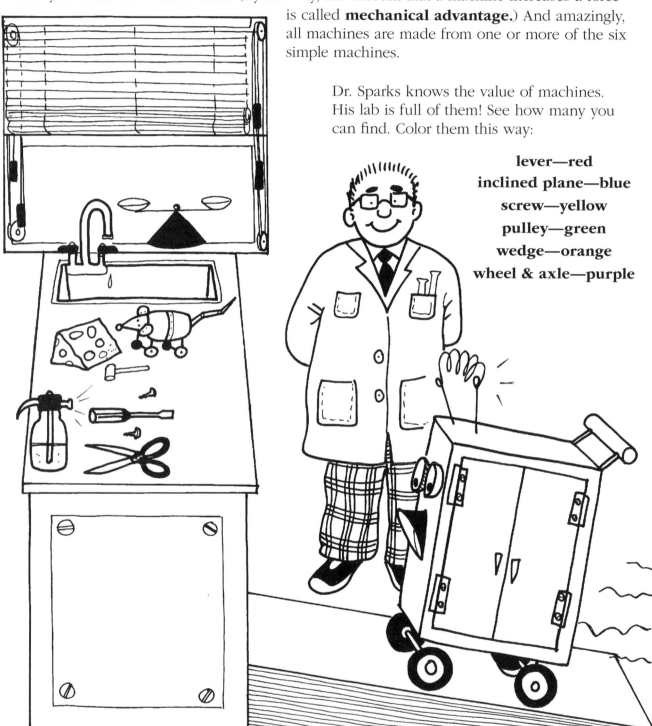

Name _____

THE GREAT BREAKUP

As a geologist, Cosmo Quake is used to breakups. He spends a lot of time observing the breakup or wearing down of rocks and minerals, but he was totally unprepared for a romantic breakup! Now, his heart is broken, and it is causing problems in his work. As he keeps notes about erosion and weathering, he keeps using the wrong words.

Cross out words that do not belong in his notes. Write the correct words that he would be writing if his life were not so disrupted by a lost romance.

1. The agents that weather and change Earth's surface are arguments, cold hearts, anger, and hurt feelings.

2. The most change is done by heartbreak.

3. Ex-girlfriends push large piles of rock and soil along and leave them piled in moraines when they melt.

4. Running tears move sediment.

5. Some minerals are dissolved in the moving sadness.

6. As rivers drag sediments along, the river romance is eroded.

7. Some sediments are discouraged as the running water slows down.

8. Rivers drop sediments when they empty into a lake or ocean. This sediment forms the down in the dumps.

9. Loose soils in the desert are easily blown away by strong wishes.

10. Plant life holds down sighs and keeps it from being eroded by wind and water.

11. Glacial hope cracks rocks and erodes soil.

12. Misery is the force that pulls material down a slope.

13. Strong winds blow sand into huge piles called desperate.

14. A large mass of valentines that covers 50,000 square kilometers or more is called a continental corsage.

15. Physical weathering is the breakup of hearts into fragments.

Name

TAKEN FOR "GRANITE"

Spewing, erupting volcanoes . . . high temperatures . . . tons of pressure . . . deposits of buried and hardened fragments . . . all of these lead to something we take for granted—the common (or not so common) ROCK! You might think rocks are pretty ordinary, not worth a lot of attention. Or you may be a serious rock hound (someone who loves, collects, and studies rocks). Whichever you are, it's good to know about rocks, because they're a pretty fundamental part of your world.

Show that you don't take rocks for granted by answering the questions on these two pages (222 and 223). You'll find some help on the rocks at the bottom of both pages. An answer may be used more than once.

1. What are the three big groups of rocks? _____

_____

2. Which rocks are formed from hardened lava that flowed from volcanoes? _____

3. What is the name of a very porous igneous rock that is so light that it floats? _____

4. What are the hollow rocks lined with crystals on their insides? _____

5. Which kind of metamorphic rocks are dense and lack banding?

_____

6. Rock fragments that are buried for a long time change because of what?

_____

7. Which rocks have a name that means "fire"? _____

8. What are the remains of once-living organisms found in sedimentary rocks?

_____

9. What are wavy features found on some sandstones?_____

10. What rocks are changed by high temperatures and high pressure?

_____

11. Name four kinds of sedimentary rocks. _____

_____

12. What term is used to describe metamorphic rocks with a banded texture?

_____

EXTRUSIVE · MARBLE · DARK · Anthracite · FOSSILS · FELSITE · CEMENTATION · RIPPLE MARKS · Quartzite · SAND-STONE · Limestone · FELDSPAR · Metamorphic · Intrusive · PUMICE · Siltstone

Use with page 223.

Name _____

13. What kinds of rocks often form in layers? _____

14. Basaltic magma would form what color of igneous rock? _____

15. Igneous rocks can change into what two groups of rocks? _____

_____

16. What class of sedimentary rocks is made of fragments of rocks, minerals, and shells?

_____

17. Which igneous rocks are coarse-grained due to slow cooling? _____

18. Name four kinds of metamorphic rocks. _____

_____

19. What kinds of rocks are caused by weathering? _____

20. Name four kinds of igneous rocks. _____

_____

21. What is the class that includes sedimentary rocks that are deposited

from a solution made by organic processes?_____

22. What metamorphic rock is commonly known as "coal"? _____

23. Which igneous rocks are fine-grained due to fast cooling? _____

24. What process happens when mud or silt is buried and water and air are

squeezed out, producing such rocks as shale? _____

25. What process happens when minerals are precipitated out of water and
hold particles of rock together? _____

26. What rocks are a mix of rounded pebbles and sand? _____

27. What rocks are a mix of sharp, angular pebbles? _____

28. What sedimentary rock is formed from thin layers of clay compacted very

tightly together? _____

29. Where is the precipitate calcite commonly found to create interesting

formations in the ground? _____

30. What animals secrete calcite around their bodies, forming massive reefs?

_____

Pressure
GEODES
BRECCIA
CONGLOMERATE
Granite
CORALS
IGNEOUS
SHALE
CAVES
SEDIMENTARY
nonfoliated
FOLIATED
COMPACTION
LIGHT
CLASTIC
SLATE
basalt
NON-CLASTIC

Use with page 222.

Name _____

GREAT QUAKES & ERUPTIONS

Can you find out about some of Earth's most devastating earthquakes, most damaging volcanoes, longest earthquakes, most active volcanoes? Get a good almanac or encyclopedia, and see what you can learn about these earthquakes and volcanoes.

EARTHQUAKES

Write what you can find out about the magnitude, length, and damage of each "quake."

1923 Tokyo _____

1927 China _____

1939 Chile _____

1970 Peru _____

1976 China _____

1980 Italy _____

1989 San Francisco _____

1992 Turkey _____

1993 India _____

1994 California _____

1995 Japan _____

VOLCANOES

Write what you can find out about these eruptions and their damage.

A.D. 79 Mt. Vesuvius, Italy _____

1669 Mt. Etna, Sicily _____

1792 Mt. Unzen, Japan _____

1815 Mt. Tambora, Indonesia _____

1883 Mt. Krakotoa, Indonesia _____

1902 Mt. Pelée, Martinique _____

1906 Mt. Vesuvius, Italy _____

1980 Mt. St. Helens, Oregon, USA _____

1984 Mt. Mauna Loa, Hawaii _____

1985 Nevado del Ruiz, Colombia _____

Name _____

A DANGEROUS ATTRACTION

Robo Rat has a big problem! He needs some new batteries, but they are lying on the other side of a pile of magnets. Since he is made of steel, the magnets will grab him and hold him forever! Fortunately, some of the magnets are "fake"—they are made of plastic. Color the fake magnets that contain false statements red. Then draw a path that touches only the fake magnets. Keep him away from the real magnets with true statements. He could get stuck!

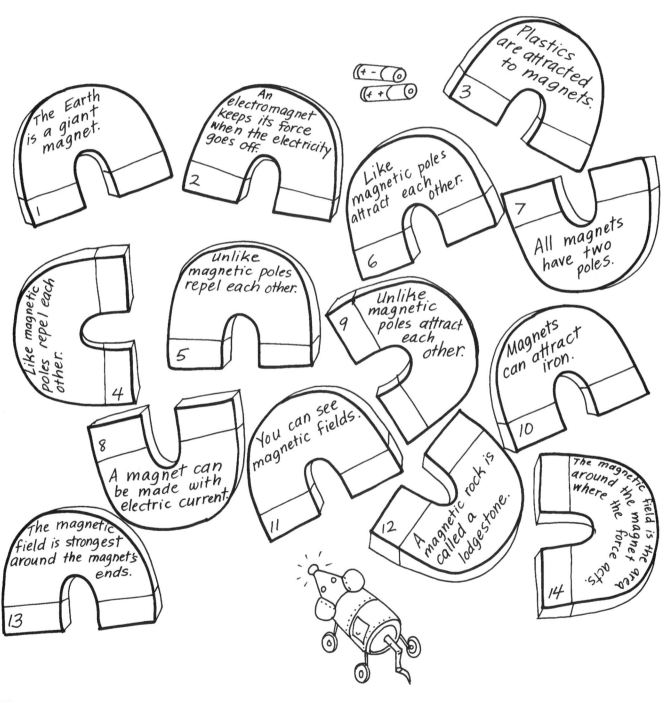

1. The Earth is a giant magnet.

2. An electromagnet keeps its force when the electricity goes off.

3. Plastics are attracted to magnets.

4. Like magnetic poles repel each other.

5. Unlike magnetic poles repel each other.

6. Like magnetic poles attract each other.

7. All magnets have two poles.

8. A magnet can be made with electric current.

9. Unlike magnetic poles attract each other.

10. Magnets can attract iron.

11. You can see magnetic fields.

12. A magnetic rock is called a lodgestone.

13. The magnetic field is strongest around the magnet's ends.

14. The magnetic field is the area around the magnet where the force acts.

Name

MATH

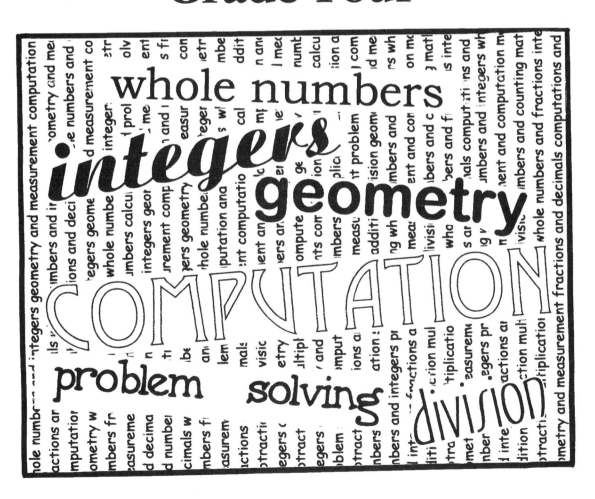

Skills Exercises
Grade Four

SKILLS CHECKLIST
Computation & Numbers and Problem Solving

✔	SKILL	PAGE(S)
	Select the proper operation for a given computation	232, 233
	Solve word problems with whole numbers	232, 233
	Solve equations with whole numbers	232, 233, 240
	Divide whole numbers	232, 233, 240, 241
	Choose among a variety of whole number operations	232, 233, 241
	Add and subtract whole numbers	232, 233, 238, 239
	Read and write whole numbers	234
	Compare and order whole numbers	235
	Round whole numbers	236
	Identify place value of whole numbers	237
	Multiply and divide by powers of ten	240
	Multiply whole numbers	240, 241
	Solve problems in long division	242, 243
	Name fractional parts of a whole or set	244
	Read and write fractional numbers and mixed numerals	244, 245
	Solve word problems with fractional and decimal numerals	244, 245
	Add and subtract fractions and mixed numerals	246, 247
	Write and solve equations with fractions and decimals	246, 247
	Read and write decimals and mixed numerals	248, 249
	Compare and order decimals and mixed numerals	249
	Identify information needed for solving a problem	250, 251
	Solve problems involving metric measurements	250, 251
	Solve problems involving U.S. customary measurements	250, 251
	Solve problems using fractions	250, 251
	Solve problems using decimals	250, 251, 258
	Solve a variety of word problems	250–254, 258
	Solve problems using information from diagrams and illustrations	253–255, 258, 259
	Solve multistep problems	256–258
	Find missing numbers for problem solutions	257
	Solve problems using money	258
	Select appropriate operation(s) for solving problems	259

SKILLS CHECKLIST
Geometry & Measurement and Graphing, Statistics, & Probability

✔	SKILL	PAGE(S)
	Identify kinds of lines: perpendicular, parallel, and intersecting	260
	Identify and describe points, lines, line segments, rays, and planes	260, 261
	Identify different kinds of angles	260, 262
	Identify plane figures	261, 263
	Identify and define kinds of triangles: scalene, equilateral, isosceles, and right	263
	Identify and define different kinds of polygons	264
	Identify properties and parts of a circle	265
	Recognize and define space figures	266
	Identify similar and congruent figures	267
	Identify various U.S. customary units for measuring	268
	Compare volume of space figures	269
	Identify various metric units for measuring	270
	Use U.S. customary measurements for measurement tasks	271
	Find the perimeter of plane figures	272, 273
	Determine time measurements	274, 275
	Read & interpret tables of statistics	276, 277
	Read & interpret a pictograph	278, 279
	Read & interpret a circle graph	280
	Read & interpret a line graph	281
	Read & interpret a bar graph	282, 283
	Find locations on a coordinate grid	284, 285, 286
	Plot locations on a coordinate grid	286, 287
	Describe possible outcomes of events	288
	Describe all the possible outcomes of one action	288
	Find probability of an event	289

THE FINAL COUNT

When the Olympic Games are over, the medals are counted. At the Summer Olympic Games in Atlanta, 842 medals were awarded. This is the way the final count looked for the top 20 medal-winning countries. Use the chart to solve the problems below.

Summer Olympic Games
Final Medal Standings for Top 20 Countries

Country	Gold	Silver	Bronze	Total Medals
United States	44	32	25	
Germany	20	18		65
Russia		21	16	63
China	16	22	12	
Australia	9		23	41
France		7	15	37
Italy	13	10	12	
South Korea	7	15		27
Cuba	9	8		25
Ukraine		2	12	23
Canada	3		8	22
Hungary		4	10	21
Romania	4		9	20
Netherlands	4	5		19
Poland	7	5	5	
Spain	5	6	6	
Bulgaria	3	7	5	
Brazil	3		9	15
Great Britain	1	8	6	
Belarus	1	6		15

1. Write the missing numbers in the spaces on the chart.

2. Which four countries won the same total number of medals? _____

   _____

3. Which two countries won 17 medals?

   _____

4. Which three countries each won 12 bronze medals? _____

   _____

   _____

5. Which country won the same number of gold and bronze medals? _____

6. Which country won 8 times as many bronze medals as gold medals? _____

7. Which country won twice as many medals as Cuba? _____

8. Which country won more bronze medals than the U.S.? _____

9. How many more gold medals did Russia win than Ukraine? _____

10. Which country won half of its medals in silver? _____

Use with page 233.

Name _____

THE FINAL COUNT, CONT.

The medal count is quite different at the Winter Olympics because there are fewer events. The chart below tells the final medal count for all medal-winning countries at the Winter Olympic Games in Lillehammer, Norway. Use the information to solve the problems below.

_____ 1. Write the missing numbers in the spaces on the chart.

_____ 2. Find the total number of medals awarded in 1994.

_____ 3. How many medals did the top 6 countries win?

_____ 4. How many medals did the other 16 countries win?

_____ 5. Which country won more gold medals than Norway?

_____ 6. Which country won more silver and bronze, but fewer gold medals than the U.S.?

_____ 7. Which country won three times the gold medals of Canada?

_____ 8. Which country won the same number of gold medals as Switzerland?

_____ 9. Which country won 17 more medals than China?

_____ 10. Which country won 22 fewer medals than Norway?

Winter Olympic Games
Final Medal Standings

Country	Gold	Silver	Bronze	Total Medals
Norway	10	11	5	
Germany	9	7		24
Russia	11		4	23
Italy	7	5	8	
United States	6		2	13
Canada		6	4	13
Switzerland		4	2	9
Austria	2	3	4	
South Korea		1	1	6
Finland	0		5	6
Japan	1	2		5
France	0		4	5
Netherlands	0	1	3	
Sweden		1	0	3
Kazakstan	1	2	0	
China	0		2	3
Slovenia	0	0		3
Ukraine		0	1	2
Belarus	0	2	0	
Great Britain	0		2	2
Uzbekistan	1	0		1
Australia		0	1	1

Use with page 232.

Name _____

A BIG RACE—A WARM POOL

At the Summer Olympics in Atlanta, 14,000 people could find seats in the Aquatic Center to watch swimming events. Swimmers could compete in 32 different events for medals. They swam from 50 meters to 1500 meters in different races. The swimming pool was 50 meters long, with water that stayed at about 78 °F to 80 °F.

There are many numbers around the Olympic Games—numbers of people and medals, scores, distances, measurements, temperatures, and amounts of money.

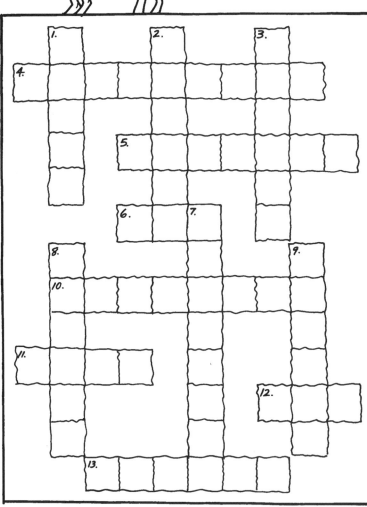

**Read these numbers written in words.
Write the numerals into the puzzle to match the clues.**

DOWN

1. forty thousand, nine hundred, seventy-three

2. one hundred fifty-one thousand, six hundred

3. nine hundred thousand, nine hundred, one

7. seventy-one million, eight hundred thousand, three

8. six hundred ten thousand, three hundred, ninety

9. four hundred fifty thousand, nine

ACROSS

4. three hundred million, fifty thousand, eight

5. two million, six hundred thousand, nine hundred

6. two hundred seven

10. twelve million, eight thousand, thirty-five

11. eight thousand, three hundred, fifty-one

12. nine hundred nine

13. three hundred thousand, three hundred

Name _____

SNATCH, CLEAN, & JERK!

Snatch, clean, and *jerk* may not sound like sports words—but they are! These strange words tell the names of the important moves in weight lifting. To perform a Snatch, the lifter brings the weight from a platform to an overhead hold in one movement. To perform a Clean & Jerk, the lifter pulls more weight, but the lift has two parts. First, the lifter brings the weight to his shoulders, and then he lifts it overhead.

1. **Look at these weights lifted by some Olympic athletes. Read the numbers and put them in order by numbering from 1 to 12 to show the numbers from smallest to largest, with 1 being the smallest.**

_____	Alexandre	462 kg
_____	Leonid	425 kg
_____	Manfred	430 kg
_____	Martin	407 kg
_____	Dean	412 kg
_____	Mario	410 kg
_____	Sulton	440 kg
_____	Jurgen	411 kg
_____	Todeuz	408 kg
_____	Vassili	441 kg
_____	Helmut	387 kg
_____	Rudolf	610 kg

2. **Number these from smallest to largest.**

_____	72,999
_____	70,859
_____	107,200
_____	17,040
_____	5,966
_____	1,000,000
_____	600,000
_____	51,030
_____	999,999

Olympic Fact

Tommy Kono was sick as a child. His parents tried to cure his asthma with powdered snakes, burned bird, and bear kidneys. During World War II, his family was sent to a Japanese-American detention camp. It was a terrible time for his family, but he was introduced to weight lifting there. Tommy won a gold medal as a weight lifter in 1952.

Name _____

THE ETERNAL FLAME

At the Summer Olympic Games in Atlanta, 10,300 athletes gathered under the Olympic flag to compete in 271 events from 31 different sports. There were 1,929 medals given. Many Olympic symbols were in view at the Opening Ceremonies. The most breathtaking symbol was the Olympic Torch. Its flame came from a torch that burns continuously in Athens, Greece. This "eternal flame" was originally ignited by the sun. Every Olympic year, the flame is carried to the host city by a torch relay. Many people take part in bringing the flame to the site of the latest Olympic Games.

When information about the Olympics is reported, the numbers are often rounded for easier repeating. Round these numbers to the digit that is underlined.

1. 10,750 _____

2. 271 _____

3. 1,933 _____

4. 357 _____

5. 891 _____

6. 7,486 _____

7. 15,426 _____

8. 4,542 _____

9. 800,426 _____

10. 754,086 _____

11. 999,999 _____

12. 101,326 _____

13. 60,600 _____

14. 774,688 _____

15. 10,987 _____

16. 766 _____

17. 98,922 _____

18. 609 _____

19. 555 _____

20. 55,555 _____

21. 923 _____

22. 18,533 _____

23. 600,001 _____

24. 1,507 _____

Name _____

CLEAN JUMPS, PLEASE!

Show jumping is the most thrilling and most televised of all the Olympic equestrian events. The rider takes the horse around a course full of obstacles at top speeds. On the way, the rider tries to keep control of the horse and to avoid trips, falls, or other faults!

Help this rider get around this course without errors. Write the place value for each underlined digit. Write the answer on each obstacle the horse must jump.

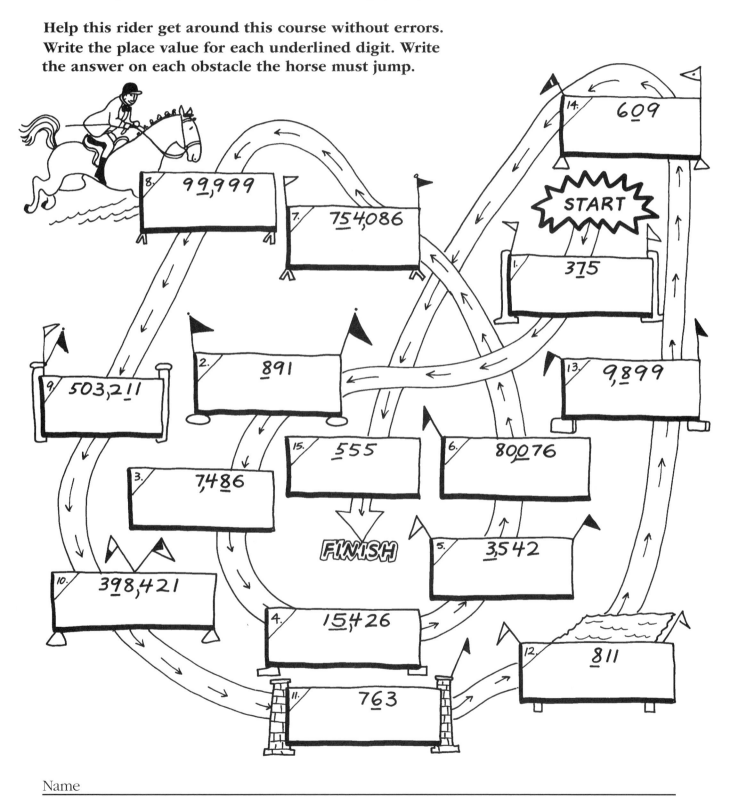

HIGH SPEEDS & TOUGH TURNS

Experts say that the giant slalom takes the most technical skill of any ski event. Skiers race down the mountain over a long, steep, fast course. They must go through a series of gates marked by flags. Spectators also love to watch the downhill slalom, where skiers make high-speed turns to go through the gates at speeds of up to 80 miles per hour!

Write a long column addition problem using all the numbers on the slalom gate flags. Use box #1 to write and solve your problem. Then solve the other column addition problems.

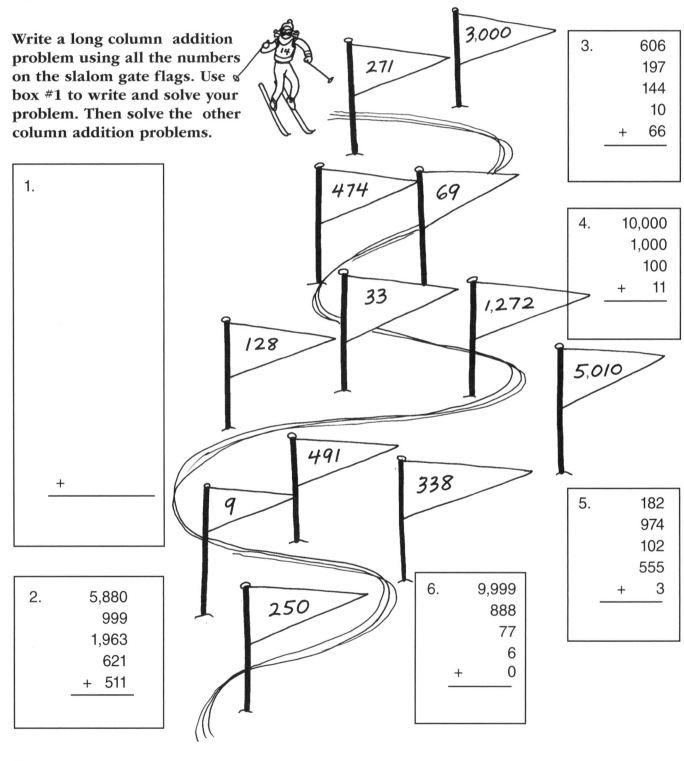

Flags: 271, 3,000, 474, 69, 33, 1,272, 128, 5,010, 491, 338, 9, 250

1.

+
_____

2.
```
    5,880
      999
    1,963
      621
  +  511
_____
```

3.
```
      606
      197
      144
       10
  +    66
_____
```

4.
```
   10,000
    1,000
      100
  +    11
_____
```

5.
```
      182
      974
      102
      555
  +     3
_____
```

6.
```
    9,999
      888
       77
        6
  +     0
_____
```

Name _____

KNOCK OUT!

Boxing was not allowed at the first modern Olympics in 1896 because it was considered too ungentlemanly and dangerous. Today it is a very popular Olympic sport. Some of the world's greatest boxers, such as Floyd Patterson, Muhammad Ali, Sugar Ray Leonard, Joe Frazier, Floyd Mayweather, and Evander Holyfield, won Olympic medals before becoming professional boxers.

See if you can knock out these subtraction problems by getting all the answers right!

1.
$$500 - 229$$

2.
$$900 - 683$$

3.
$$40 - 26$$

4.
$$300 - 258$$

5.
$$407 - 133$$

6.
$$90 - 55$$

7.
$$800 - 393$$

8.
$$5,500 - 203$$

9.
$$9,050 - 5,348$$

10.
$$7,001 - 6,420$$

11.
$$6,110 - 456$$

12.
$$8,006 - 731$$

13.
$$800,321 - 79,001$$

14.
$$32,000 - 19,862$$

Olympic Fact

One of the most memorable moments of the 1996 Summer Olympic Games in Atlanta was when boxing legend and 1960 gold medal-winner Muhammad Ali (who suffers from Parkinson's disease) lit the Olympic torch.

Name _____

SAILING WITHOUT A SAIL

It's spectacular . . . breathtaking . . . awesome! Crowds at the Winter Olympics always love to watch the ski jumpers sailing through the air. Spectators hold their breath until the skier lands safely on the ground! Skiers gain points for strong take-offs, smooth flights, clean landings, and distance. Skiers take off into the air from jumps as high as 120 meters and sail for hundreds of feet.

Use multiplication to figure out these distances.

1. 23 meters x 10   = _____

2. 23 meters x 100   = _____

3. 31 meters x 30   = _____

4. 111 meters x 1,000   = _____

5. 505 meters x 10   = _____

6. 2,222 meters x 400   = _____

7. 717 meters x 10,000   = _____

8. 4,024 meters x 20   = _____

9. 70 meters x 40   = _____

10. 250 meters x 1,000   = _____

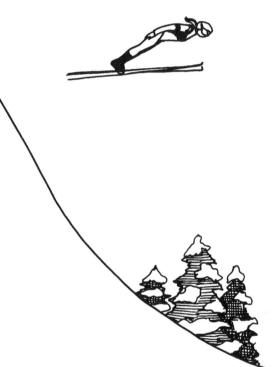

Use division to figure out these distances.

11. 4,400 meters ÷ 10   = _____

12. 4,400 meters ÷ 100   = _____

13. 4,400 meters ÷ 200   = _____

14. 1,000 meters ÷ 10   = _____

15. 1,000 meters ÷ 100   = _____

16. 330 meters ÷ 10   = _____

17. 880,000 meters ÷ 1,000   = _____

18. 700 meters ÷ 70   = _____

19. 5,600 meters ÷ 80   = _____

20. 61,070 meters ÷ 10   = _____

Olympic Fact

Judges stand at one-meter intervals along the edge of the hill and watch to see where the ski jumpers land. They decide the distances with their eyes instead of measuring with any tools.

Name _____

HOLD YOUR BREATH!

Can you imagine doing a complicated routine underwater in perfect timing with other athletes for $3\frac{1}{2}$ minutes, while holding your breath for most of the time? Synchronized swimmers do just that. In this Olympic sport, swimmers spend 60% of the routine time underwater. They must do difficult, synchronized movements, and touching the bottom or side of the pool is not allowed!

In each row of these problems, one problem is not synchronized with the others! The answers to all the problems in each row are the same—except for one. Find the different answer in each row, and write that answer on the swim cap of the swimmer at the end of the row.

> **Olympic Fact**
>
> Synchronized swimming used to be called water ballet. The U.S. team won the gold in this event at the 1996 Olympics.

1. $2\overline{)400}$ $\begin{array}{r} 40 \\ \times\ 5 \\ \hline \end{array}$ $\begin{array}{r} 1,400 \\ -\ 1,200 \\ \hline \end{array}$ $\begin{array}{r} 197 \\ +\ \ \ 4 \\ \hline \end{array}$ $\begin{array}{r} 1,654 \\ -1,454 \\ \hline \end{array}$

2. $\begin{array}{r} 88 \\ \times\ \ 9 \\ \hline \end{array}$ $\begin{array}{r} 655 \\ +\ 137 \\ \hline \end{array}$ $\begin{array}{r} 1,000 \\ -\ \ \ 205 \\ \hline \end{array}$ $5\overline{)3,960}$ $1,584 \div 2$

3. $\begin{array}{r} 99 \\ +\ 45 \\ \hline \end{array}$ $3\overline{)288}$ $\begin{array}{r} 4,791 \\ -4,647 \\ \hline \end{array}$ $5\overline{)720}$ $\begin{array}{r} 36 \\ \times\ 4 \\ \hline \end{array}$

4. $6\overline{)3,036}$ $\begin{array}{r} 894 \\ -\ 388 \\ \hline \end{array}$ $\begin{array}{r} 311 \\ +\ 195 \\ \hline \end{array}$ $\begin{array}{r} 98 \\ \times\ 6 \\ \hline \end{array}$ $\begin{array}{r} 2,000 \\ -\ 1,494 \\ \hline \end{array}$

5. $\begin{array}{r} 6,670 \\ -\ 6,000 \\ \hline \end{array}$ $2\overline{)1,340}$ $\begin{array}{r} 1,200 \\ -\ \ 530 \\ \hline \end{array}$ $\begin{array}{r} 210 \\ \times\ \ 3 \\ \hline \end{array}$ $\begin{array}{r} 158 \\ 111 \\ +401 \\ \hline \end{array}$

Name

WEIGHTY CALCULATIONS

Sumo wrestling is a sport for athletes with strong, large bodies. Some sumo wrestlers on Earth have measured over 6 feet tall and weighed about 700 pounds. On the imaginary planet Zebulan, creatures of all heights and weights enjoy sumo wrestling Every year, Zebulan holds a competition to find the best wrestler on the planet.

Use your division skills to calculate the average weights of the Zebulan sumo wrestlers who competed in this year's competition. Write the answers in the correct spaces to solve the crossword puzzle.

Find the average weight of the athlete in each group.

Across

1. Total 4,981 lb ÷ 17 wrestlers = _____ lb each

4. Total 1,484 lb ÷ 4 wrestlers = _____ lb each

5. Total 680 lb ÷ 20 wrestlers = _____ lb each

7. Total 930 lb ÷ 10 wrestlers = _____ lb each

9. Total 1,212 lb ÷ 3 wrestlers = _____ lb each

10. Total 4,554 lb ÷ 1 wrestler = _____ lb each

12. Total 3,107 lb ÷ 13 wrestlers = _____ lb each

15. Total 9,260 lb ÷ 10 wrestlers = _____ lb each

Down

2. Total 4,200 lb ÷ 12 wrestlers = _____ lb each

3. Total 4,190 lb ÷ 10 wrestlers = _____ lb each

4. Total 35,400 lb ÷ 100 wrestlers = _____ lb each

5. Total 6,020 lb ÷ 20 wrestlers = _____ lb each

6. Total 2,952 lb ÷ 8 wrestlers = _____ lb each

8. Total 738 lb ÷ 2 wrestlers = _____ lb each

11. Total 48,600 lb ÷ 100 wrestlers = _____ lb each

13. Total 306,000 lb ÷ 1,000 wrestlers = ___ lb each

14. Total 4,470 lb ÷ 10 wrestlers = _____ lb each

Name _____

PEDALING FOR MEDALS

Olympic biker Jeannie Longo of France holds the record for the most world titles. Along with her Olympic gold medal, she has won 13 world titles and has set many biking records.

Jeannie has probably ridden thousands of miles to practice for her competitions. Here are some practice times of other bikers. Use division skills to find the missing numbers.

1. Olga: 10,000 miles in 20 weeks =

   _____ miles a week

2. MaryLou: 12,000 miles in 30 weeks =

   _____ miles a week

3. Chen Su: 5,985 miles in 7 weeks = _____ miles a week

4. Loretta: 555 miles in _____ days = 111 miles in one day

5. Katarina: 19,250 miles in 250 days = _____ miles in a day

6. Elaine: 22,000 miles in _____ weeks = 1,000 miles a week

7. Andrea: 1,650 miles in 6 months = _____ miles a month

8. Serena: 13,600 miles in _____ days = 68 miles a day

9. Tasha: 39,000 miles in _____ months = 3,000 miles a month

10. Sonja: 900 miles in 50 days = _____ miles a day

11. Helen: 2,000 miles in 40 weeks = _____ miles a week

12. Latitia: 600 miles in _____ days = 24 miles a day

13. Who rode the most in a day—Latitia, Sonja, Katarina, or Loretta? _____

Name

FROSTY SPORTS

Most sports at the Winter Olympics are outdoor sports. Even if the competitions are held indoors, the temperatures are usually cold to keep the ice from melting. You'll need to be good with fractions to solve these puzzles with facts about the Winter Olympics.

QUESTION: *Which event has brought the most Winter Olympic medals to the U.S.?*

1. Write the second $\frac{1}{6}$ of SKIING.   **K** _____

2. Write the first $\frac{1}{4}$ of ATTITUDE. _____

3. Write the first $\frac{1}{3}$ of SPECTATOR. _____

4. Write the first $\frac{1}{4}$ of GOLD. _____

5. Write the last $\frac{1}{5}$ of SNOWBOARDS. _____

6. Write the first $\frac{1}{10}$ of ICE DANCING. _____

7. Write the last $\frac{1}{4}$ of GAME. _____

8. Write the last $\frac{1}{8}$ of BIATHLON. _____

ANSWER: *Unscramble the letters to find the sport*: _____

QUESTION: *Which ski event brought U.S. skier Lindsey Vonn a gold medal in 2010?*

1. Write the first $\frac{1}{6}$ of NAGANO. _____

2. Write the first $\frac{1}{4}$ of LUGE. _____

3. Write the second $\frac{1}{5}$ of SNOWBOARDS. _____

4. Write the second $\frac{1}{8}$ of OLYMPICS. _____

5. Write the third $\frac{1}{5}$ of MEDAL. _____

6. Write the first $\frac{1}{5}$ of HIGHLIGHTS. _____

ANSWER: *Unscramble the letters to find this event:*

_____

Olympic Fact

Olympic gold medal–winner Dan Jansen has skated over 100,000 miles on his speed skates. This is more than 4 times the distance around the world.

Name _____

BE CAREFUL NOT TO SWING!

Some of the most difficult moves a male gymnast must do are done while he hangs from rings. Gymnasts show amazing skill and strength as they hold their bodies in tough positions. The rings are not supposed to swing or wobble as the gymnast does the moves! The gymnast's body and arms are not supposed to wobble, sag, or shake!

Keep these rings from wobbling by identifying the ones with lowest term fractions. If a ring holds a fraction in lowest terms, color the inside of the ring with a marker or colored pencil. If the fraction is not in lowest terms, write the lowest term fraction in the ring.

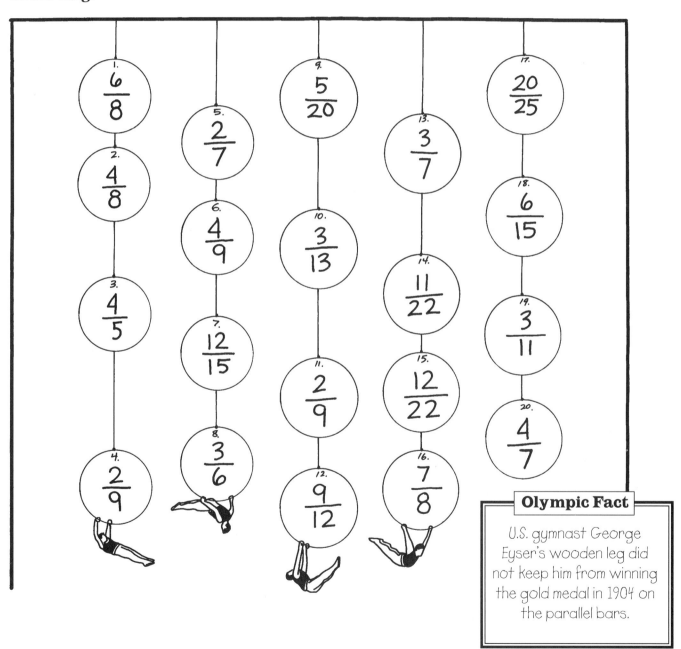

Olympic Fact

U.S. gymnast George Eyser's wooden leg did not keep him from winning the gold medal in 1904 on the parallel bars.

Name _____

PENTATHLON CALCULATIONS

Penta means five, so athletes who compete in the pentathlon have to be good at five different sports. The modern pentathlon is based on the duties of a warrior who must deliver a message across enemy lines. He has to ride a horse around many obstacles, defend himself with a sword and gun, run great distances, and swim across rivers and streams. Olympic competitors must complete contests in equestrian riding, fencing, pistol shooting, running, and swimming.

Each of these calculations also has five parts. You need to be good at each step in order to get the right answer!

1. $\frac{9}{10} - \frac{1}{10} + \frac{7}{10} + \frac{5}{10} - \frac{1}{10} =$ _____

2. $\frac{7}{9} - \frac{3}{9} - \frac{2}{9} + \frac{6}{9} - \frac{2}{9} =$ _____

3. $\frac{2}{13} + \frac{5}{13} - \frac{4}{13} + \frac{10}{13} - \frac{6}{13} =$ _____

4. $\frac{5}{6} - \frac{2}{6} + \frac{6}{6} - \frac{2}{6} - \frac{3}{6} =$ _____

5. $\frac{3}{20} - \frac{1}{20} + \frac{15}{20} - \frac{4}{20} + \frac{2}{20} =$ _____

6. $\frac{1}{11} + \frac{55}{11} + \frac{8}{11} - \frac{9}{11} + \frac{1}{11} =$ _____

7. $\frac{1}{5} - \frac{1}{5} + \frac{2}{5} + \frac{9}{5} - \frac{6}{5} =$ _____

8. $\frac{4}{16} - \frac{2}{16} + \frac{7}{16} + \frac{5}{16} + \frac{1}{16} =$ _____

9. $\frac{5}{25} - \frac{3}{25} + \frac{9}{25} - \frac{2}{25} + \frac{1}{25} =$ _____

10. $\frac{6}{12} - \frac{5}{12} + \frac{7}{12} - \frac{7}{12} + \frac{1}{12} =$ _____

11. $\frac{9}{6} - \frac{2}{6} + \frac{10}{6} - \frac{3}{6} + \frac{15}{6} =$ _____

12. $\frac{11}{100} + \frac{15}{100} - \frac{4}{100} + \frac{50}{100} - \frac{1}{100} =$ _____

13. $\frac{3}{30} + \frac{8}{30} + \frac{14}{30} - \frac{7}{30} - \frac{2}{30} =$ _____

14. $\frac{0}{10} + \frac{8}{10} + \frac{14}{10} - \frac{2}{10} + \frac{5}{10} =$ _____

Name _____

WHEN IS A SHELL A SCULL?

An exciting sport in the Summer Olympic Games is rowing. Boats used for competitive rowing are called shells. Some of the shells are sculls, but some are not! It depends on how the oars are arranged. In sculls, each crew member rows with two oars instead of one—that's the main difference! The boats are very light and move quickly over the 2000-meter course.

Solve each row of problems as quickly as the crews row the shells. Don't be sloppy, or it will take longer to correct your mistakes! Can you tell which boat is the scull?

1. $5\frac{3}{8} + 6\frac{3}{8} =$ _____

2. $17\frac{2}{8} + 9\frac{3}{8} =$ _____

3. $22\frac{4}{5} - 5\frac{2}{5} =$ _____

4. $15\frac{2}{4} - 5\frac{1}{4} =$ _____

9. $7\frac{2}{5} - 6\frac{3}{5} =$ _____

10. $30\frac{3}{11} - 20\frac{2}{11} =$ _____

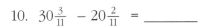

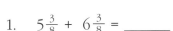

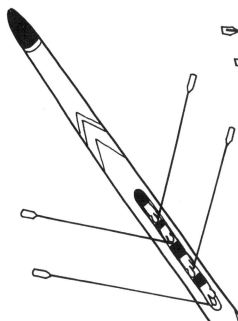

11. $2\frac{3}{9} + 4\frac{1}{9} =$ _____

12. $16\frac{2}{5} + 3\frac{2}{5} =$ _____

5. $10\frac{1}{4} + 1\frac{3}{4} =$ _____

6. $8\frac{1}{5} - 5\frac{2}{5} =$ _____

7. $5\frac{2}{3} + 5\frac{1}{2} =$ _____

8. $18\frac{2}{3} - 8\frac{1}{6} =$ _____

13. $32\frac{1}{5} - 7\frac{2}{5} =$ _____

14. $20\frac{1}{6} - 5\frac{5}{6} =$ _____

15. $\frac{1}{10} + 5\frac{9}{10} =$ _____

Name _____

TAKE THE PLUNGE!

Can you imagine jumping off a three-story building into a pool of water? This is what platform divers do. Olympic divers either jump off high platforms, where they begin at a standstill, or they jump off a bouncy spring-board. Seven judges watch each dive and score it between 0 and 10. Scores for eleven dives are added together. The diver with the highest score wins. In 1996, Mary Ellen Clark got a bronze medal for the USA with a score of 472.95.

Find a decimal in the pool to match each of the decimal words below.

1. one hundred eighty-three ten thousandths

_____

2. one and eighty-three thousandths

_____

3. one hundred fifteen thousandths

_____

4. fifty-five hundredths

_____

5. ninety-nine and seven tenths

_____

6. thirteen and four tenths

_____

7. five hundred and five thousandths

_____

8. nine and seventy-eight hundredths

_____

9. ninety-seven hundredths

_____

10. ten and eighty-three hundredths

_____

11. one hundred eight and three tenths

_____

12. two hundred thirty-four thousandths

_____

13. five and five hundred fifty-five thousandths

_____

14. nine hundred seventy-eight thousandths

_____

15. nine hundred seventy-eight and three tenths

_____

16. eleven and five hundred one thousandths

_____

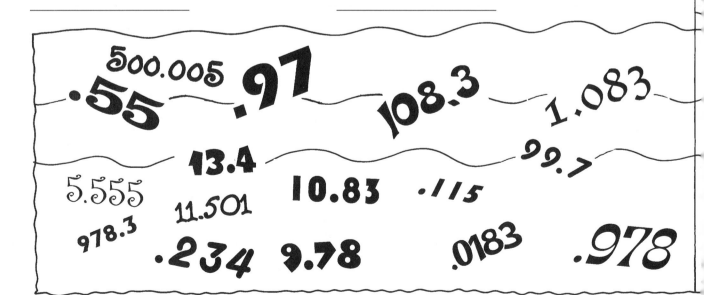

500.005 .55 .97 108.3 1.083

13.4 99.7

5.555 11.501 10.83 .115

978.3 .234 9.78 .0183 .978

Name _____

NOSE ROLLS & FAKIES

This must be the sport with the wildest names for moves and tricks! On a snowboard you can do Halfpipes, Nose Rolls, Wheelies, McTwists, Chicken Salads, and Ollies—and many more tricks with wild, wacky names! 1998 was the first time snowboarders could take part in the Olympic Games. The boarders were ready to do all these fancy tricks in Japan!

To finish each of these tricks with a good score, read the decimals on each card. Then number them in order from the largest to the smallest.

Trick #1   FAKIE

_____ 0.11103   _____ 1.7

_____ 0.103   _____ 11.3

_____ 10.370   _____ 13.01

_____ 11.370   _____ 0.13

Trick #2   NOSE ROLL

_____ 15.02   _____ 15.21

_____ 1.5   _____ 1.51

_____ 0.005   _____ 55.5

_____ 0.05   _____ 5.5

Trick #3   BACKSCRATCHER

_____ 4.5   _____ 4.7

_____ 0.451   _____ 44.5

_____ 0.45   _____ 4.4

_____ 0.06   _____ 0.44

Trick #4   McTWIST

_____ 5.28   _____ 5.6

_____ 9.97   _____ 0.009

_____ 0.8   _____ 5.8

_____ 0.99   _____ 0.08

Trick #5   CHICKEN SALAD

_____ 2.6   _____ 6.2

_____ 2.7   _____ 2.9

_____ 2.006   _____ 22.6

_____ 26.6   _____ 2.999

Trick #6   OLLIE

_____ 7.2   _____ 7.7

_____ 0.72   _____ 77.27

_____ 0.072   _____ 0.07

_____ 72.1   _____ 0.007

Trick #7   TAIL WHEELIE

_____ 0.0001   _____ 0.000001

_____ 0.001   _____ 0.01

_____ 101.1   _____ 10.11

_____ 1.1   _____ 0.00011

Name

WINTER SPORTS FEST

Every winter the Bigtown Middle School has a big Winter Sports Fest. Students can take part in all kinds of sports—from ski races and ice carving contests to elaborate snowball throwing competitions. To solve the problems about this event, you will have to decide which pieces of information are needed. For each problem on pages 250 and 251, circle the letters of the information items that are needed to find the answer. Solve the problems on a separate piece of paper, and write the answers after each problem.

1. How many cups of hot chocolate did the skaters drink? _____

    a. 500 cups of hot chocolate were gulped or sipped by all the students this year.
    b. 40 cups were drunk by the sledders and the skiers.
    c. The ice skaters drank $\frac{1}{10}$ of the hot chocolate.

2. What is Jenny's record distance for a snowball throw? _____

    a. Jenny's snowball was $2\frac{1}{2}$ inches in diameter.
    b. Joe's snowball was 3 inches in diameter.
    c. Jenny's record distance for a snowball throw is 6 meters farther than Joe's.
    d. Joe's record throw is 58.4 meters.

3. What was the difference between the highest and lowest temperatures during the 2016 Winter Sports Fest? _____

    a. On the warmest day of the 2016 Winter Sports Fest, the highest temperature was 31 °F.
    b. Water freezes at 32 °F.
    c. The coldest temperature during the 2016 Winter Sports Fest was 18 °F.
    d. The wind blew at 21 mph.
    e. The lowest temperature in 2016 was −6 °F.

4. How many spectators watched the events in the afternoon? _____

    a. There were 196 spectators attending before noon.
    b. The crowd dwindled to 53 at lunchtime.
    c. The crowd in the afternoon was $1\frac{1}{2}$ times the size of the morning crowd.

Use with page 251.

Name

5. How much faster than Wanda and Will were the sled run winners? _____

   a. Water freezes at 32 °F.

   b. Wanda and Will finished the sledding run in 1 minute 22 seconds.

   c. The slowest sled run time was 1 minute 41 seconds.

   d. Erin and Erika won the sled race with a time of 1 minute 15 seconds.

   e. The slowest sled run was 26 seconds longer than the fastest time.

6. About how many snowballs did each kid throw? _____

   a. 704 snowballs were thrown during the snowball fight competition.

   b. There were 16 kids on each of two teams.

   c. There was an equal number of fourth graders on each team.

7. What fraction of the ski team wore goggles? _____

   a. The ski team had 30 members.

   b. $\frac{1}{5}$ of the team members wore sunglasses.

   c. There were 16 girls and 14 boys on the team.

   d. 25 of the kids on the team wore goggles.

8. How many fewer times did the 6th graders fall than the 8th graders? _____

   a. There were 74 falls on the 7th-grade snowboard team.

   b. There were 88 falls on the 8th-grade snowboard team.

   c. There were 50 falls on the 6th-grade team.

   d. There were 7 members on the 8th-grade team.

9. Who was the fastest of the three racers, and what was his or her time? _____

   a. The speed skating competition was for a 500-meter distance.

   b. Sara skated the race in 65 seconds.

   c. James took 5 seconds longer than Sara.

   d. Barry's race time was 2 seconds faster than Sara's.

10. How many awards were given all together? _____

   a. The trophies and medals were awarded at the end of the Sports Fest.

   b. Awards were given for 28 events.

   c. Four awards were given for each event.

   d. Speed skaters won 16 of the awards.

Use with page 250.

Name

SPORTS TRIVIA

Solve these problems and learn some fun sports facts that you can use to impress your friends! Surprise them with your knowledge of sports trivia!

1. Yuki the sumo wrestler loves to eat ice cream before he wrestles. From January to November, he ate 19 kg of ice cream every month. In December, he ate only 16 kg. How many kg did he eat last year? _____ kg (the average weight of a sumo wrestler)

2. Mac the weightlifter packed his duffel bag carefully. He weighed each item: black belt—8 lb, spandex suit—1 lb, liniment—3 lb, protein powder—9 lb, and an old trophy—23 lb. How much does the stuff in the bag weigh? _____ lb (weight of a lifting bar)

3. Lincoln and Jefferson Middle Schools held a basketball shoot-out marathon. The Lincoln students made 920 baskets. The Jefferson kids shot 971. How many baskets were made in all? _____ (the year basketball was invented)

4. Keri entered 4 events at the gymnastics meet. She won 1 medal. Her 3 teammates each won 3 medals. How many medals did the whole team win? _____ (the width in centimeters of a balance beam)

5. Juan's swim team swims laps in a small pool. The coach counts every two lengths as 1 lap. If Juan swims 30 lengths, how many laps has he gone? _____ (number of colored balls in a billiards game)

6. Jason is 14 holes short of finishing his 22nd golf game this month. He plays 18 holes during each game. How many holes has he played this month? _____ (the number of dimples on a golf ball)

7. The Philly Freeze hockey team lost $\frac{1}{3}$ of their games last season. They played 9 games. How many did they lose? _____ (the number of points in a hockey "hat trick")

8. The state track meet was held at Feeble Stadium. It holds 12,000 spectators in 4 equal sections of seats. How many fans will fit into each section? _____ (number of meters in a cross-country race)

Name _____

LOST IN THE TREES

For this sport, equipment is everything! What is this important piece of equipment? Find out by solving the problems in your head or on a separate piece of paper. Then find the space in the puzzle with the correct answer and color that space with the color given.

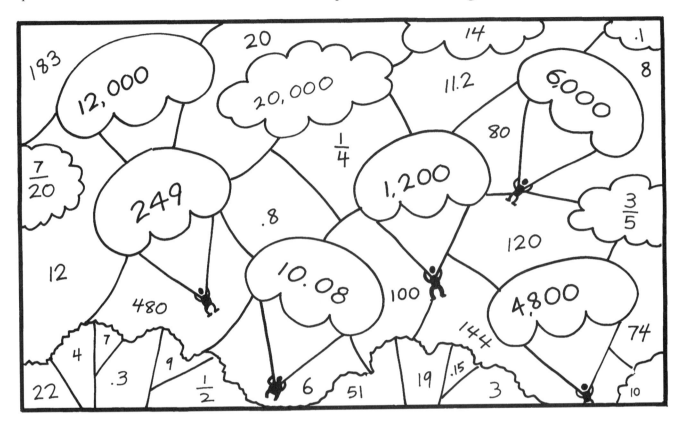

Blue

1. seventeen less than two hundred
2. twenty-one more than fifty-three
3. one-eighth of sixty-four
4. ten squared
5. half of one-half
6. ten times forty-eight
7. half of one hundred sixty
8. twelve dozen

Red

9. twice six thousand
10. ten and eight-hundredths

White

11. $\frac{1}{20}$ less than $\frac{8}{20}$
12. one hundred times two hundred
13. $\frac{1}{2}$ of twenty-eight
14. one minus nine-tenths
15. one minus $\frac{2}{5}$ Yellow

Yellow

16. five hundred dozen
17. fifty-one less than three hundred

Purple

18. seventy more than fifty
19. two-tenths plus six-tenths

20. greatest common factor of eighteen and twelve
21. least common multiple of three and four
22. least common denominator of $\frac{1}{4}$ and $\frac{7}{10}$
23. twelve minus eight-tenths

Orange

24. four hundred tripled
25. one hundred times forty-eight

Green

All spaces with other answers.

Name

TUGGING PROBLEMS

Take a close look at the team members in this tug-of-war game, so that you can finish the picture accurately. After you have worked each problem, fill in the blank next to it with the number of things you colored or drew.

1. Draw muscles on 10% of the team members. _____

2. Color 0.25 of the girls' hair orange. _____

3. Color 50% of the flowers yellow. _____

4. Color 75% of the hats green. _____

5. Color $\frac{7}{20}$ of the shoes red. _____

6. Color 0.1 of the shoes blue. _____

7. Color $\frac{4}{9}$ of the shirts blue. _____

8. Color $\frac{10}{20}$ of the rope red. _____

9. Draw stars on $\frac{2}{18}$ of the shirts. _____

10. Color 60% of the socks purple. _____

11. Color 0.6 of the shorts orange. _____

12. Draw stripes on $\frac{1}{9}$ of the shirts. _____

13. Color 0.5 of the long pants brown. _____

14. Color bruises on 5% of the elbows. _____

15. Draw bandages on 15% of the knees. _____

16. Put a new hat on 0.1 of the team members. _____

17. Draw mud under $\frac{4}{5}$ of the team members. _____

18. Draw bees stinging 0.2 of the team members. _____

19. Draw untied shoelaces hanging off $\frac{15}{100}$ of the shoes. _____

20. Draw a dog pulling on the shirt of $\frac{10}{100}$ of the team members. _____

RAH, RAH, RAH!

The Slicksville Sluggers' fans are all wound up today. Their team is on a 20-game winning streak! Solve their baseball game problems. Be sure to pay close attention! These problems will take more than one step to solve.

1. Bud, the hot dog vendor, sells 2 sizes of dogs. At Friday's game he sold 14 junior dogs at $1.50 each and 56 jumbo dogs at $2.00 each. How much money did he bring in?

_____

2. Red McGrew had a great game on Saturday. He hit a single, a double, and a home run. If the bases are 90 feet apart, how far did he run on his own hits?

_____

3. Loki's grandpa took his family to the game today. He started with $50. He bought a senior ticket for $5, two adult tickets for $7 each, and four children's tickets at $2.50 each. How much money was left for snacks?

_____

4. It rained at yesterday's game. Luckily, Rosa had brought 3 umbrellas, 2 slickers, and a plastic garbage bag. If 3 can stay dry under each umbrella, how many friends can she help out?

_____

5. Sadie and her 18 friends all wanted to sit together in the bleachers. They found 2 rows with 4 seats each and 2 rows with 3 seats each. How many more seats will they need to find?

_____

6. The booster club sells programs at 20 home games. They need to raise $6,400 for a new scoreboard. At $4 a program, how many will they need to sell at each game?

_____

Name _____

FLIPPING OVER NUMBERS

The Baker kids have been having a great time doing flips on their backyard trampoline. In order to keep track of everyone's total flips, Biff made a chart. By mistake, he left out some numbers. Finish the chart and answer the questions.

	Front Flips	Back Flips	Straddle Flips	Twist Flips	Totals
Biff	4		3	7	18
Bob	2	8	4	4	
Ben		1	6	10	22
BUD	3		3	3	12
Barb	7	9	1	1	
Bonnie	8	6		7	21
Totals					

1. Total Front Flips? _____

2. Who did the most flips? _____

3. Three kids who tied? _____

   _____ _____

4. Who did the most Front Flips? _____

5. Who did the least Straddle Flips? _____

6. Who did the same number of all four kinds of flips? _____

7. Who did the most Twist Flips? _____

8. Who tied in Twist Flips? _____

9. Kind of flip done most? _____

10. Kind of flip done least? _____

11. Barb's most successful flip? _____

12. Bonnie's least successful flip? _____

13. Whose total was 10 more than Bud's?

   _____

14. What flip total was $\frac{1}{3}$ of Bonnie's total flips? _____

15. Who flipped 3 more than Barb? _____

16. Total of all flips? _____

Name _____

THE MISSING SNACKS

Oops! Twelve people walked away from the snack stand without one of the snacks for which they had paid. Which snack is missing? You should be able to tell from looking at the total bill what food item or items they've left behind!

Write the name of the missing food (or souvenir) in the blank for each problem.

Hey! You forgot your change!

HOT DOGS $1.00	ICE CREAM $1.25
HOT PRETZELS .... 65¢	PIZZA $2.00
DRINKS .... 90¢	LICORICE .... 30¢
CANDY .... 50¢	NACHOS $1.30
POPCORN .... 60¢	COFFEE .... 75¢
PENNANTS .... 20¢	HOT CHOCOLATE .... 80¢

1. 1 hot dog _____
   1 drink _____
   1 _____ _____
   Total   **$3.90**

2. 1 pizza _____
   2 _____ _____
   1 nachos _____
   Total   **$4.80**

3. 1 _____ _____
   1 hot chocolate _____
   1 popcorn _____
   Total   **$2.65**

4. 1 _____ _____
   1 candy _____
   1 licorice rope _____
   1 drink _____
   Total   **$2.35**

5. 1 drink _____
   1 _____ _____
   1 ice cream _____
   Total   **$3.45**

6. 4 _____ _____
   1 drink _____
   Total   **$8.90**

7. 1 _____ _____
   1 hot dog _____
   1 ice cream _____
   Total   **$2.45**

8. 2 hot chocolates _____
   2 _____ _____
   Total   **$2.80**

9. 1 coffee _____
   1 hot chocolate _____
   2 _____ _____
   Total   **$2.85**

10. 1 popcorn _____
    1 _____ _____
    1 hot pretzel _____
    Total   **$2.15**

11. 2 licorice ropes _____
    2 popcorn _____
    2 _____ _____
    Total   **$3.60**

12. 4 _____ _____
    4 drinks _____
    Total   **$7.60**

Name

HORSING AROUND

Lucy E. Quine loves horses. She has saved $300 from her job at the stables, and she's thrilled to find a sale at the tack shop. Pay attention to the prices to help her get some good deals on riding clothes and equipment!

BLANKET $65.00 44.50

GIRTH $39.00 27.60

HELMET $95.00 55.90

HALTER $30.00 20.00

BRIDLE $59.00 43.25

BIT $25.00 18.80

BREECHES $80.00 39.90

LEAD ROPE $15.00 11.50

SADDLE $300.00 250.10

DRESS BOOTS $110.00 $75.00

CURRY BRUSH $10.00 $5.25

1. Could she afford to buy a horse blanket, boots, and a bridle?

_____

2. If she buys the saddle, how much will be left for other items?

_____

3. What three articles are each close to $40?

_____

_____

4. How much would she pay for the boots, helmet, and breeches?

_____

5. How much less is a halter than a bridle?

_____

6. How many lead ropes can she get for $30?

_____

7. What will it cost if she buys the most expensive item and the least expensive item together?

_____

8. Which item is about $50 less than the helmet?

_____

9. Will she pay more for a curry brush, blanket, and bit or a bridle and helmet?

_____

10. Choose the articles you would buy if you had $300 to spend. Don't go over $300!

_____

_____

_____

Name

_____

UP & OVER

Horses can leap over the most troublesome obstacles. Don't let these obstacles stop the horse from a great race. Fill in the correct signs on each jump to get the answer shown. Write + or – or x or ÷ in each of the blanks. (The first one is done for you!)

1. 17 – 4 + 10 = 23

2. 4 __ 2 __ 2 = 16

3. 56 __ 6 __ 2 = 25

4. ½ __ 1 __ 2 = 3

5. 5 __ 2 __ 3 = 6

6. 1 __ 2 __ 3 = 9

7. 8 __ 3 __ 4 = 20

8. 10 __ 2 __ 3 = 15

9. 20 __ 4 __ 80 = 0

10. 29 __ 10 __ 13 = 26

11. 100 __ 100 __ 1 = 10,001

12. 55 __ 50 __ 5 = 25

13. 13 __ 13 __ 13 = 13

14. 81 __ 9 __ 6 = 54

LOCKER ROOM MYSTERY

The lockers in the Ashland Middle School locker room have unusual names on them! Can you figure out which locker belongs to which athlete?

Write the letter of the locker that matches each clue.

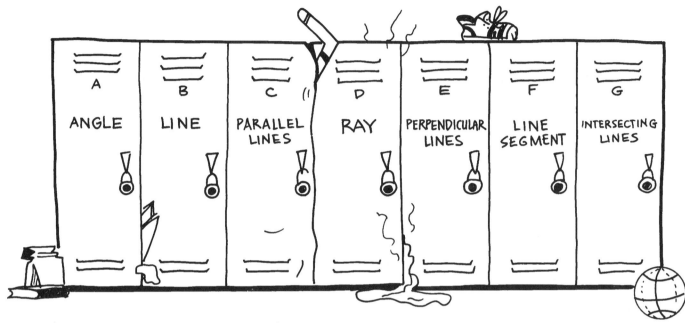

Clues

_____ 1. Ashley's Locker   I'm part of a line that has only one endpoint.

_____ 2. Sara's Locker   We are lines in the same plane, but we never met.

_____ 3. Gina's Locker   I am made of two rays that have the same end point.

_____ 4. Kate's Locker   I am part of a line that has two endpoints.

_____ 5. Gayle's Locker   I extend in opposite directions without end.

_____ 6. Kayla's Locker   When I meet another line, it is always at a right angle.

_____ 7. Megan's Locker   The two of us meet and cross each other.

8. Draw a pair of perpendicular lines.	9. Draw a pair of intersecting lines.	10. Draw a pair of parallel lines.

Name _____

GEOMETRY AT THE BALL PARK

Take your markers to the ballpark for the first home game, and search the scene for geometric places and spaces.

Color or trace at least three of each figure.
Use the color chart to find the right color for each one.

FIGURE	COLOR
point	blue
plane	green
line segment	red
angle	yellow

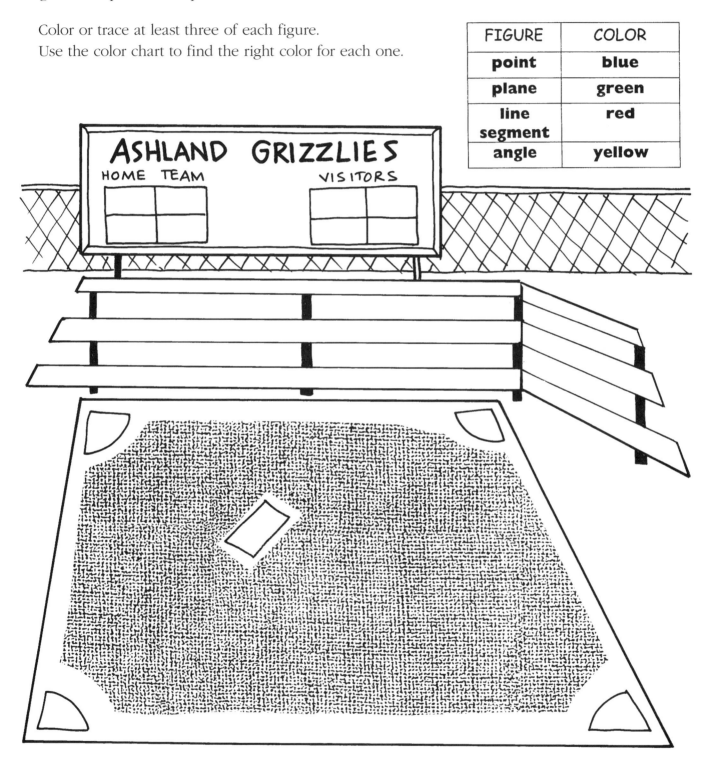

ASHLAND GRIZZLIES

HOME TEAM   VISITORS

Name

Identify Kinds of Angles

NEW ANGLE ON CHEERS

The cheerleaders are practicing for the first pep rally. They're practicing some new tricks and routines.

1. Name all the acute angles.

____

____

2. Name all the right angles.

____

____

3. Name at least two obtuse angles.

____

____

Name ______________________________

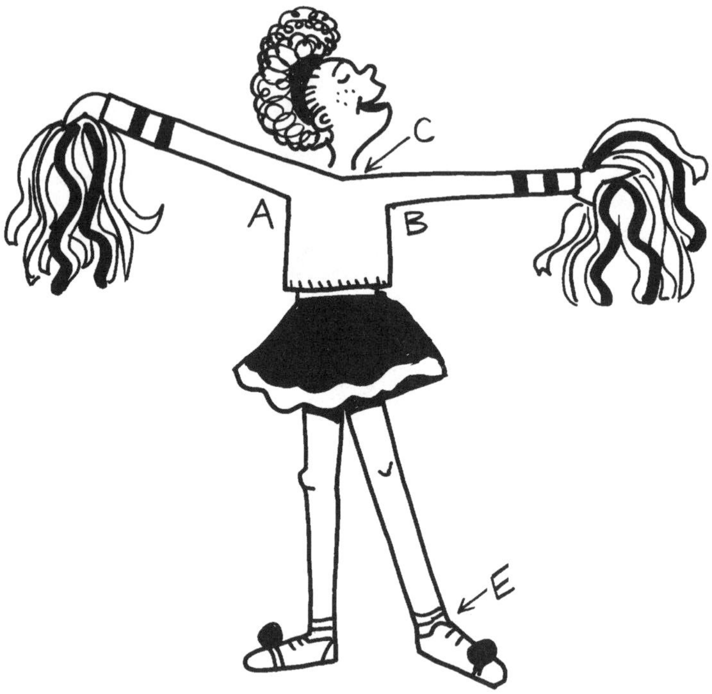

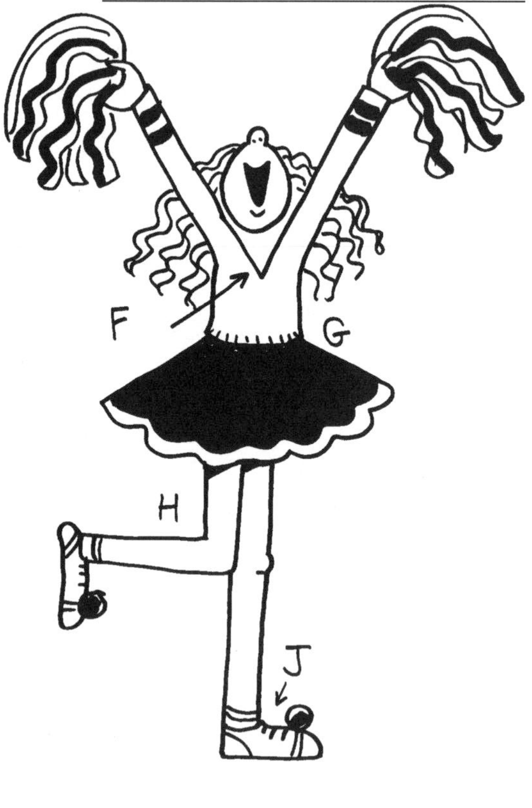

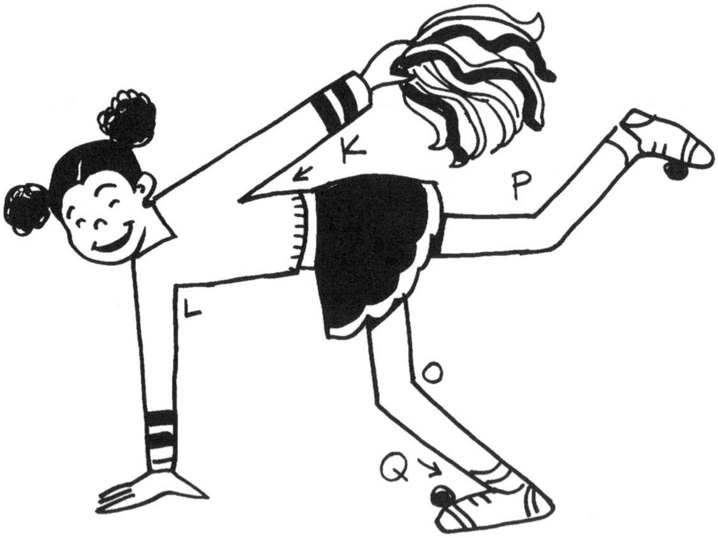

GYM FLOOR GEOMETRY

Kind of Triangle	Color
right triangles	blue
isosceles triangles	green
scalene triangles	purple
equilateral triangles	red
other shapes	yellow

The Booster Club spent a year collecting money for a new gym floor. What a job! Student groups were asked to submit designs for the floor. Here is the prizewinning design. It's full of triangles. Can you find them all? Follow the chart to color the floor design.

Prize Winning Design

We did it!

BOOSTER CLUB

SHARP EYES FOR SHAPES

There is a piece of hidden sports equipment in this picture. Do you know what it is?

To find out, follow the color chart to color each figure. Because some shapes fit more than one definition, color each shape in the order indicated on the chart.

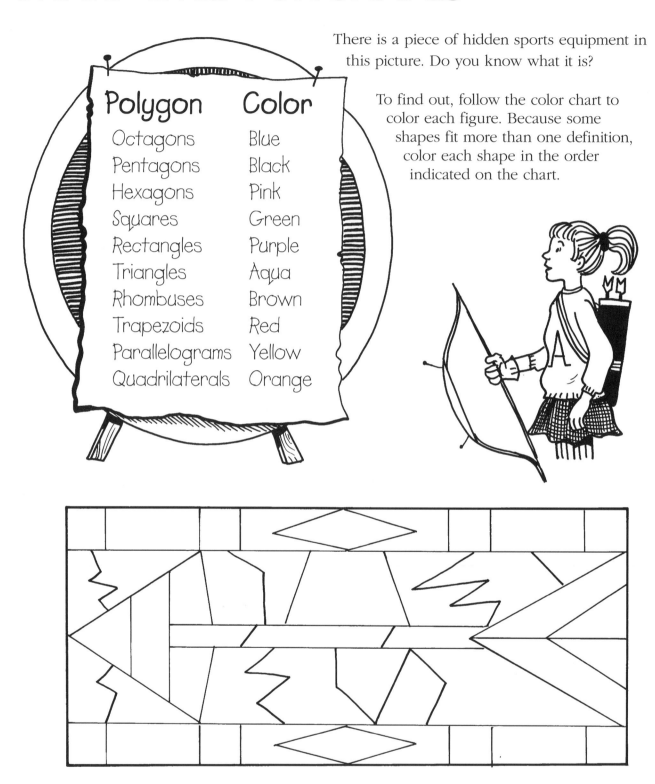

Polygon	Color
Octagons	Blue
Pentagons	Black
Hexagons	Pink
Squares	Green
Rectangles	Purple
Triangles	Aqua
Rhombuses	Brown
Trapezoids	Red
Parallelograms	Yellow
Quadrilaterals	Orange

1. What is it? _____

2. In what sport is this object used? _____

Name _____

GOING IN CIRCLES

The wrestling team is warming up for their big match against their rivals, the Crescent City Cougars. The athletes will show off their wrestling skills on a circular mat with a diameter of 11 meters.

Use the circle diagram of the mat to show off your geometry skills and knowledge about the parts of a circle.

1. The team captain, Will, will stand at the center. What point is this? _____

2. Jason and Dan warm up by jogging back and forth on the diameters. Name the diameters.

   _____

3. Geoff will warm up by jogging back and forth on each radius. Name the radii.

   _____

4. Chris will jump rope along 2 chords. Name 2 chords.

   _____

5. Travis will skip along 4 arcs. Name 4 arcs.

   _____

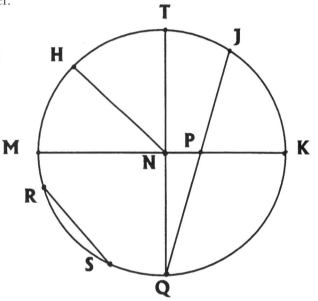

Draw another wrestling mat. Make sure it contains all parts of the circle listed below. Trace them with the colors shown.

   1 center (black)

   2 radii (red)

   2 chords (green)

   2 diameters (orange)

   2 arcs (blue)

Name _____

GEOMETRY ON WHEELS

FIGURE	COLOR
cubes	red
spheres	blue
cones	green
rectangular prisms	yellow
cylinders	purple
triangular prisms	brown
pyramids	orange

The practice course for the skating team is loaded with geometric space figures. Skaters practice jumps and turns over and around the figures.

Color or outline the figures to identify them. Use the color chart.

Use a red line to draw a path for this skater: First, he skates between 2 spheres, then between 2 cylinders and over the top of a pyramid. Then he curves between the pyramid and a cone, past the lower corner of a rectangular prism, between a cone and a sphere, and over the top of a triangular prism. He circles around the outside of the prism and jumps over a cube to the finish line.

STEP UP

SIZE 20 HIGH TOPS

CHALK

TENNIS BALLS

2000#

STOP!

GRIZZLIES

BALANCE BEAM

REFRESHMENT TENT

ENERGY BARS

FINISH

Name

A CLOSE LOOK AT FIGURES

Wrestlers must get weighed before each match. In wrestling, opponents are matched as closely as possible in size and weight. It doesn't matter if they look similar or have similar figures—it's the exact weight that counts!

Geometric figures must be exactly the same size and shape to be called congruent. If they are the same shape, they are similar, no matter what their size.

How would you describe the figures of these two wrestlers? (Circle one answer.)

congruent   similar   neither

Label each pair of figures C (congruent)

 1. _____

 2. _____

 3. _____

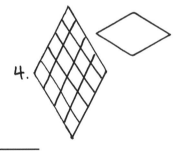 4. _____

5. _____

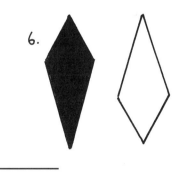 6. _____

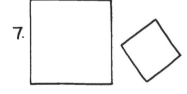 7. _____

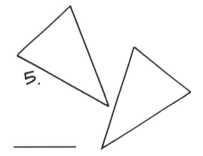 8. _____

 9. _____

Name _____

GET A JUMP ON VOLUME

The skateboard club has some very talented competitors. They practice year-round on ramps and jumps in the new skateboard park. Here are some of the structures they have built to jump over.

Examine each structure to find its volume. (Count the cubic units.) Then answer the questions.

1. Which has 9 cubic units? _____

2. Which jump's volume is 8 cubic units? _____

3. Which jump's volume is 5 cubic units? _____

4. Which jump's volume is 3 cubic units? _____

5. How many cubic units are in jump F? _____

6. Which jumps have more cubic units than H? _____

7. Which jumps have fewer cubic units than A? _____

8. Are there any jumps with 2 cubic units? _____

9. Are there any jumps with 7 cubic units? _____

10. Which jump's volume is 4 cubic units? _____

11. How many have 6 cubic units? _____

12. Which stands have the same number of cubic units? _____

Name _____

COURTSIDE MEASUREMENTS

Search the tennis court puzzle for U.S. customary measurement units.

```
O  F  A  E  K  R  F  E  E  T  P  I  N  T  S
T  U  D  E  G  R  E  E  S  R  R  N  B  I  R
A  I  O  U  N  C  E  S  R  R  A  U  O  N  C
B  Y  A  C  Y  T  O  N  S  U  M  N  R  C  U
L  P  Y  Y  E  A  R  S  L  Q  Q  A  F  H  P
E  O  A  N  I  B  C  R  O  M  M  I  L  E  S
S  U  R  M  G  A  L  E  N  R  O  O  B  S  Q
P  N  D  R  H  A  H  O  U  R  S  L  O  E  U
O  D  S  E  C  O  N  D  S  E  P  W  D  I  A
O  S  U  N  D  A  G  A  L  L  O  N  S  R  R
N  Y  H  A  M  I  N  U  T  E  S  E  T  X  T
S  D  R  A  Y  S  T  E  A  S  P  O  O  N  S
```

Circle a term in the puzzle to fill each of these blanks. (One is written backwards.)

1. The tennis players are 13 _____ old.

2. Sheri jogs 2 _____ to the tennis court.

3. An hour equals 60 _____ .

4. A glass of Thirst Blaster holds 14

   _____ .

5. Jordan is exactly 5 _____ tall.

6. Four cups of milk is one _____ .

7. Danielle weighs 83 _____ .

8. Suzie practices for 3 _____ after school.

9. 1 cup of juice holds 16 _____ .

10. Six feet equals 2 _____ .

11. The temperature is 77 _____ today.

12. The match lasted 30 minutes, 10 _____ .

13. One quart of drink equals 2 _____ .

14. One quart of drink equals 4 _____ .

15. Jeri's height is 5 feet, or 60 _____ .

16. The tennis bus weighs one _____ .

17. One tablespoon equals 3 _____ .

18. The team drank 40 quarts—that's
    10 _____ .

Name _____

PASSING THE TEST

In most schools, athletes must keep good grades in order to play a school sport. How is Tom doing on his measurement test? He needs to have 9 correct in order to pass the test.

Circle the numbers of the correct answers. Cross out the wrong answers and replace them with the correct answers.

I'm sure I'll pass the test.

Measurement Test

Student Name: **Tom**   Date: **January 6**

1. Liquids are measured in ___*meters*___ .

2. Would 5 millimeters of water fill a cup? yes (no)

3. Circle the greater amount: (10 kilograms)   100 grams

4. Could someone's hand be 1 decimeter long? (yes)   no

5. Circle the larger amount: 2 kilometers   (200 meters)

6. 1 meter = ___*100*___ centimeters.

7. 1 kilometer = ___*1000*___ meters.

8. ___*100*___ milliliters = 1 liter.

9. 100 meters = ___*1*___ decimeter(s).

10. 5 grams = ___*5000*___ milligrams.

11. 20 meters = ___*2*___ centimeters.

12. ___*300*___ centimeters = 3 meters.

13. 1 metric ton = ___*1000*___ kilograms.

14. 1 gram = ___*100*___ milligrams.

15. 10 kilometers = ___*500*___ meters.

16. 10,000 milligrams = ___*10*___ grams.

Will Tom pass? _____

Name _____

UNIFORM MEASUREMENTS

It's time to order uniforms for the soccer team. Matt is getting measured to find out exactly what size he needs.

Look at the measurements needed for Matt. Find a measuring tape or ruler and a friend or classmate. Use U.S. customary units to find these measurements on your friend. Round all the measurements to the nearest whole unit.

circumference of head = _____

circumference of neck = _____

shoulder to tip of fingers = _____

distance around waist = _____

length of longest finger = _____

distance around thigh = _____

width of kneecap = _____

knee to ankle = _____

total leg length = _____

distance around ankle = _____

foot length heel to toe = _____

Name _____

AROUND THE EDGE

The sports at Ashland Middle School take place in all kinds of places and spaces. But it seems that no matter where the practices are located, one thing is always the same. At every practice, every coach asks the athletes to warm up by running around the outside of the field, room, mat, or court!

Figure out how far the athletes have to run at each of these locations. Find the perimeter of each sports area shown. Write the perimeter inside the area. Write P = _____.

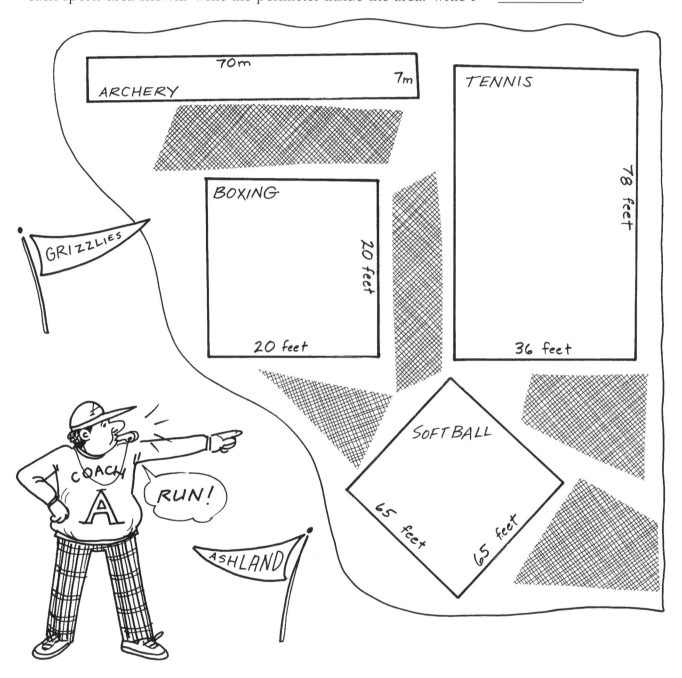

Use with page 273.

Name

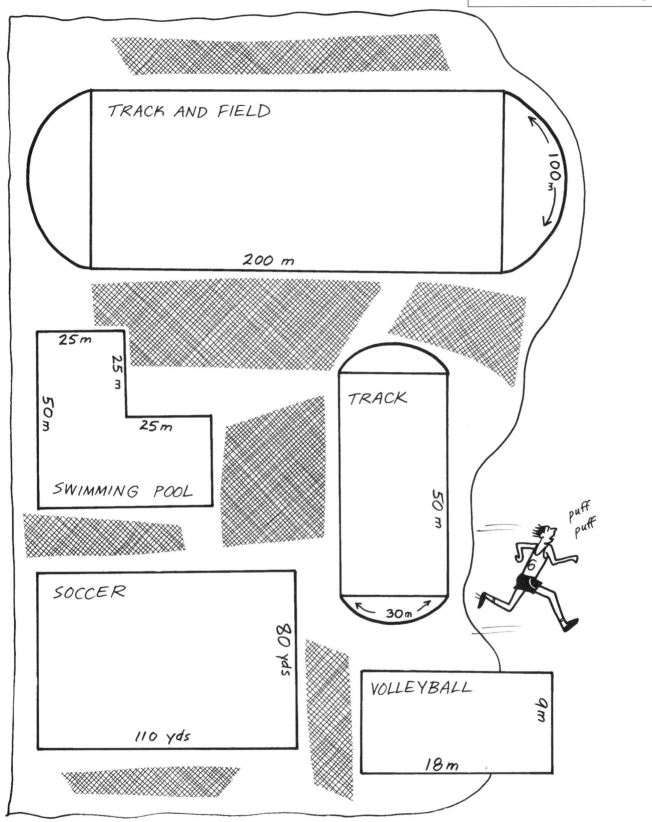

TRACK AND FIELD

100 m

200 m

25 m

25 m

50 m

25 m

SWIMMING POOL

TRACK

50 m

30 m

puff puff

6

SOCCER

80 yds

110 yds

VOLLEYBALL

9 m

18 m

In which sport do the athletes run the farthest to warm up? _____

Use with page 272.

Name _____

JUGGLING THE SCHEDULE

Brianna is trying to juggle a very heavy schedule.
She is busy with basketball, school, and other
activities. Use the calendar on the next page to
answer questions about her schedule.

1. What is the longest time Brianna has between
   basketball games in February?

   _____

2. Team pictures will be taken 1 week and 1 day
   after her big math test. What day will that be?

   _____

3. If Brianna's history project was assigned 2
   weeks and 3 days before it was due, on what
   day did her teacher assign it?

   _____

4. How many weeks are there between her
   mom's birthday and her baby-sitting job?

   _____

5. How many days before the Valentine Dance did she ask Jay to be her date?

   _____

6. Is Brianna available to baby-sit in the evening 21 days after the team pizza party?

   _____

7. If soccer practice begins 2 weeks and 4 days after the tryouts, on what date
   will Brianna begin soccer practice?

8. Brianna plans to start studying for her math test 5 days ahead of time. On what date will
   she begin her studying?

9. A dentist appointment is scheduled for 15 days after the Science Fair. What day of the
   week will that be?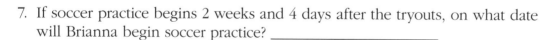

10. What is the longest number of days that Brianna went without a basketball practice in
    February? _____

Use with page 275.

Name _____

FEBRUARY

Sunday	Monday	Tuesday	Wednesday	Thursday	Friday	Saturday
1	2 Ask Jay to go to the Valentine Dance. • Practice – 3:00 – 4:30	3 Game! 6:00 – 8:00	4 • Basketball • Practice – 3:00 – 4:30	5 MOM'S BIRTHDAY • Basketball • Practice – 3:00 – 4:30	6	7 Basketball Team's PIZZA PARTY 7:00 PM
8	9 • Basketball • Practice – 3:00 – 4:30	10 Game! 6:00 – 8:00 Math Test	11 BB • Practice 3:00 – 4:30	12 • Basketball • Practice 3:00 – 4:30	13 Game! 6:00 – 8:00	14 ♥ Valentine Dance ! ♯ ! ♥
15 Go Shopping	16 NO SCHOOL Presidents' Day	17 • Basketball Practice – 3: – 4:30	18 • Basketball • Practice – 3:00 – 4:30	19 History Project Due !! (uh oh) • Practice 3: – 4:30	20 Sleep over at Katie's Dance Practice	21 BIG GAME
22	23 Science Fair Basketball Practice 3: – 4:30	24 Game 6: – 8:00	25 • Basketball Practice 3: – 4:30	26 babysit for the myers – 6:00 – 8:00 • BB practice 3: – 4:30	27 REPORT CARDS GAME 6: – 8:00	28 Soccer tryouts 9 am.

11. How long after Brianna's math test will she get a report card? _____

12. From the date of the Science Fair, in how many days will it be March 17? _____

13. What day of the week will it be 2 weeks and 6 days from February 27? _____

14. What will the date be 3 weeks and 4 days from February 16? _____

Use with page 274.

Name _____

OUTRAGEOUS COLLECTIONS

What strange things some people collect! Many people have collections, but some take it to extremes. People who collect thousands of magnets, clovers, mousetraps, or airsickness bags may do this for the love of collecting. Or they may do it to get in the record books!

The table below shows **data** (numerical information) for some outrageous collections. Use the information on the table to answer the questions.

1. Which collection is the largest?

   _____

2. Which collection is the smallest?

   _____

3. Who has more items, Hugh or Ted?

   _____

4. How many clovers are in George's collection? _____

5. Who collected four times as many items as Sonja? _____

6. Who collected about five times as many items as Louise?

   _____

7. Which 3 collections are very close to 2,000?

   _____

   _____

OUTRAGEOUS COLLECTIONS

Collection	Collector	Record Number Collected
mousetraps	Reinhard Hellwig	2,334
golf balls	Ted J. Hoz	43,824
items of underwear	Imelda Marcos	1,700
shoes	Sonja Bata	10,000
watches	Florenzo Barindelli	3,562
light bulbs	Hugh Hicks	60,000
airsickness bags	Nick Vermeulen	2,112
gnomes & pixies	Anne Atkin	2,010
bandages (unused)	Brian Viner	3,750
refrigerator magnets	Louise J. Greenfarb	21,500
clovers	George Kaminski	13,382 four-leaf 1,336 five-leaf 78 six-leaf 6 seven-leaf
bubble gum	Thomas & Volker Martins	1,712
parking meters	Lotta Sjölin	292
nutcrackers	Jürgen Löschner	2,200
ballpoint pens	Angelika Unverhau	108,500
piggy banks	Ove Nortstrom	3,575
jet fighters	Michel Pont	100
marbles	Sam McCarthy-Fox	40,000

8. Which collection has about the same number as the bubble gum collection? _____

9. How many collections are larger than the underwear collection? _____

10. How many collections are smaller than the piggy bank collection? _____

11. Whose collection is about the same in number of items as the watches? _____

12. Which collection surprises you most? _____

   Why?_____

Use with page 277.

Name _____

OUTRAGEOUS COLLECTIONS, CONT.

Curious visitors come to see many of the collections described on page 276. This table is about visitors to some other collections that have not set any records. Use the table to answer the questions.

Use with page 276.

CURIOUS VISITORS
Numbers of Visitors May-June

Collection Visited	May	June	July	August
Elvis souvenirs	666	900	1,001	768
ski poles	89	320	465	345
shoes	1,000	1,590	1,899	1,200
marbles	707	933	955	700
safety pins	30	66	71	14
stuffed animals	4,500	4,811	5,736	4,801
spoons	691	699	741	366
gum wrappers	190	580	711	533
cash registers	1,101	2,801	4,138	3,100
lightbulbs	1,400	1,451	1,478	1,410
shoelaces	57	84	99	150

1. For which collection was the number of visitors about the same over all four months?

_____

2. Which month was the best for most of the collections?

_____

3. Most collections had (more, fewer) visitors in June than July.

_____

4. Which collection had fewer visitors in July than in August?

_____

5. Most collections had (more, fewer) visitors in August than in July.

_____

6. How many collections had fewer visitors in August than in May?

_____

7. Which collection had the least interest from visitors over the summer?

_____

8. Which collection seems to have had the most visitors over the summer?

_____

9. How many collections had more visitors in July than the shoe collection did?

_____

10. How many collections had fewer visitors in May than the marble collection did?

_____

11. Which collection had about 2,000 more visitors in August than it did in May?

_____

12. How many more visitors saw the safety pin exhibit in June than in August?

_____

Name _____

LOTS & LOTS OF LOOPS

Eddy McDonald of Canada spent three hours performing loops with his yo-yo. Someone was counting as he was doing loops, and they counted 21,663 complete loops. He must have had a tired arm!

The **pictograph** uses pictures to show numbers of yo-yo loops done by some less expert yo-yo spinners. Use the graph to tell whether each statement is true or false.

COUNT THE YO-YO LOOPS   KEY: ⊚ = 500 YoYo Loops

COMPETITORS	LOOPS IN TWO HOURS
Yolanda	⊚ ⊚ ⊚ ⊚ ⊚ ⊚ ⊚ ◖
Yang-Lei	⊚ ⊚ ⊚ ⊚ ⊚ ⊚ ⊚ ⊚
Yvette	⊚ ⊚ ⊚ ⊚ ⊚ ⊚ ⊚ ◖
Yazzi	⊚ ⊚ ⊚ ⊚ ⊚ ⊚
Yacko	⊚ ⊚ ⊚ ⊚
Yuri	⊚ ⊚ ⊚ ⊚ ⊚ ⊚ ⊚ ⊚ ⊚ ◖
Yanni	⊚ ⊚ ⊚

Write T or F for each statement.

_____ 1. Yacko did 4,500 loops.

_____ 2. All seven did over 30,000 loops.

_____ 3. Yanni did half the loops of Yazzi.

_____ 4. Yang-Lei did twice the loops as Yacko.

_____ 5. Yolanda did 1,000 less loops than Yvette.

_____ 6. Yolana and Yazzi together did 6,750 loops.

_____ 7. Yacko and Yvette together did 7,000 loops.

_____ 8. Yvette did three times as many loops as Yanni.

_____ 9. Yuri did more than three times as many as Yanni.

_____ 10. All seven put together did less than Eddy McDonald when he set his record.

Name _____

BODACIOUS BALANCING

This must take years of practice. People actually balance stacks of glasses on their chins! Ashrita Furman is the record-holder for this amazing trick. He set the record by balancing a stack of 81 glasses on his chin for ten seconds. DON'T try this at home with real glasses! Only practice with plastic cups!

Here's a graph that another glass-balancer kept as she practiced her skill. The **pictograph** uses pictures to show the amounts of glasses successfully balanced each day for a week.

Use the graph to fill in then blanks below.

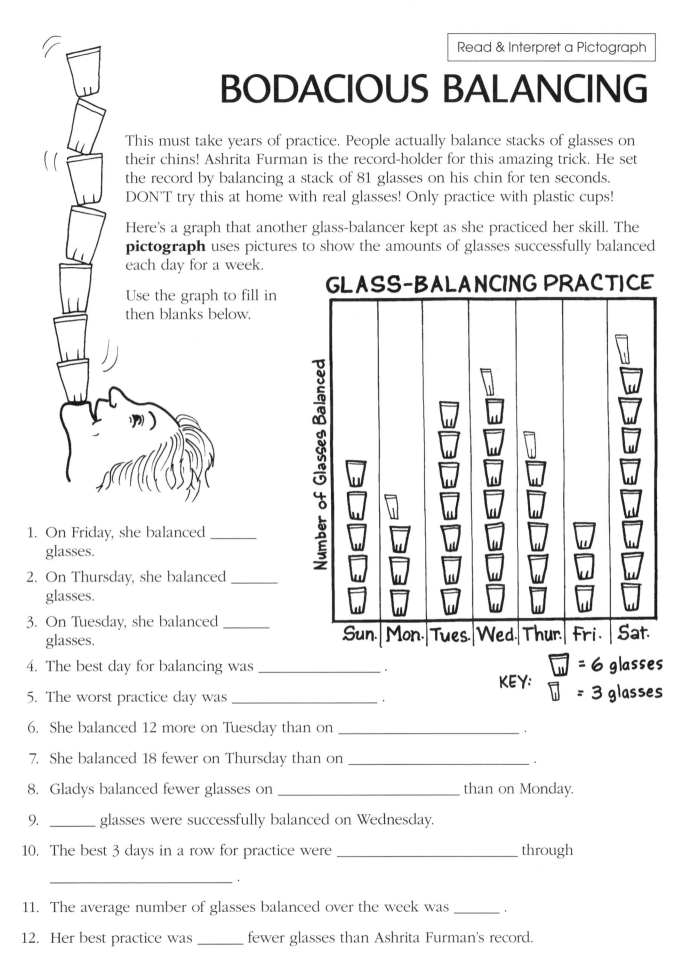

GLASS-BALANCING PRACTICE

KEY: 🥤 = 6 glasses 🥃 = 3 glasses

1. On Friday, she balanced _____ glasses.

2. On Thursday, she balanced _____ glasses.

3. On Tuesday, she balanced _____ glasses.

4. The best day for balancing was _____ .

5. The worst practice day was _____ .

6. She balanced 12 more on Tuesday than on _____ .

7. She balanced 18 fewer on Thursday than on _____ .

8. Gladys balanced fewer glasses on _____ than on Monday.

9. _____ glasses were successfully balanced on Wednesday.

10. The best 3 days in a row for practice were _____ through

    _____ .

11. The average number of glasses balanced over the week was _____ .

12. Her best practice was _____ fewer glasses than Ashrita Furman's record.

Name

TATTOOS, TREES, AND FAST TALKING

Which record do you wish you had set: the highest hot air balloon flight, the most ice cream eaten, the fastest bathtub race, the deepest ocean dive, or the longest distance spitting a watermelon seed?

Two hundred kids were asked about six records. They were asked which of the six records they would like to have set themselves. The survey gave the results shown on the circle graph. Use the graph information to answer the questions.

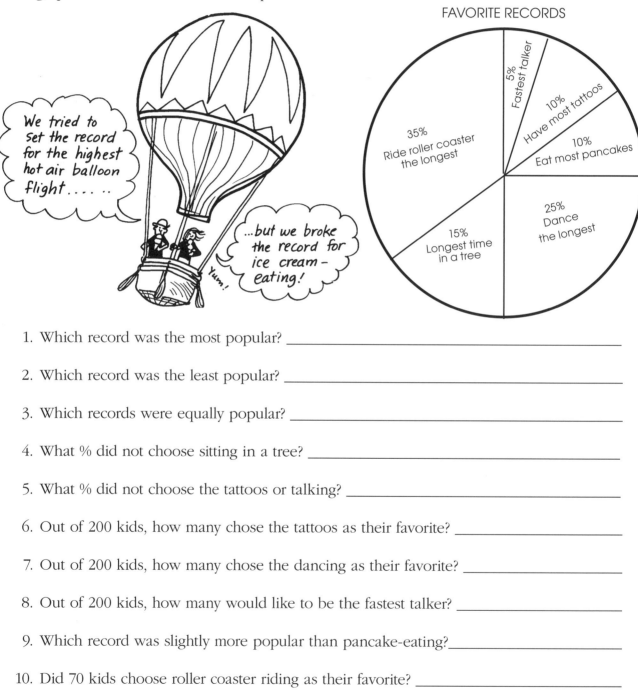

1. Which record was the most popular? _____

2. Which record was the least popular? _____

3. Which records were equally popular? _____

4. What % did not choose sitting in a tree? _____

5. What % did not choose the tattoos or talking? _____

6. Out of 200 kids, how many chose the tattoos as their favorite? _____

7. Out of 200 kids, how many chose the dancing as their favorite? _____

8. Out of 200 kids, how many would like to be the fastest talker? _____

9. Which record was slightly more popular than pancake-eating? _____

10. Did 70 kids choose roller coaster riding as their favorite? _____

Name _____

PLAYING WITH FIRE

Anthony Gatto, of the United States, set the record for flaming torch juggling by keeping seven flaming torches moving in the air at once. This is a record you should not try practicing in your home or back yard!

The line graph shows the results of one juggler's practice for a year. It shows the most torches she successfully juggled at any time during each month. Use the graph to find information about Jasmine's juggles.

JUGGLING FLAMING TORCHES

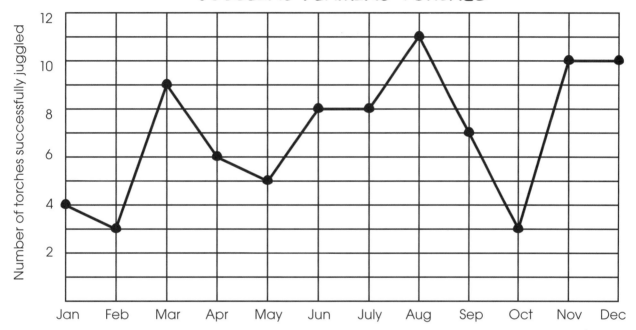

Write . . .

1. Number juggled in March _____

2. Number juggled in November _____

3. Number juggled in May _____

4. Best month _____

5. Worst month _____

6. Difference between August and September

   _____

7. Difference between November and December

   _____

8. Greatest drop between which 2 months?

   _____ _____

9. Greatest increase between which 2 months?

   _____

10. Difference between least and greatest numbers?

    _____

11. Difference between March and April?

    _____

12. Difference between January and December?

    _____

Name _____

RECORD-SETTING SWALLOWING

Large amounts of food items are swallowed in extremely fast times to set food-eating records. Pancakes, spaghetti, raw eggs, whole lemons, pickled onions, and other interesting foods are gobbled up for the sake of competition.

The graph shows the number of food items that were eaten to set some speed-eating records. Use the graph to solve the problems on the next page.

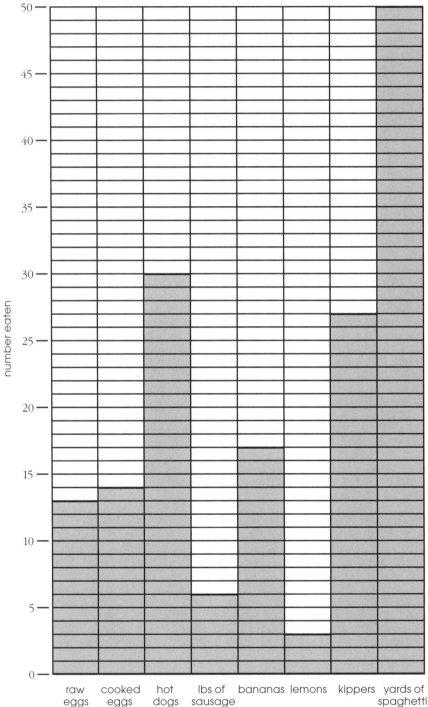

RECORD-SETTING SWALLOWING

number eaten

raw eggs — 13
cooked eggs — 14
hot dogs — 30
lbs of sausage — 6
bananas — 17
lemons — 3
kippers — 27
yards of spaghetti — 50

Use with page 283.

Name

RECORD-SETTING SWALLOWING,
CONTINUED

1. How many eggs were eaten to set the two egg records?

_____

2. How many fewer bananas than kippers were eaten to set the record?

_____

3. The raw eggs were eaten in 1 second. The cooked eggs took 14.42 seconds. How much longer did the cooked eggs take?

_____

4. How many more bananas were eaten for the banana record than lemons were eaten for the lemon-eating record?

_____

5. It took 2 minutes to set the banana record. At this rate, how many bananas could be eaten in 10 minutes?

_____

6. It took 3 minutes and 10 seconds to eat the amount of sausage shown on the graph. At the same rate, how long would it take to eat 30 pounds?

_____

7. It took 64 seconds to eat the hot dogs for the record. About how much time did it take per hot dog?

_____

8. It took one second to set the raw egg record. At this rate, how many raw eggs could be eaten in a minute?

_____

9. The actual spaghetti-eating record was set by eating 100 yards of spaghetti. If the amount on the chart took 6.01 seconds, how long did the actual record take?

_____

10. The lemons were eaten whole—skins, seeds, and all—in 15.3 seconds.

At the same rate, how long would it take to eat 9 lemons? _____

Use with page 282.

Name _____

SWATTING TO SET A RECORD

Yes, there really is a World Championship of Mosquito Killing. It is held every year in Finland. Henri Pellonpää holds the record for the most of the pesky insects killed in five minutes. His record is 21 mosquitoes.

Follow the directions below to locate Henri's mosquitoes on the coordinate grid.

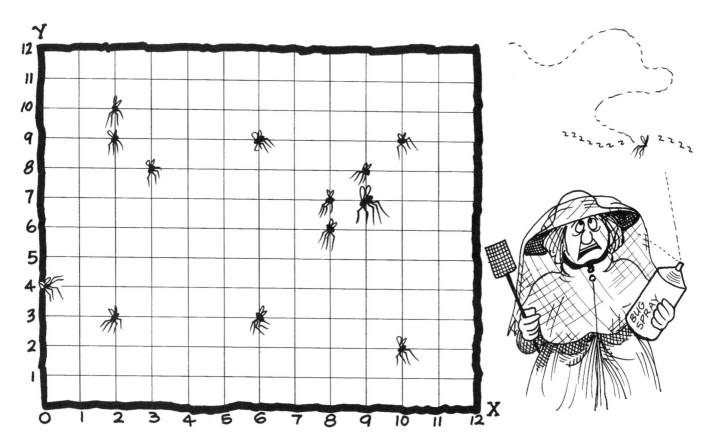

Remember that coordinates of a location are written (x, y). X is the location on the horizontal line. Y is the location on the vertical line.

1. Is there a mosquito at (8, 6)? _____

2. Is there a mosquito at (2, 10)? _____

3. Is there a mosquito at (9, 4)? _____

4. Is there a mosquito at (10, 8)? _____

5. Is there a mosquito at (12, 0)? _____

6. Is there a mosquito at (9, 7)? _____

7. Is there a mosquito at (8, 7)? _____

8. Is there a mosquito at (3, 6)? _____

9. Is there a mosquito at (6, 3)? _____

10. Where is the largest mosquito? _____

11. Draw a mosquito at (12, 3).

12. Draw a mosquito at (3, 6).

13. Draw a mosquito at (9, 4).

14. Draw a mosquito at (8, 0).

Name _____

THE THINGS PEOPLE THROW

It's amazing what things get thrown, tossed, and spit in an effort to set a record! Some of the world records include spitting cherry pits and crickets, tossing pancakes and cow pies, and catching tossed grapes in the mouth.

Find the tossed items on the coordinate grid below. Answer the questions about their locations.

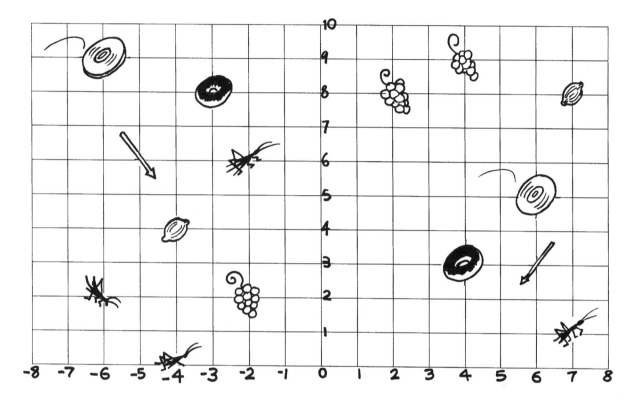

Write the locations where these are found. Write the coordinates like this: (x, y).

1. The are found at _____ , _____ , and _____ .

2. The are found at _____ and _____ .

3. The are found at _____ and _____ .

4. The are found at _____ and _____ .

5. The are found at _____ and _____ .

6. The are found at _____ , _____ , _____ , and _____ .

Name _____

A RECORD-HOLDING CRAWLER

The largest one of this animal was 15.5 inches (39 centimeters) long. Follow the directions to plot and connect the points on the grid. You'll find out what type of animal holds this record.

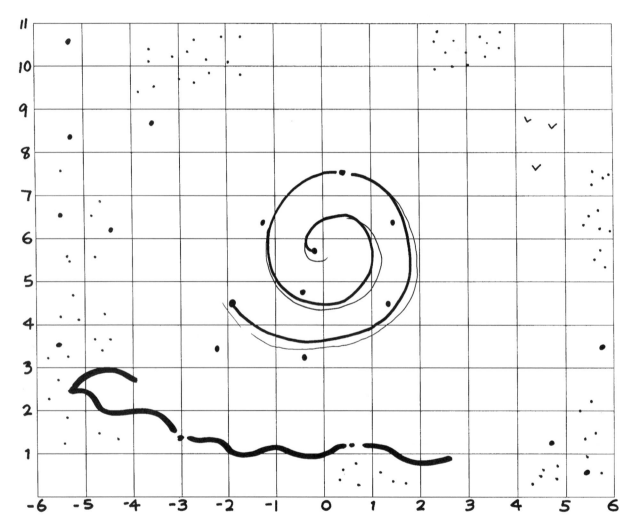

Plot these points. Then connect them in this order with a line.

A. (3, 1)	F. (5, 9)	K. (2, 2)	P. (−3, 7)
B. (4, 2)	G. (4, 11)	L. (−2, 2)	Q. (−2, 9)
C. (4, 3)	H. (4, 9)	M. (−3, 3)	R. (0, 10)
D. (5, 8)	I. (3, 7)	N. (−4, 4)	S. (2, 9)
E. (6, 10)	J. (3, 4)	O. (−3, 5)	T. (3, 7)

Name _____

EIGHT HOURS OF SHOE-SHINING

Imagine shining almost 15,000 shoes! A team of four teenagers set the record for shoe-shining by polishing 14,975 shoes in London, England.

Decide what some of those shoes looked like. Draw them on the grid in the locations that are described below.

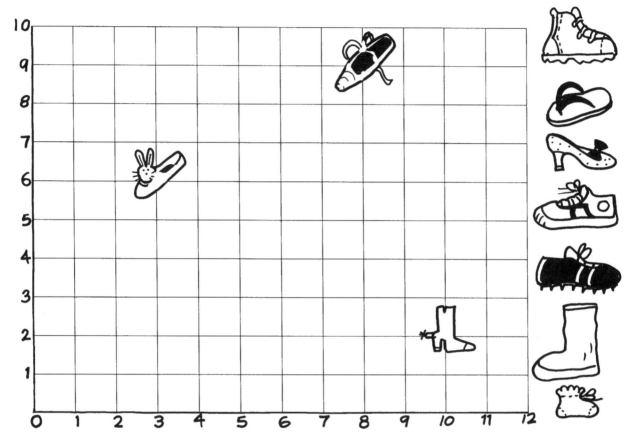

1. Is the bunny slipper at (3, 6)? _____

2. Where is the ballet shoe? _____

3. Where is the boot? _____

4. Draw a clown shoe at (0, 3).

5. Draw a tennis shoe at (2, 9).

6. Draw a baby shoe at (4, 3).

7. Draw a blue dancing shoe at (6, 7).

8. Draw a brown hiking boot at (1, 9).

9. Draw a green slipper at (5, 7)

10. Draw a red high heel at (9, 5).

11. Draw one of your shoes at (8, 4).

12. Draw a loafer at (8, 0).

13. Draw any yellow shoe at (11, 1).

14. Draw any purple shoe at (5, 0).

15. Draw any orange shoe at (7, 5).

16. Draw a fancy shoe at (11, 6).

17. Draw any shoe at (2, 2).

18. Draw any shoe at (1, 6).

Name _____

RECORD-BREAKING SNAKE-SITTING

A Texas man named Jackie Bibby set the record for sitting in a bathtub with the greatest number of poisonous snakes. There were 195 rattlesnakes in that tub with Jackie! Can you imagine sitting in the tub with even one snake?

What are the possibilities of getting bit if you're sitting with a snake that's known to bite? There are two equal possibilities: you get bit, or you don't get bit.

Probability is the chance that something will happen. This chance is 1 out of 2.

Outcomes are the possibilities of a chance event.
    There are TWO possible outcomes of this experiment. Let's hope the outcome is no bite.

1. You flip a coin. How many possible outcomes are there for this action? _____
    What are they? _____

Tell the number of possible outcomes for these events.

2. Toss of one 6-sided die _____

3. Being born in a month
    beginning with J _____

4. Being born in a month
    beginning with M _____

5. Being born on a day
    beginning with T _____

6. Being born on a day beginning with W _____

7. Being born in a U.S. state
    that is an island _____

8. Choosing a 1-digit number that is
    an even number _____

9. Choosing a 1-digit number that is
    a prime number _____

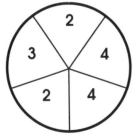

10. How many possible outcomes are there from
     spinning this spinner? _____

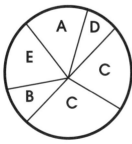

11. How many possible outcomes are there from
     spinning this spinner? _____

12. Which is the most likely? _____

13. Which is the least likely? _____

14. Which outcomes are equally likely? _____

Name _____

TATTOO OR NOT TATTOO?

To break this record, you would need to get most of your body covered with tattoos. The record for the most tattoos is held by Bernie Moeller, who has 14,002 individual tattoos.

Several diners are at a restaurant with five waiters. Three of the waiters have tattoos. All of the waiters are working today.

The diners have an **equal probability** of being served by any of the waiters. What is the probability (chance) that their waiter will have a tattoo?

Here's how to decide. Write a fraction as shown.

P (T) **probability of a tattoo** = $\dfrac{\text{number of waiters with tattoos}}{\text{total number of waiters}}$. So, P (T) = $\frac{3}{5}$.

- The probability of an event that is impossible is 0.

- The probability of an event that is certain is 1.

- When you don't know the **outcome,** the probability is somewhere between 0 and 1, usually expressed in a fraction.

Find the probability of each of these. Write 0, 1, or a fraction between 0 and 1.

1. The sun will rise tomorrow. _____

2. A coin toss will yield **heads.** _____

3. 2 odd numbers will have an even sum._____

4. The sun will set in the east. _____

5. You'll turn one year younger today. _____

6. If you toss one die, you will get a 6. _____

7. 2 even numbers will have an even sum. _____

8. You will have homework today. _____

9. Spring will follow summer. _____

10. If you toss one die, you will get an even number. _____

11. You will be 11 on your next birthday.

_____

Name _____

APPENDIX

CONTENTS

LANGUAGE ARTS SKILLS TEST

Part One: Reading Comprehension

Give a title to each article.

1. _____

   The largest painting ever done by one artist is *Mother Earth*. David Aberg finished it in 2006. It's 86,000 square feet (7,990 square meters). No wonder it took over two years to paint!

2. _____

   Wolfgang Amadeus Mozart started composing music at age 4. Even though he died at the young age of 35, he wrote more than 600 pieces of music in his lifetime.

3. _____

   The largest supply of sunken treasure in the world lies on the bottom of the Atlantic Ocean off the coast of the Bahamas. There are about 2,000 Spanish galleons that sank in this area in the 1500's.

4. _____

   The Spanish painter Picasso is one of history's most productive painters. He painted over 13,000 paintings. In addition, he did many sculptures, book illustrations, and engravings in his 91 years of life.

5. _____

   The heaviest cake ever baked weighed 619 pounds (281 kilograms). It was baked in Bucharest, the capital of the eastern European nation of Romania, in 2008.

6. What do all the articles have in common?

   _____

   _____

   _____

GREAT DANCE RECORDS

KIND of RECORD	The Dance or Dancers	Date	Number or length
Largest Twist Dance	Salvation Army Pearl, MS	2014	3,040 people
Largest Hula Dance	Miyakojima City, Okinawa, Japan	2015	1,509 dancers
Longest Dance Line	Walkway Over The Hudson, Poughkeepsie, NY	2012	2,569 dancers in a line
Longest Dancing Dragon	Three groups in Ontario, Canada	2012	18,269 feet (5,568 meters)
Most Exhausting Dance	Mike Ritof & Edith Boudreaux Chicago, IL	1930-1931	5,152 hours
Lowest Height Limbo Stick Anyone Danced Under	Shemika Charles New York, NY	2010	8.5 inches (21.5 centimeters)

7. Which record was set outside of the USA in 2015?

   _____

8. Which record was set by one person?

   _____

9. Which record included the most people?

   _____

10. Which record took longest?

    _____

11. What year was the limbo record set?

    _____

12. What state was the site of the Longest Dance Line?

    _____

13. Which record surprises you most?

    _____

14. Why? _____

    _____

    _____

Name _____

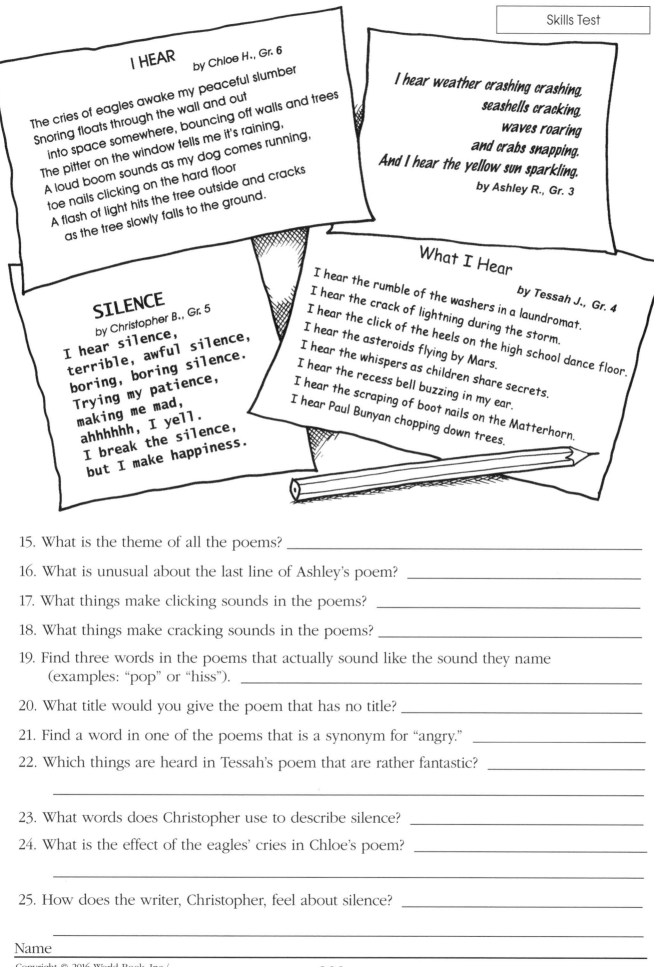

I HEAR by Chloe H., Gr. 6

The cries of eagles awake my peaceful slumber
Snoring floats through the wall and out
into space somewhere, bouncing off walls and trees
The pitter on the window tells me it's raining,
A loud boom sounds as my dog comes running,
toe nails clicking on the hard floor
A flash of light hits the tree outside and cracks
as the tree slowly falls to the ground.

I hear weather crashing crashing,
seashells cracking,
waves roaring
and crabs snapping.
And I hear the yellow sun sparkling.
by Ashley R., Gr. 3

SILENCE
by Christopher B., Gr. 5
I hear silence,
terrible, awful silence,
boring, boring silence.
Trying my patience,
making me mad,
ahhhhhh, I yell.
I break the silence,
but I make happiness.

What I Hear
by Tessah J., Gr. 4
I hear the rumble of the washers in a laundromat.
I hear the crack of lightning during the storm.
I hear the click of the heels on the high school dance floor.
I hear the asteroids flying by Mars.
I hear the whispers as children share secrets.
I hear the recess bell buzzing in my ear.
I hear the scraping of boot nails on the Matterhorn.
I hear Paul Bunyan chopping down trees.

15. What is the theme of all the poems? _____

16. What is unusual about the last line of Ashley's poem? _____

17. What things make clicking sounds in the poems? _____

18. What things make cracking sounds in the poems? _____

19. Find three words in the poems that actually sound like the sound they name
    (examples: "pop" or "hiss"). _____

20. What title would you give the poem that has no title? _____

21. Find a word in one of the poems that is a synonym for "angry." _____

22. Which things are heard in Tessah's poem that are rather fantastic? _____

_____

23. What words does Christopher use to describe silence? _____

24. What is the effect of the eagles' cries in Chloe's poem? _____

_____

25. How does the writer, Christopher, feel about silence? _____

_____

Name _____

Read the poem and the sentences below. Next to each one, write the code letters of the literary devices that have been used. There may be more than one.

| P = personification | I = idiom | M = metaphor |
| A = alliteration | S = simile | E = exaggeration |

_____ 26. Read the poem *The Wind* and write the code letters.

_____ 27. **The queen is quite quick at quilting!**

_____ 28. *You are driving me up a wall with your constant complaining!*

_____ 29. **Today the clouds are dragons breathing fires of stinging raindrops.**

_____ 30. A sneaky fog stretched out its long, silvery fingers, reaching for me.

_____ 31. My calculator is like an annoying little brother.

_____ 32. **It was so hot that the chickens laid scrambled eggs.**

The Wind
by Joseph Z., Gr. 4

The wind is a crystal clear icy breeze.
It is a strong giant, a gentle child,
a furious volcano,
a steady moving thing.
    It has feelings like us,
    like a rushing person,
    like a curious child,
    like a patient, waving person.
Sometimes it dies,
Sometimes it's alive—faster than you and me.
The wind shakes us, calms us, freezes us,
It's a dirty job
    but <u>something</u> has to do it.

33. The limerick is out of order! Number the lines in the right order.

____Of the dragons so near,

____It's just that his suit was too tight!

____For months kept refusing to fight.

____He didn't have fear

____It's strange that Sir Guilford, the Knight

34. Read the poem. Write two more lines with the same form the writer has used.

What I WAS and What I AM
by Sophie D., Gr. 2

I was a tree but now I'm paper
I was wheat but now I'm bread
I was a stream but now I'm a river
I was a chick but now I'm a chicken
I was a sprout but now I'm the biggest tree
in the world
I was nothing but now I am something
I was a loaf of bread but now I'm a crumb

I was _____ but now I'm _____

I was _____ but now I'm _____

Name _____

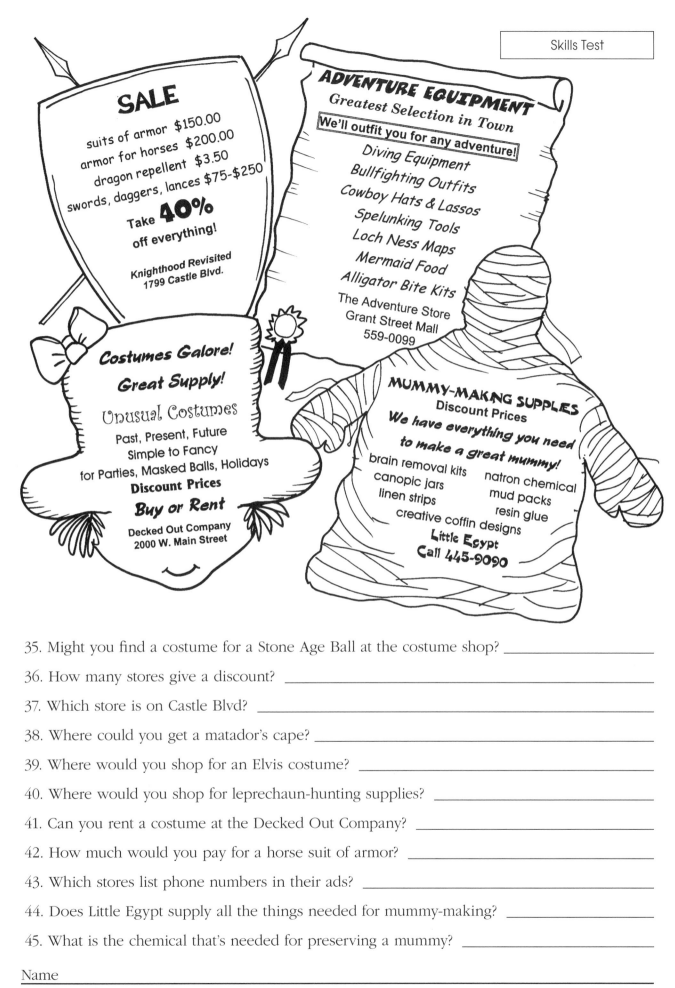

SALE

suits of armor $150.00
armor for horses $200.00
dragon repellent $3.50
swords, daggers, lances $75-$250

Take **40%** off everything!

Knighthood Revisited
1799 Castle Blvd.

ADVENTURE EQUIPMENT
Greatest Selection in Town

We'll outfit you for any adventure!

Diving Equipment
Bullfighting Outfits
Cowboy Hats & Lassos
Spelunking Tools
Loch Ness Maps
Mermaid Food
Alligator Bite Kits

The Adventure Store
Grant Street Mall
559-0099

Costumes Galore!
Great Supply!
Unusual Costumes
Past, Present, Future
Simple to Fancy
for Parties, Masked Balls, Holidays
Discount Prices
Buy or Rent

Decked Out Company
2000 W. Main Street

MUMMY-MAKNG SUPPLES
Discount Prices

We have everything you need to make a great mummy!

brain removal kits
canopic jars
linen strips
natron chemical
mud packs
resin glue
creative coffin designs

Little Egypt
Call 445-9090

35. Might you find a costume for a Stone Age Ball at the costume shop? _____

36. How many stores give a discount? _____

37. Which store is on Castle Blvd? _____

38. Where could you get a matador's cape? _____

39. Where would you shop for an Elvis costume? _____

40. Where would you shop for leprechaun-hunting supplies? _____

41. Can you rent a costume at the Decked Out Company? _____

42. How much would you pay for a horse suit of armor? _____

43. Which stores list phone numbers in their ads? _____

44. Does Little Egypt supply all the things needed for mummy-making? _____

45. What is the chemical that's needed for preserving a mummy? _____

Name _____

Are You Ready?

If you ever plan to do any adventuring in space, you will need to know how astronauts get along. When you head into space, the ordinary environment of life is gone. There is no air, sunshine, day or night, or gravity. When your shuttle takes off, your body will feel squished and squashed. Everything in the world of the astronaut is without gravity. You will have to sleep, move, eat, and stay healthy in a place where everything floats around.

Fortunately, you'll have a space suit made of 15 plastic layers that supplies you with oxygen and removes carbon dioxide and other waste products. The suit keeps the atmospheric pressure right for your body and keeps you warm. It has a special drink bag and a camera for sending pictures to the cockpit. You'll also have to be hooked up to a portable lavatory to take care of body wastes!

Living without gravity is quite a bit different from your normal life! You'll have to be tied to your bunk at night or use a sleeping suit. Your dinner would float away if it were not securely wrapped in a package. Living without day and night is strange, too. Someone will have to tell you when it's time for you to sleep.

So, what do you think? Sounds thrilling, doesn't it? Do you still want to head off into space?

46. Find two statements that give details to support the idea that living without gravity is strange. Underline them.

47. The author's purpose in writing this was
    a. to give information
    b. to tell about a particular space trip
    c. to warn you not to go to space

48. The main idea is
    a. Space travel is dangerous.
    b. Astronauts need special equipment to deal with different life in space.
    c. Space travel is great fun.

49. Write a title for this piece.

_____

(Title)

Slowly, stealthily, soundlessly she crept across the balcony. Her tip-toe steps were soft as air. No one must see her! No one must hear her! The hush of the night was so huge that any sound would be like crashing thunder splitting the air. Oh, so smoothly, she pulled herself over the railing. Tying the precious bundle to her long rope, she lowered it cautiously to the ground. With just as much care, she eased over the top of the balcony rail and slid herself after it. Once on the ground, she tied the bundle around her waist and vanished into the dark tangles of the vines and bushes. She was never seen again.

Number these in the order they occurred.

____ 50. She tied up the bundle.

____ 51. She vanished.

____ 52. She climbed over the balcony.

____ 53. She lowered the bundle.

54. One characteristic of the main character that the piece shows is:
    a. She is sinister.
    b. She is a hero.
    c. She is careful.

55. The setting of the story is _____

    _____

56. What will happen next?_____

    _____

    _____

57. Write a short summary of the piece.

    _____

    _____

    _____

Name _____

Part Two: Words & Vocabulary

Answer the questions. Each question is worth 1 point.

Write the letter of the word on the right that matches each definition.

_____ 58. whirlpool

_____ 59. odor

_____ 60. to lie

_____ 61. friendly

_____ 62. on time

_____ 63. scold

_____ 64. very hungry

_____ 65. dictionary

_____ 66. puppet

_____ 67. enemy

_____ 68. fear of germs

_____ 69. gloomy

a. annual
b. minuscule
c. chide
d. microphobia
e. morose
f. scoundrel
g. prevaricate
h. famished
i. shriek
j. maelstrom
k. aroma
l. foe
m. martinet
n. cordial
o. lexicon
p. punctual
q. claustrophobia
r. aggravate

Circle the best answer.

70. Which of these would you eat?

    vessel   jetsam   foible   borscht

71. Which would you be likely to find in a church?

    a vicar   a gam   a subpoena   a barracuda

72. Which would you find in the ocean?

    sequoia   flotsam   eclipse   bungalow

73. Which would you choose to help you sail a ship?

    a mariner   a novice   a manatee   a euphonium

74. Would you **aggravate** a villain?   yes   no

75. Which word means **tasty?**

    lunar   tortuous   morose   savory

Name

Circle the word that best fits the blank in each sentence.

76. Amy's _____ remarks hurt everyone's feelings.

      courteous   crude   careful   creative

77. Jake was _____ when he saw how close the shark was to his surfboard.

      horrific   satisfied   terrified   horrible

78. I was surprised by the _____ of a lifeguard on this crowded beach.

      presence   hairdo   tan   absence

79. We laughed when the crab _____ Josie's sunglasses.

      disappeared   snatched   returned   crawled

Tell what you think the words in bold mean as they are used in these sentences.

80. I had never seen a bathing suit quite like the **peculiar** one she wore yesterday.

    I think this word means _____.

81. The **ambidextrous** girl wrote one letter with her left hand and one with her right hand.

    I think this word means _____.

Write the letter of the word on the right that matches each definition.

_____ 82. to make friends

_____ 83. a creature with five feet

_____ 84. to read wrong

_____ 85. full of fear

_____ 86. one who sails

_____ 87. to cause terror

_____ 88. state of being sharp

_____ 89. to make afraid

_____ 90. fear of water

_____ 91. without hope

_____ 92. full of danger

a. hoping   l. phobophobia

b. hopeless   m. aquaphobia

c. reread   n. frightful

d. misread   o. frighten

e. dangerous   p. sharpness

f. friendly   q. sharply

g. befriend   r. sharper

h. pentapod   s. terrify

i. octopod   t. sailor

j. fearless   u. terrible

k. fearful   v. hopeful

Write the letter of the word that has a root that means . . .

_____ 93. flee

_____ 94. burn

_____ 95. carry

_____ 96. act or do

_____ 97. climb

_____ 98. see

a. dynamic   f. fugitive

b. flammable   g. visible

c. transport   h. telegram

d. descend   i. defend

e. action   j. minivan

Name _____

Write the letter of a synonym for each word below.

_____ 99. novice

_____ 100. cease

_____ 101. foible

_____ 102. valiant

_____ 103. conceal

_____ 104. stationary

_____ 105. tremulous

_____ 106. chide

_____ 107. obstinate

a. scold

b. stop

c. victory

d. stubborn

e. flaw

f. tremendous

g. fearful

h. shriek

i. immovable

j. brave

k. hide

l. beginner

Write the letter of an antonym for each word below.

_____ 108. temporary

_____ 109. sturdy

_____ 110. careless

_____ 111. accelerated

_____ 112. cordial

a. permanent

b. flimsy

c. rude

d. speedy

e. friendly

f. heavy

g. cautious

h. agony

i. slowed

Choose the correct homophone to complete each sentence.

113. Who would like to be _____ (buried, berried) in the sand?

114. I _____ (heard, herd) about your surfing accident.

115. Let's clean up the junk that people _____ (through, threw) on the beach today.

116. My boat's motor died, so my friends _____ (toad, towed) it back to shore.

117. Oh, no! She's headed _____ (strait, straight) for the shark!

Use each of these words to make two compound words.

118. down _____   _____

119. out   _____   _____

120. light _____   _____

121. fish   _____   _____

Name _____

Answer the following questions about denotations and connotations.

122. Circle the connotation of the word **pirate.**

    a. one who robs ships at sea

    b. a mean, ruthless man with a patched eye and a wooden leg who makes people walk
       the plank

123. Circle the denotation of the word **surf.**

    a. the foamy, breaking waves that are such fun for swimming and jumping

    b. the swelling of the sea that breaks on the shore

124. Read the denotation and connotation. Tell what the word is. _____

    Denotation: the breaking up of a sea-going vessel

    Connotation: crashing into rocks on a wild sea and splitting apart

125. Read the denotation and connotation. Tell what the word is. _____

    Denotation: irritation or blistering caused by exposure to the sun

    Connotation: miserable, painful, red skin that you can't stand to touch

Circle the word that correctly completes each sentence.

126. When they heard about the hurricane coming, Jerod's family decided to buy flood
     (insurance, assurance).

127. When the ship reached port, the captain dropped the (buoy, anchor).

128. The lifeguard station used a (barometer, anemometer) to measure the speed of the wind
     at the beach.

129. I've played in the (annual, biennial) beach volleyball tournament every year for the past
     10 years.

130. Hurry! Run! A (meteor, meteorite) has just hit the beach!

131. I can see through this (translucent, transparent) piece of sea glass.

132. Juna was offered a job as a lifeguard, but she decided not to (except, accept) it.

Name

Choose three of these words. Write two meanings for each word you choose.

fly   trunk   pen   quarter   date   fence   run   light   down   saw   spot   box   fire

word   *meanings*

133. _____   (1) _____

                                    (2) _____

134. _____   (1) _____

                                    (2) _____

135. _____   (1) _____

                                    (2) _____

Write the letter of the figurative language expression that matches each meaning below.

_____ 136. calm down

_____ 137. make you mad

_____ 138. give away a secret

_____ 139. take a chance

_____ 140. start too soon

_____ 141. say something embarrassing

_____ 142. fool around

_____ 143. an argument to have

_____ 144. a bad deal, full of problems

_____ 145. is very expensive

a. spill the beans
b. go bananas
c. cost an arm and a leg
d. red-letter day
e. the last straw
f. a bone to pick
g. drive you up a wall
h. go out on a limb
i. scream bloody murder
j. put a lid on it
k. put your foot in your mouth
l. ham it up
m. jump the gun
n. a real lemon

Cross out the word that does not belong.

146. anemone   barracuda   lobster   crocodile   squid

147. sunshine   flashlight   boardwalk   butterfly   camera

148. mice   artichoke   rainbows   keys   babies

Finish these analogies.

149. legs : crab *as* _____ : octopus

150. motorcycle : motorcycles *as* _____ : geese

151. melt : _____ *as* compliment : criticize

152. _____ : blizzard *as* rain : monsoon

153. argue : _____ *as* excite : excitement

154. calculator : mathematician as surfboard : _____

Name _____

Part Three: Spelling

Fill in _ie_ or _ei_ for each word.

155. bel _____ ve

156. n _____ ghbor

157. fr _____ nd

158. rec _____ ve

159. w _____ ght

160. ach _____ ve

Write the correct ending for each word.

161. nerv _____ (ous, eous, ious)

162. pleas _____ (ent, int, ant)

163. imposs _____ (able, ible, ibel)

164. rad _____ (ous, ious, ius, us)

165. compl _____ (eat, ete, ate)

166. trav _____ (al, el, il, le)

167. import _____ (ence, ince, ance)

168. vaca _____ (cian, shun, tion, sion)

169. carniv _____ (al, el, il, le)

170. chocol _____ (ete, ate, eat)

Which words on Freddy's poster do NOT have silent letters? Write them below.

171. _____

stalk   bridge

ghost   honest

envy   sword

combing   erupt

wriggle   knife

shhhhh

Which words on Pierre's poster are NOT correct? Write them on the lines correctly.

firecracker   celery   enerjy

couffed   surprice   phone

skuba   sider   babisitter

172. _____

173. _____

174. _____

175. _____

176. _____

177. _____

Are these words spelled correctly? Write yes or no next to each word.

_____ 178. tommorrow

_____ 179. Tennessee

_____ 180. memmory

_____ 181. bannana

_____ 182. terrible

_____ 183. annimal

_____ 184. syllable

Name _____

Write each word in its plural form.

185. radio _____

186. monkey _____

187. loaf _____

188. mess _____

189. butterfly _____

190. goose _____

Circle the correctly-spelled word in each group.

191. Atlantic, Antartica, Brasil

192. Lincon, Warshington, Jupiter

193. Checago, Michigan, Las Angelas

194. Wednesday, Tuseday, Saterday

195. Chrissmas, Haloween, Thanksgiving

Circle the word in each group that is NOT spelled correctly.

196. tomatoes
     torpedoes
     pianoes
     volcanoes
     solos

197. wierd
     ancient
     their
     height
     beige

198. homework
     bookkeeper
     roommate
     notbook
     somebody

199. completely
     magecal
     favorable
     accidental
     dentist

200. subbmarine
     transport
     exclude
     semicircle
     antiwar

201. terrifick
     agreement
     dangerous
     explosion
     tropical

202. arithmatic
     caterpillar
     Pennsylvania
     hippopotamus

203. stubborn
     elegent
     comical
     curious

204. galaxy
     astronot
     rotation
     atmosphere

Name _____

Which words on the chef's shopping list are spelled INCORRECTLY? Write them correctly below.

SHOPPING LIST

vegtables
custard
suger
macaroni
spaghetti
chocolate
lettuse
onions
sausage
tomatos
noodels

205. _____

_____

These words are all misspelled. Write them correctly.

206. pilat _____

207. peopel _____

208. cought _____

209. molacule _____

210. lama _____

211. lafter _____

212. agin _____

213. appeer _____

214. enugh _____

Write these misspelled words correctly.

215. toung _____

216. mosquitoe _____

217. oder _____

218. oppisite _____

219. lonleyness _____

220. lenth _____

221. pleeze _____

222. allmost _____

223. nesessary _____

224. **Circle the correctly spelled words on Sheriff Frog's poster.**

WANTED

wieght   wreath   wisper

expel   tragady   seize

apologize   wepons   satasfy

prise   oxygen   serious

rhithm   exercize   excellent

quisses   stomack   quartet

strength   explane   gravity

squeaze   zero   buzy

Name _____

304

Write the correct word to finish each sentence.

225. _____ (Adopt, Adept) a pet today!

226. I _____ (except, accept) your apology.

227. Count the _____ (angels, angles) in your rectangle.

228. Did you do a _____ (through, though, thorough) job of cleaning?

229. I write in my _____ (dairy, diary) every day.

230. For breakfast, I ate bran _____ (cereal, serial) today.

231. My library book has been _____ (overdue, overdo) for a week.

232. My cat actually _____ (pried, pride) open the cat food box!

233. My _____ (hoarse, horse) is too old to ride anymore.

234. Don't _____ (break, brake) any bones!

Re-write each headline, spelling all the words correctly.

235. **FRIEK AXIDENTS REPORTTED ON PUBLIK BEECHES**

_____

236. *DOCTER DOES SUPRIZE OPARATION*

_____

237. **SKI SESON CANCELLED DUE TO DANGROUS ICE STORM**

_____

238. **TWO HUNRERD HOMES LOST IN TORNADOE**

_____

239. **ELAPHANT RECIEVES GOLD MEDDLE**

_____

Name _____

Part Four: Grammar & Usage

Identify the following sentences by writing . . .

S for **simple sentence**   **R** for **run-on sentence**

C for **compound sentence**   **F** for **sentence fragment**

_____ 240. Going over the waterfall.

_____ 241. Eat your breakfast and clean your cabins.

_____ 242. Turn left at the stump take three steps north enter the cave.

_____ 243. What a cute squirrel in your tent!

_____ 244. Did you step in the poison ivy?

Write the simple subject for each sentence on the line.

_____ 245. Sam raced us to the diving board.

_____ 246. Were the bears eating your marshmallows?

_____ 247. The biggest chipmunk took my backpack.

Write the simple predicate for each sentence on the line.

_____ 248. Falling rocks crashed into the campsite.

_____ 249. Could crafty coyotes catch cunning campers?

_____ 250. We watched while the wind blew our tent away.

Identify the parts of speech in the sentence below by writing . . .

N for **noun**   **ADJ** for **adjective**   **V** for **verb**   **ADV** for **adverb**

Three hungry campers gobbled pancakes greedily.

_____ 251. Three   _____ 253. campers   _____ 255. pancakes

_____ 252. hungry   _____ 254. gobbled   _____ 256. greedily

Read the following sentence, and look for the nouns. Decide if the nouns are common or proper.

Last Friday, Billy put spiders in the beds and hot pepper in the soup.

_____ 257. Write the common nouns from the sentence.

_____ 258. Write the proper nouns from the sentence.

Write a possessive noun phrase (two words) to fit each description.

_____ 259. teeth belonging to one fox

_____ 260. teeth belonging to more than one fox

_____ 261. shirts belonging to three campers

_____ 262. tail of one skunk

Write the subject pronoun from each sentence.

_____ 263. They couldn't decide where to pitch their tent.

_____ 264. She said that the task was too hard.

Name _____

Write the object pronoun from each sentence.

_____ 265. Don't ask him for help.

_____ 266. We gave them a ride on the donkey.

Write the correct form (tense) of the verb needed in the sentence.
Find the verb at the end of each sentence.

_____ 267. Yesterday, Carl _____ boats for a contest. (row)

_____ 268. This morning, Lisa _____ away from the sinking boat. (swim)

_____ 269. Oh, no! Matt _____ off his raft into the river! (fall)

_____ 270. Tomorrow our cabin _____ kites. (fly)

_____ 271. Who _____ my green pajamas last night? (wear)

_____ 272. How many campers _____ to their parents this week? (write)

_____ 273. She _____ when she saw the lizard in her shoe. (faint)

_____ 274. Last night we _____ to replace the cook. (vote)

Write the helping verb from each sentence.

_____ 275. He is playing with matches.

_____ 276. Tom should start getting wood for the campfire.

_____ 277. Bigfoot is coming!

_____ 278. Is it true that you have seen a spaceship?

Identify each part of speech shown at the end of the sentence by writing . . .

N for **noun**   **V** for **verb**   **ADJ** for **adjective**   **ADV** for **adverb**

_____ 279. Eat your grilled cheese sandwich. (Eat)

_____ 280. Watch the song leader closely. (closely)

_____ 281. Don't you just love the beautiful camp theme song? (beautiful)

_____ 282. Who won the frog jumping contest? (contest)

_____ 283. Counselor Wacky fell out of the canoe. (fell)

_____ 284. That meat loaf was the most terrible food yet! (terrible)

_____ 285. Back away slowly from the rattlesnake. (slowly)

Write the correct form of the adjective that should be placed in the blank.
The adjectives are shown at the end of the sentence.

_____ 286. Karl's race was _____ than Isaac's. (fast)

_____ 287. Whose frog jumped to the _____ lily pad? (farther)

_____ 288. This is the _____ lunch meat I've ever seen! (slimy)

Write the adjective form that will correctly fill in the blank.

_____ 289. This is the _____ pizza I have ever eaten. (better, best)

_____ 290. I have eaten a lot, but it is still _____ than you've eaten. (less, least)

_____ 291. My score was the _____ of all the runners. (worse, worst)

Name _____

Write the adverb form that will correctly fill in the blank.

_____ 292. Billy gets up _____ than the other campers. (early)

_____ 293. He plays pranks _____ than the other campers. (often)

_____ 294. Nick can climb the flagpole the _____ of all of the campers. (quickly)

Choose the word that will show the correct use of a negative.

_____ 295. No one (would, wouldn't) want to miss the shooting stars.

_____ 296. The campers have not gotten (any, no) mail today.

_____ 297. Won't (anyone, no one) come to the haunted cabin with me?

_____ 298. We don't (never, ever) want to go there again.

Write the preposition from each sentence.

_____ 299. Just what do you have hidden under your bed?

_____ 300. Let's push the counselors into the pool.

_____ 301. I will race you across the campground.

Write the prepositional phrase from each sentence.

_____ 302. Bigfoot is standing behind you.

_____ 303. Please walk around the flowers.

_____ 304. There's some rotten food beneath your bed.

Write the two words used to form each contraction.

_____ 305. won't   _____ 307. I've

_____ 306. they're   _____ 308. we'd

Find the misspelled words in the sentences, and write them correctly on the line.

The cook at are camp allways creats the most delichus meels.
We have our faverite pizza wunce a weak and marshmellows every day for desert!

309. _____

_____

Circle the words that should have capital letters in each sentence.

310. camp begins on sunday and ends on friday each week in july.

311. counselor joe told lisa to write to her parents.

Add the missing punctuation to the letter below.

312.
Dear Mom and Dad   July 15 1999
I am having the best time at this camp You won't believe how well Im doing We have terrible food lots of mosquitoes and grumpy counselors Doesn't it sound great I think I saw an alien and I fell out of the canoe three times
How much longer can I stay

Your loving son
Manuel

Name _____

Part Five: Writing

Circle the letter of the word that is most effective for each blank.

313. The elephant _____ along heavily in the parade.

    a. pranced   d. lumbered

    b. skipped   e. walked

    c. slid

314. Jana's best friend was _____ by her sudden and mysterious disappearance.

    a. amused   c. troubled

    b. bored   d. satisfied

315. Someone or something is _____ in the dark shadows, staring out at me with piercing eyes.

    a. hiding   c. standing

    b. lurking   d. playing

316. The sunset threw a _____ orange glow across the rippling lake.

    a. glamorous   c. nice

    b. spectacular   d. cute

Circle the letter(s) of the correct answer(s).

317. Which example shows an active voice?

    a. The peppers on my sandwich were very hot and spicy.

    b. The spicy peppers bit my tongue.

    c. Pepper juice was spicy on my tongue.

318. Which sentence(s) contain(s) a comparison that is a metaphor and not a simile?

    a. My little sister is a peach of a kid.

    b. This homework is going as slowly as an opera.

    c. Little twin brothers are like double hurricanes.

319. Which sentence(s) contain(s) a simile?

    a. Tom is as salty as a potato chip.

    b. Life is like a puzzle with some of the pieces missing.

    c. My dad's meat loaf tastes like sawdust.

    d. The teakettle hisses at me.

320. Which sentence does NOT contain a metaphor?

    a. The raging river gobbles up boats and swallows them whole.

    b. The wind is a playful kitten.

    c. Math is as slippery as wet spaghetti.

321. Which mood would these words help to set?

    hurry, scurry, fast, zip, bustle, quick, dart, dash, race

    a. curious

    b. playful

    c. quiet

    d. rushing

322. Which would be a **persuasive** piece of writing?

    a. advertisement convincing someone to buy a new basketball shoe

    b. wild imaginative tale about the future

    c. description of an unusual character

    d. directions for building a kite

323. Which would be an **expository** piece?

    a. a tall tale

    b. an explanation of how you earn interest on your savings account at the bank

    c. a poster encouraging you to try the new lemon liver yogurt

    d. a description of a surfing trip

Name _____

324. Which sentence appeals to your sense of hearing?

    a. The scream of the red sirens splits through the black night.

    b. The flashing ambulance lights make my eyes squeeze shut.

    c. My heart pounds wildly in my chest as I wait for the ambulance.

325. Which sentence creates a strong visual image?

    a. The moon is not shining tonight.

    b. Last night's moon shimmered like a slice of silver ribbon in a black sky.

    c. What is it like to walk on the moon?

326. Which sentence does NOT create a strong visual image?

    a. Dripping red juices slowly slide across the road from the wrecked tomato truck.

    b. Fluffy, sugary, golden meringue tops the thick, yellow, lemon cream of the pie.

    c. The cracking and popping sound of her gum hurt my ears.

WRITING TASKS: For each writing task below, follow the directions given.

Task 1: Number these sentences (1–7) in an order that makes sense.

_____ When it was over, we found our car in the neighbor's swimming pool.

_____ Our car was hurled across the street like a plastic toy.

_____ The tornado struck at dawn.

_____ Suddenly the roar stopped and everything was still.

_____ Slowly, we crept out of the shelter.

_____ We hurried into the shelter.

_____ A whirling, black funnel headed straight for our house.

Task 2: Replace each ordinary word with a more colorful or interesting word. Write a new word above the <u>underlined</u> word.

It was a <u>bad</u> idea to ride the roller coaster when I was feeling <u>sick</u>. The Triple Loop looked <u>scary</u>. Once I got on, my stomach <u>hurt</u> as the roller coaster <u>moved</u> up and down and <u>went</u> from side to side. I have never felt so <u>awful</u>!

Task 3: Write a more active word above each underlined word.

1. The parade <u>went</u> on for four miles.

2. Did you really <u>have</u> six eclairs for lunch?

3. Don't you think she <u>was</u> on the trampoline too long?

Task 4: Rewrite the following sentences to make the meaning clear.

1. Sitting on the top shelf of the closet, I found an old sandwich.

_____

2. We heard about the robber who was caught on the radio.

_____

Name

Task 5: Cross out any unneeded or repetitive ideas.

1. She totally ate the whole pizza.

2. Jason drew seven three-sided triangles in his geometry design.

3. In my opinion, I think that snowboards are not at all dangerous even a bit.

Task 6: Write a strong beginning for one of these topics.

- learning to tame a lion
- a dog who can read
- a strange disappearance
- lizards who can dance
- a visit with Bigfoot
- a shocking letter
- an accident
- a terrible flood
- a memory

_____

_____

_____

Task 7: Circle the examples of figurative language in this letter.

Dear Genoa,

You are one bad apple. I am so burned up at you! I went out on a limb to help you with a problem, and now you've let the cat out of the bag about my secret. I thought I could trust you not to spill the beans. Your goose is cooked, girl! No matter how hard you try, I don't think you'll be able to get your foot out of your mouth any time soon.

Sincerely,

Your mad-as-a-hatter ex-friend

Task 8: Write a clear, complete, interesting sentence about one of these topics.

- a bothersome bumblebee
- a wild thunderstorm
- a dark, spooky night
- a slithery snake
- a disappointment
- a tough science test

_____

_____

_____

Task 9: Choose one of the people below, and write two good questions that you would ask him or her.

- your favorite author
- a heart surgeon
- a gorilla trainer
- a Supreme Court justice
- someone who climbed Mt. Everest
- someone who rode a roller coaster for 14 days straight

1. _____

_____

2. _____

_____

Name _____

Task 10: Rewrite the conversation from the cartoon. Write it in a paragraph that includes dialogue. Use correct punctuation for the dialogue.

> Georgia, what time is it when a gorilla knocks on your door?

> It's time to run out the back door, Dan!

_____

_____

_____

_____

_____

_____

Editing task 11 is worth 10 points.

Task 11: Correct the spelling, punctuation, capitalization, and grammar in the following letter. Also, eliminate excess words or phrases. Cross out the errors
and write the corrections above each line.

Dear editor

   In my opinion, I beleeve that the new minature golf corse which the city has built owned by the city should change its rules. It does not make sens to refuse kids under 18 to come unless they are with adults I thought the city bilt this corse to atract kids and give them something good to do in the evenings. this is a wunderful activity for kids, but you are keeping them away. Most teenagers want to go out for an activity with their friends, not their parents Whose bad idea was this! I protest I hope this rule will be changed soon

                              Sincerely,

                                 Adam

Writing task 12 is worth 15 points.

Task 12: Write a description, story, or tall tale to go along with the picture.
Make sure your piece of writing has:

- a good title
- a strong beginning
- a strong middle
- a strong ending
- details to explain the main idea

_____

_____

_____

_____

_____

Name _____

SOCIAL STUDIES SKILLS TEST

Part One: Geography of the U.S.

Write the name of each numbered state and body of water shown on the map.

1. _____

2. _____

3. _____

4. _____

5. _____

6. _____

7. _____

8. _____

9. _____

10. _____

11. _____

12. _____

13. _____

14. _____

15. _____

Match the capitals with the states.

_____ 16. Washington   _____ 21. Massachusetts   A. Tallahassee   F. Santa Fe   K. Olympia

_____ 17. Nebraska   _____ 22. Georgia   B. Madison   G. Little Rock   L. Boston

_____ 18. Florida   _____ 23. Idaho   C. Des Moines   H. Lincoln   M. Seattle

_____ 19. Iowa   _____ 24. New Mexico   D. Pierre   I. Omaha

_____ 20. Arkansas   _____ 25. Wisconsin   E. Atlanta   J. Boise

26. Circle states that can be found in the Pacific Region of the United States.
    Alaska   Colorado   Oregon   Arizona   California

27. Circle states that can be found in the Mountain Region of the United States.
    Texas   Nebraska   Montana   Utah   Colorado

28. Circle states that can be found in the Plains Region of the United States.
    Iowa   Oklahoma   Nebraska   North Dakota   Oregon

29. Circle states that can be found in the Southwest Region of the United States.
    Missouri   Illinois   New Mexico   Arizona   Texas

30. Circle states that can be found in the Middle Atlantic Region of the United States.
    Vermont   Pennsylvania   Alabama   New York   New Jersey

31. Circle states that can be found in the Southeast Region of the United States.
    Mississippi   Arkansas   Ohio   Texas   Louisiana   South Carolina   Virginia

32. Circle states that can be found in the New England Region of the United States.
    Michigan   Maine   Massachusetts   New Hampshire   Connecticut

33. Circle states that can be found in the Great Lakes Region of the United States.
    Minnesota   Ohio   West Virginia   Indiana   Colorado   Michigan

34. Circle cities that are state capitals.
    Baton Rouge   Chicago   Cheyenne   Denver   Seattle   Juneau   Boise

35. Circle cities that are not state capitals.
    Los Angeles   Boston   Indianapolis   Chicago   Detroit   Nashville   Miami

Write the letter that shows the location of each U.S. feature on the map.

_____ 36. Great Basin

_____ 37. Rocky Mts.

_____ 38. Appalachian Mts.

_____ 39. Mississippi River

_____ 40. Rio Grande

_____ 41. Mojave Desert

_____ 42. Great Salt Lake

_____ 43. Lake Michigan

_____ 44. Great Plains

_____ 45. Sierra Nevada Mts.

Name

Write the letter of the U.S. region that contains the features or places listed.

A. Pacific   B. Mountain   C. Southwest   D. Middle Atlantic
E. New England   F. Southeast   G. Plains   H. Great Lakes

_____ 46. Rocky Mountains   Yosemite Park   Las Vegas   Montana   Denver
_____ 47. Indianapolis   Detroit   Chicago   auto capital   famous cheese   Ohio
_____ 48. New York   Niagara Falls   Liberty Bell   Washington, D.C.   Delaware
_____ 49. Georgia   Memphis   Kentucky Derby   Mammoth Cave   New Orleans
_____ 50. Crater Lake   volcanoes   Seattle   Juneau   redwood forests   50th state
_____ 51. lobsters   Rhode Island   maple sugar   Boston   Cape Cod   Vermont
_____ 52. North Dakota   Mt. Rushmore   Gateway Arch   Kansas City
_____ 53. Oklahoma   oil and gas   Carlsbad Caverns   Grand Canyon   cliff dwellings

Match the features to the cities.

_____ 54. Country Music Capital
_____ 55. Lincoln Memorial
_____ 56. Golden Gate Bridge
_____ 57. Liberty Bell
_____ 58. Alamo
_____ 59. Statue of Liberty
_____ 60. Gateway Arch
_____ 61. Kentucky Derby
_____ 62. Willis Tower
_____ 63. Space Needle

A. San Francisco   F. Louisville
B. St. Louis   G. Washington, D.C.
C. Philadelphia   H. Seattle
D. San Antonio   I. New York
E. Nashville   J. Chicago

Write the letter that matches each country shown on the map.

_____ 64. Panama
_____ 65. Cuba
_____ 66. Honduras
_____ 67. Mexico
_____ 68. Puerto Rico
_____ 69. Guatemala
_____ 70. Haiti

Match these important U.S. sites to the states.

_____ 71. Arlington National Cemetery
_____ 72. Grand Canyon
_____ 73. Cape Cod
_____ 74. Valley Forge
_____ 75. Glacier National Park
_____ 76. Tallest active volcano
_____ 77. Yosemite
_____ 78. Mammoth Cave
_____ 79. Niagara Falls
_____ 80. Mt. St. Helens

A. Montana   F. Kentucky
B. California   G. Massachusetts
C. Virginia   H. Hawaii
D. Arizona   I. New York
E. Pennsylvania   J. Washington

Name _____

81. The U.S. Constitution and other historical documents can be found in:

    The Smithsonian Institute   The Supreme Court   The National Archives

82. Circle the hemispheres where the United States lies:

    Northern   Southern   Eastern   Western

83. Circle the continents that are totally or partly in the Northern Hemisphere:

    Asia   Europe   Antarctica   South America   North America   Australia   Africa

84. Circle the oceans that are in the Eastern Hemisphere:

    Arctic Ocean   Indian Ocean   Atlantic Ocean   Pacific Ocean

85. A place that holds 14 different museums is:

    The White House   The Smithsonian Institute   The Capitol   The Library of Congress

86. The line of latitude at $66\frac{1}{2}°$ south is

    Tropic of Cancer   Arctic Circle   Antarctic Circle   Tropic of Capricorn   Equator

87. Which line of latitude runs through the United States?

    89°N   5°N   26°S   80°S   40°N

88. What is at 0° latitude? _____

89. What is at 0° longitude? _____

90. What is at 90° north latitude? _____

91. Circle the Canadian cities.   Toronto   Buffalo   Montreal   Vancouver   Detroit

92. Circle the Canadian provinces.   Alberta   Yukon   Quebec   Manitoba   Saskatchewan

93. Circle the names of two Mexican peninsulas.

    Yucatan   Everglades   Honduras   Baja California   Sierra Madre

94. Circle the items that are natural resources of Mexico.

    bananas   silver   beans   coffee   cacao   diamonds   automobiles

95. Circle the features or places that can be found in Mexico.

    Tropic of Cancer   Rio Grande River   Dallas   Central Plateau   mountains

96. Which South American country is close to Antarctica?

    Brazil   Venezuela   Argentina   Suriname

97. Circle the countries that the Andes Mountains pass through.

    Argentina   Paraguay   Guyana   Chile   Peru   Uruguay   Ecuador   Colombia

98. It is 4:00 P.M. Eastern Time. What time is it in Mountain Time? _____

99. It is noon Pacific Time. In what time zone is it 3:00 P.M.? _____

100. It is 9:00 P.M. in California. What time is it in Boston? _____

Name _____

Part Two: Map Skills & Geography

Write the letter of the location on the world map that matches each of these countries.

_____ 101. Egypt

_____ 102. Mexico

_____ 103. Brazil

_____ 104. Spain

_____ 105. India

_____ 106. Canada

_____ 107. New Zealand

_____ 108. Norway

_____ 109. Kenya

_____ 110. China

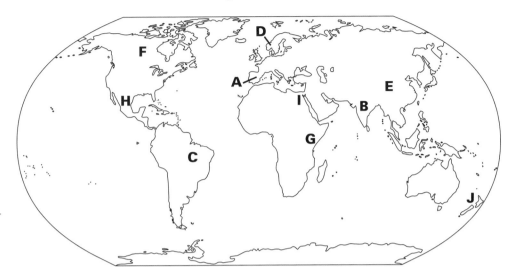

Write the letter of the map term that matches each description.

_____ 111. tells what the map is about

_____ 112. shows amount of rainfall

_____ 113. explains map symbols

_____ 114. shows height of landforms

_____ 115. gives directions on the map

_____ 116. shows cities, states, and countries

_____ 117. shows rivers, lakes, and mountains

_____ 118. tells about distances on a map

_____ 119. shows things a country produces

_____ 120. shows rooms in a building

a. title
b. population map
c. political map
d. elevation map
e. scale
f. product map
g. floor plan
h. physical map
i. weather map
j. road map
k. map key
l. time zone map
m. compass rose

Circle the correct answer or answers.

121. If the scale of a park map is 1 inch = 20 feet, a measurement on the map of 6 inches stands for how much distance in the actual park?

    a. 3.5 feet   b. 12 feet   c. 120 feet   d. 1,200 feet   e. 12,000 feet

122. An island that is 60 miles long is 3 inches long on a map. The map's scale is

    a. 1 in. = 10 miles   b. 1 in. = 3 miles   c. 1 in. = 600 miles   d. 1 in. = 20 miles

123. Which continents does the equator pass through?

    a. Europe   b. South America   c. North America   d. Africa   e. Australia

Name _____

124. Which continent is entirely south of the equator?
    a. Australia   b. Africa   c. Asia   d. South America

125. Which continents are entirely north of the equator?
    a. Europe   b. South America c. Asia   d. North America

Circle the correct answer or answers.

126. Which continents are entirely in the Eastern Hemisphere?
    a. Asia   b. North America c. Europe   d. Africa   e. Australia

127. Which continents are entirely in the Western Hemisphere?
    a. Europe   b. North America c. South America d. Antarctica

128. Which country does the Tropic of Cancer pass through?
    a. Greenland   b. Brazil   c. South Africa   d. Mexico

129. Which countries does the Arctic Circle pass through?
    a. Spain   b. Norway   c. India   d. United States

Write the letter of the location on the map that matches each of these states.

_____ 130. Wyoming

_____ 131. New Mexico

_____ 132. Texas

_____ 133. Tennessee

_____ 134. Alabama

_____ 135. Kansas

_____ 136. Virginia

_____ 137. Oregon

_____ 138. Vermont

_____ 139. Wisconsin

140. Circle the oceans that touch South America.
    a. Atlantic   b. Arctic   c. Indian   d. Pacific

141. Circle the countries that touch the Arctic Ocean.
    a. Russia   b. Canada   c. Norway   d. France   e. Mexico

142. Which U.S. states are on the Gulf of Mexico? Circle them.
    a. Texas   b. Missouri   c. Florida   d. Louisiana e. Virginia   f. Arkansas

143. Circle the state that is east of Ohio.
    a. Illinois   b. Wisconsin   c. Kansas   d. Pennsylvania

144. Circle the states that are west of Minnesota.
    a. Tennessee b. Arizona   c. Wyoming   d. Oklahoma

145. Circle the states that border California.
    a. Nevada   b. New Mexico c. Oregon   d. Utah   e. Arizona

Name

Fantasy Village

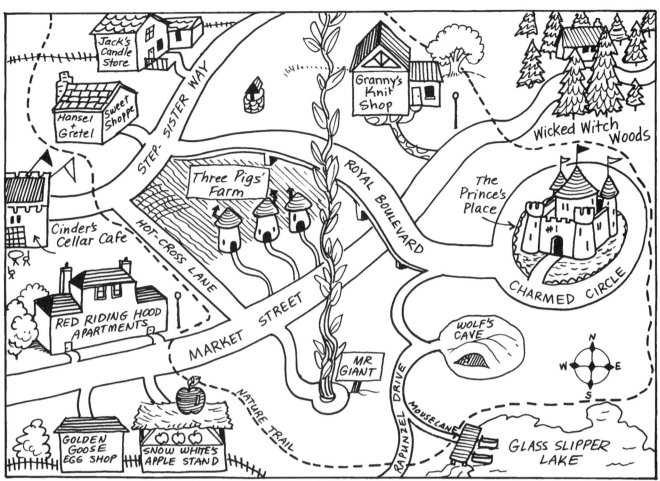

Scale 1 inch = 500 feet

Use the Fantasy Village map (and a ruler) to answer these questions.

_____ 146. Which street does the nature trail cross twice?

_____ 147. Wicked Witch Woods is what direction from Mr. Giant's home?

_____ 148. How tall is Mr. Giant's beanstalk (as much as is shown on the map)?

_____ 149. How far apart are the pigs' driveways?

_____ 150. What direction is Jack's Candle Store from the castle?

_____ 151. How long is Royal Boulevard?

_____ 152. How many streets border the pigs' farm?

_____ 153. Does the wolf live closer to Granny, the pigs, or Red Riding Hood?

_____ 154. What direction is Snow White's Apple Stand from the Sweet Shoppe?

155. Describe the shortest route (on streets and trails) the wolf could take to get to Granny's shop.

_____

_____

Name

Write the letter of the term that matches each definition.

_____ 156. a deep, narrow valley with steep sides

_____ 157. narrow strip of land that connects two larger pieces of land
and is bordered on both sides by water

_____ 158. a high, flat landform that rises steeply above surrounding land

_____ 159. an area of very low precipitation

_____ 160. a body of land mostly surrounded by water

_____ 161. place where a river empties into a large body of water

_____ 162. the study of the Earth's surface and everything on it

_____ 163. an area of low land between mountains or hills

_____ 164. part of an ocean or sea that extends into land; larger than a bay

a. geography

b. gulf

c. mouth

d. plateau

e. desert

f. valley

g. canyon

h. isthmus

i. peninsula

j. source

_____ 165. If it is noon in California (PT), what time is it in Colorado (MT)?

_____ 166. What time does a 3-hour flight leaving New York (ET) at 9 A.M.
land in Oregon (PT)?

_____ 167. What time is it in Kansas (CT) when it is midnight in Seattle (PT)?

_____ 168. What time did a 6-hour flight arriving in New Jersey at 1:30 P.M.
(ET) leave Denver (MT)?

Write the direction you would travel if you were taking the shortest way . . .

_____ 169. from Japan to Iraq

_____ 170. from Canada to Mexico

_____ 171. from New Zealand to Spain

_____ 172. from Italy to Algeria

_____ 173. from Kenya to Canada

_____ 174. from Germany to China

Name

SCIENCE SKILLS TEST

Write the letter that matches each flower part.

_____ 1. petal

_____ 2. sepal

_____ 3. ovary

_____ 4. pollen grains

_____ 5. pistil

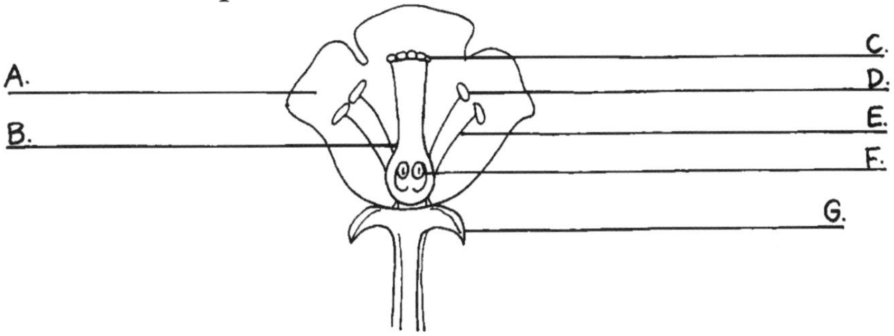

Write the answer on the line.

_____ 6. In what process does a green plant use sunlight to make food?

_____ 7. In what process does a plant break down food and release energy?

_____ 8. What gas is given off during respiration?

_____ 9. What gas is given off during photosynthesis?

_____ 10. What chemical in plants helps trap light energy to make food?

11. Circle the seed plants.

   pine tree   moss   daisy   lily   apple tree   fern

12. Circle the animals pictured at the right that are NOT arthropods.

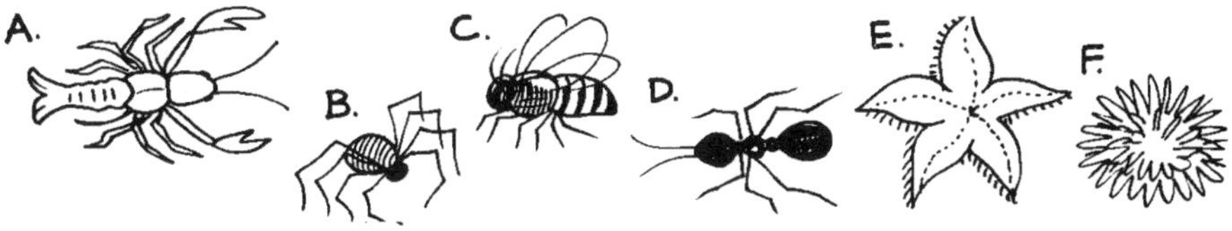

13. Circle the animals pictured at the right that are mollusks.

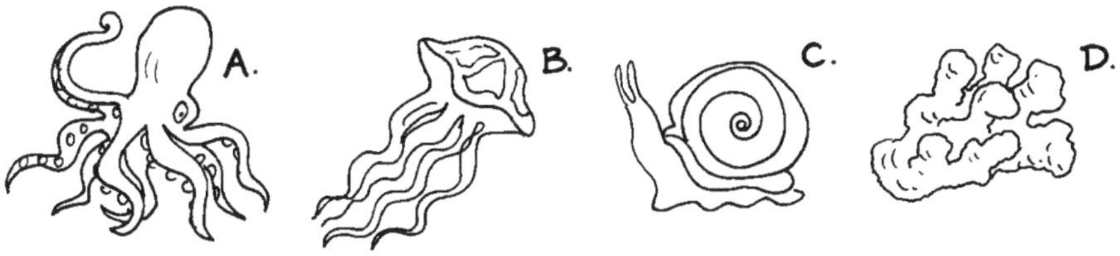

14. Circle the animals pictured at the right that are vertebrates.

Name _____

Write the letter of the animal group that matches the description.

_____ 15. cold-blooded with scales, lays eggs

_____ 16. has eight legs, two body sections, no antennae

_____ 17. warm-blooded, has wings and hollow bones

_____ 18. warm-blooded, covered with hair or fur

_____ 19. has six legs, one pair antennae, three body sections

_____ 20. thick sack of cells that forms pores or chambers

A. birds
B. sponges
C. amphibians
D. insects
E. mammals
F. arachnids
G. echinoderms
H. reptiles

Write the letter of the correct answer.

_____ 21. An animal that feeds off dead organisms is

      a. a predator   b. a producer   c. a scavenger   d. a parasite

_____ 22. All the organisms that live together in a certain place are

      a. a community   b. a biome   c. a habitat   d. producers

_____ 23. When a tick feeds on your dog, the tick is

      a. a producer   b. a scavenger   c. a parasite   d. a predator

24. Circle the organisms in the picture at the right that are consumers.

A.   **B.**   **C.**

For each body part or system, write the letter of the correct description.

_____ 25. tendons

_____ 26. esophagus

_____ 27. femur

_____ 28. joint

_____ 29. gastrocnemius

_____ 30. radius

_____ 31. scapula

_____ 32. diaphragm

_____ 33. cornea

_____ 34. stirrup

_____ 35. digestive

A. calf muscle
B. covering of the eye
C. tube from mouth to stomach
D. a bone of the upper arm
E. system for using food in the body
F. largest bone in the human body
G. collarbone
H. bands of fiber that attach muscles to bones
I. place where bones come together
J. a bone of the middle ear
K. a bone of the lower arm
L. large muscle that helps move air in and out of body
M. shoulder blade
N. system for using air in the body

Write the answer on the line.

_____ 36. What kind of exercise strengthens the heart muscle?

_____ 37. What is increased by lifting weights?

_____ 38. What gains flexibility with stretching exercises?

Name _____

_____ 39. Circle the part of an atom that has a negative electrical charge.

      a. nucleus   b. electron   c. proton   d. neutron

_____ 40. Circle the word that describes the change in state from a liquid to a gas.

      a. evaporation   b. melting   c. freezing   d. condensation

_____ 41. Change in matter that results in a different substance is a

      a. physical change   b. a mixture   c. condensation   d. a chemical change

_____ 42. A substance that contains atoms of two or more elements chemically combined is a

      a. liquid   b. a compound   c. an element   d. a solid

_____ 43. At which temperatures does water change to ice?

      a. 100 °C and 32 °F   b. 200 °F and 100 °C

      c. 0 °C and 32 °F   d. 0 °F and 32 °C

Write the chemical formula for each compound shown below.

_____ 44.

_____ 45.

_____ 46.

_____ 47.

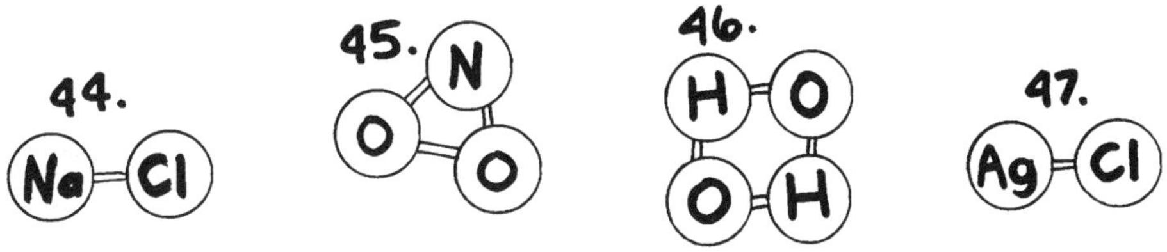

For each event below, write P for physical change or C for chemical change.

_____ 48. burning toast   _____ 49. a rusting bicycle   _____ 50. mixing lemonade and sugar

_____ 51. whipping cream   _____ 52. spoiling food

Write the answer on the line.

_____ 53. the force that slows or stops moving objects when they move across each other

_____ 54. the tendency for an object at rest to remain at rest

_____ 55. what like poles of magnets do to each other

_____ 56. the loudness or softness of a sound

Write the name of each simple machine.

_____ 57. A

_____ 58. B

_____ 59. C

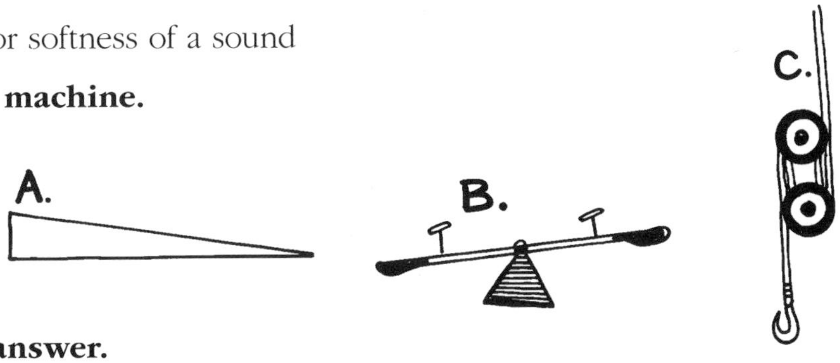

Write the letter of the correct answer.

_____ 60. A device used to measure the speed of wind is

      a. a barometer   b. a seismograph

      c. an anemometer   d. a thermometer

_____ 61. A major storm with high winds that develops over warm, tropical water is a

      a. hurricane   b. blizzard   c. tornado   d. tsunami

Name _____

_____ 62. The part of the continent that is just below the ocean water is the

      a. continental slope   b. trough   c. continental shelf   d. plain

_____ 63. The planets closest to the sun are

      a. Mercury & Venus   b. Mercury & Mars c. Uranus & Neptune   d. Jupiter & Mars

_____ 64. Water vapor condensing into little drops near the ground that freezes on grass and other objects is

      a. fog   b. dew   c. frost   d. snow   e. hail

_____ 65. Fragments of rocky matter that float in space are

      a. meteors   b. meteorites   c. meteoroids   d. comets

_____ 66. Comets are usually named after

      a. their discoverers   b. the planets they are near   c. famous astronomers

_____ 67. The four major agents of change on Earth's surface are

      a. gravity, ice, wind, water   b. air, water, pollution, heat

      c. lightning, glaciers, animals, radiation

_____ 68. Rocks that are formed from volcanic activity are

      a. igneous   b. minerals   c. metamorphic   d. sedimentary

_____ 69. In the diagram below, what is being shown?

      a. a solar eclipse

      b. a lunar eclipse

      c. Earth's rotation

      d. sunspots

Write the letter of the correct matching definition.

_____ 70. physiology

_____ 71. core

_____ 72. troposphere

_____ 73. barometer

_____ 74. antibody

_____ 75. reflection

_____ 76. caldera

_____ 77. vaccination

_____ 78. translucent

_____ 79. plankton

_____ 80. moraines

_____ 81. front

A. device to measure earthquakes

B. shot that helps the body develop defenses against a disease

C. layer of Earth's atmosphere closest to Earth

D. boundary that separates two air masses

E. hole created when the top of a volcano collapses

F. device to measure air pressure

G. bending of a ray of light as it passes through water

H. science that studies human body structure and function

I. innermost layer of the Earth

J. deposits left by melting glaciers

K. bouncing of a wave or ray off a surface

L. science that studies Earth's surface

M. a substance in body fluids that kills diseases

N. life found at the ocean bottom

O. can't see through an object, but light can pass through it

P. sea life found floating at ocean surface

Name _____

MATH SKILLS TEST

Part One: Computation & Numbers

Write the numerals to match these words.

_____ 1. ten thousand, five hundred

_____ 2. three billion

_____ 3. fifty-five thousand, nine hundred, twenty

_____ 4. six hundred thousand, six hundred

_____ 5. eight thousand, thirty

6. Number these numerals in order from smallest to largest.

_____ 500,005   _____ 25,500   _____ 3,005   _____ 5,505

_____ 7. Round this number to the nearest ten: 5,976

_____ 8. Round this number to the nearest thousand: 24,130

_____ 9. Round this number to the nearest ten thousand: 278,166

_____ 10. Round this number to the nearest hundred: 555

_____ 11. Write the factors of 24.

_____ 12. Write the factors of 49.

_____ 13. Write the common factors of 12 and 32.

_____ 14. Write the greatest common factor of 50 and 15.

Solve these problems. Write the answer on the line.

_____ 15. $8\overline{)709}$ 20. $5,500 \div 100 =$ _____

_____ 16. $\begin{array}{r} 5,961 \\ +\ 288 \\ \hline \end{array}$ 21. $65 \times 100 =$ _____

_____ 17. $\begin{array}{r} 710,621 \\ -\ 25,009 \\ \hline \end{array}$ 22. $900 \times 1,000 =$ _____

23. $2,400 \div 10 =$ _____

_____ 18. $\begin{array}{r} 279 \\ \times\ 18 \\ \hline \end{array}$ 24. $(75 + 5) \div 2 - 20 =$ _____

_____ 19. $648 \div 2$ 25. $(1,000 - 800) \times 4 \div 160 =$ _____

Name _____

Write a decimal numeral to match the words.

_____ 26. fifty-five and five tenths

_____ 27. three hundred forty-four thousandths

28. Circle the largest fraction: $\frac{2}{3}$ $\frac{7}{8}$

29. Circle the largest fraction: $\frac{2}{12}$ $\frac{3}{9}$

30. Write the fractions in order from smallest to largest. $\frac{14}{16}$ $\frac{7}{12}$ $\frac{2}{3}$ $\frac{6}{8}$

_____

31. Circle the fractions that are equivalent to $\frac{3}{4}$. $\frac{12}{16}$ $\frac{9}{12}$ $\frac{6}{12}$ $\frac{2}{3}$ $\frac{6}{8}$

32. Circle the fractions that are in lowest terms. $\frac{7}{9}$ $\frac{12}{15}$ $\frac{6}{12}$ $\frac{2}{3}$ $\frac{6}{8}$

_____ 33. Write this fraction in lowest terms: $\frac{18}{24}$

_____ 34. Write this fraction in lowest terms: $\frac{12}{16}$

_____ 35. Write this fraction as a mixed numeral: $\frac{50}{20}$

_____ 36. Write this fraction as a mixed numeral: $\frac{37}{5}$

_____ 37. Write this fraction as a mixed numeral: $\frac{44}{10}$

_____ 38. Write this mixed numeral as a fraction: $7\frac{1}{8}$

_____ 39. Write this mixed numeral as a fraction: $30\frac{5}{7}$

Choose the decimal numeral that matches the words.

_____ 40. seven and seven tenths   A. 0.05

_____ 41. five thousandths   B. 7.09

_____ 42. five hundredths   C. 0.0007

_____ 43. seven and nine hundredths   D. 0.005

_____ 44. seven ten thousandths   E. 7.7

_____ 45. seven and seven hundredths   F. 7.07

_____ 46. Round to the nearest thousandth: 0.48075

_____ 47. Round to the nearest ten thousandth: 1.86537

_____ 48. Round to the nearest hundredth: 1.6326

_____ 49. Round to the nearest tenth: 5.886

Name _____

50. Write these decimals in order from smallest to largest.   0.03   3.003   0.3   3.3   33.33

51. Circle the largest decimal numeral.   0.555   0.5   0.05   0.5005

Solve these problems.

52. $\frac{6}{7}$ x $\frac{2}{3}$ = _____

53. $\frac{7}{8}$ – $\frac{2}{4}$ = _____

54. $\frac{6}{12}$ + $\frac{2}{3}$ = _____

55. $\frac{7}{10}$ – $\frac{4}{10}$ = _____

56. $\frac{3}{5}$ x $\frac{6}{9}$ = _____

57. $\frac{3}{4}$ ÷ $\frac{2}{5}$ = _____

58. $\frac{5}{12}$ ÷ $\frac{5}{6}$ = _____

59. $2\frac{1}{2}$ + $5\frac{1}{2}$ = _____

60. $1\frac{1}{2}$ x $2\frac{1}{3}$ = _____

61. $\frac{12}{5}$ – $\frac{4}{3}$ = _____

62. 16.5 – 4.2 + 2.1 = _____

63. 15.4 + 1.2 – 4.1 = _____

64. $ 200.40
      –   15.80

65. $ 1600.99
    + 743.86

66. $ 29.50
    x   7

67.
    3 $\overline{)\$75.00}$

_____ 68. Change $\frac{3}{4}$ to a decimal.

_____ 69. Write 72.3% as a decimal.

_____ 70. Write 47.36 as a percent.

_____ 71. Write 0.53 as a percent.

_____ 72. Write 0.60 as a fraction.

_____ 73. Change $\frac{2}{5}$ to a percent.

_____ 74. Change 80% to a fraction.

75. Write these integers in order from smallest to largest: 5,   – 8,   3,   0,   –2,   8,   –5,   1

Solve these problems:

76. – 60 + 15 = _____   77. 13 – 7 + 4 + – 8 = _____   78. 25 + 5 + –18 = _____

_____ 79. Seven skaters need new skates. The skates cost $159.00 a pair. How much will the skates cost all together?

_____ 80. Of the 42 boxers at the arena, had parents watching the matches. How many boxers is this?

_____ 81. 10,300 athletes attended the Atlanta Olympics. About 8,100 fewer attended the Nagano Winter Games. How many athletes were in Nagano?

_____ 82. The thirsty runners drank 24,375 gallons of water during the week. There were 8,125 athletes. On the average, how much did each one drink?

_____ 83. 37,077 fans watched one basketball game. There were only 34,825 seats. How many fans had to stand?

Name

Part Two: Geometry & Measurement

(You will need a protractor and centimeter/inch ruler.)

Use this diagram for questions 84-90.

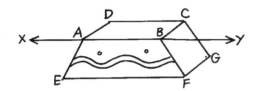

84. $\overleftrightarrow{XY}$ is: a line segment   a ray
                 a line   a plane

85. Which ones of these are line segments?
    $\overline{AB}$ $\overline{BF}$ $\overline{EA}$ $\overline{AC}$ $\overline{FY}$ $\overline{CG}$

86. $\overrightarrow{AY}$ is: a line segment   an angle
                 a line   a ray

87. B is: a line   a point   a ray

88. Which pairs of line segments are parallel?
    $\overline{AB}$ & $\overline{CD}$ $\overline{CD}$ & $\overline{BF}$ $\overline{EF}$ & $\overline{AB}$
    $\overline{AD}$ & $\overline{BC}$ $\overline{BC}$ & $\overline{FG}$ $\overline{DC}$ & $\overline{FG}$

89. EAB is: a plane   a line
             an angle   a line segment

90. BCGF is: a line segment   an angle
             a plane   a line

Use these angles for questions 91–93.

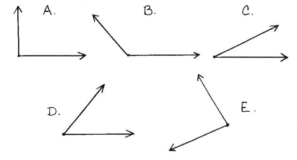

91. Which angles are right angles?

_____

92. Which angles are obtuse angles?

_____

93. Which angles are acute angles?

_____

Use the diagram below for questions 94-99.

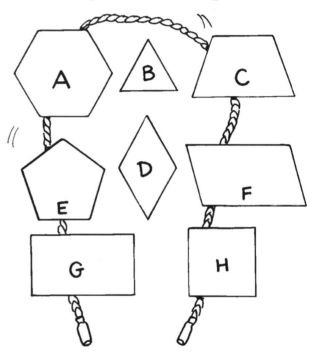

_____ 94. How many figures are rhombuses?

_____ 95. Which figure is a hexagon?

_____ 96. Which figures are parallelograms but not rectangles?

_____ 97. Which figure is a pentagon?

_____ 98. Which figure is a trapezoid?

_____ 99. Which figures are rectangles?

Name _____

Use the diagram below for questions 100–103.

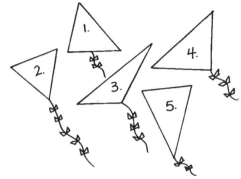

_____ 100. Which ones are scalene triangles?

_____ 101. Which are isosceles triangles?

_____ 102. Which are right triangles?

_____ 103. Which are equilateral triangles?

Use the diagram below for questions 104–107.

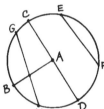

_____ 104. Name the diameter.

_____ 105. Name three chords.

_____ 106. Name three radii.

_____ 107. Is EA an arc?

Use the pictures below for questions 108–110.

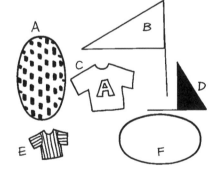

Answer true or false.

_____ 108. F is congruent to A.

_____ 109. D is congruent to B.

_____ 110. E is similar to C.

Use this figure for questions 111–112.

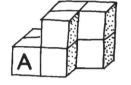
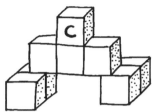
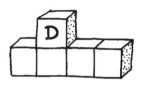

_____ 111. Which figure has a volume of 8 cubic units?

_____ 112. Which has a greater volume: D or A?

Use these figures for question 113.

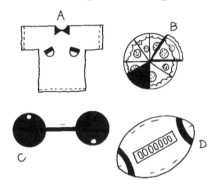

_____ 113. List the symmetrical figures.

Use these figures for questions 114–119.

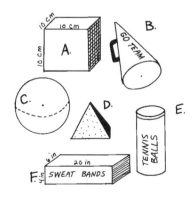

_____ 114. Which figure is a cylinder?

Name

Copyright © 2016 World Book, Inc./
Incentive Publications, Chicago, IL

_____ 115. Which figure is a cone?

_____ 116. Which figure is a sphere?

_____ 117. Which figure is a pyramid?

_____ 118. Find the volume of the cube.

_____ 119. Find the volume of the rectangular prism.

_____ 120. Measure to find the perimeter of this figure in centimeters. Round to the nearest whole centimeter.

_____ 121. Measure with centimeters to find the area of this figure.

Circle the correct answer for questions 122–124.

122. A triangle with two equal sides is:
   a. an equilateral triangle   b. an isosceles triangle   c. a scalene triangle

123. Lines in a plane that do not touch each other are:
   a. intersecting lines   b. perpendicular lines   c. parallel lines

124. A four-sided polygon is:
   a. a pentagon   b. an octagon   c. a quadrilateral   d. a hexagon

Write T (*true*) or F (*false*) for statements 125–129.

_____ 125. A rhombus is always a square.

_____ 126. All rectangles have 4 right angles.

_____ 127. An octagon has 6 equal sides.

_____ 128. A square is a rectangle.

_____ 129. A rectangle is a quadrilateral.

Name

Part Three: Graphing, Statistics, & Probability

Use this graph for questions 130–134.

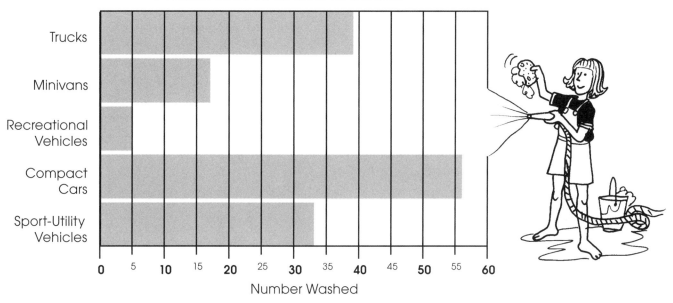

1-HOUR CAR-WASHING RECORDS

Number Washed

130. The most vehicles washed were _____ .

131. The car-washers washed 33 of what kind? _____ .

132. They washed 17 _____ .

133. They washed about 20 more _____ than minivans.

134. They washed about 50 fewer recreational vehicles than _____ .

Use this graph for questions 135–139.

135. Who swallowed the most swords?

_____

136. Which day did Leo and Leslie swallow the same number?

_____

137. Who swallowed more on Wednesday?

_____

138. Who swallowed more on Friday?

_____

139. What was the best day for Leo?

_____

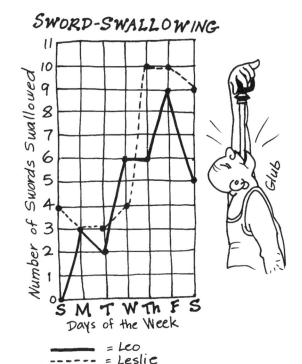

SWORD-SWALLOWING

Number of Swords Swallowed

Days of the Week

_____ = Leo
------ = Leslie

Name

Use this graph for questions 140–142.

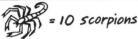
SCORPION HANDLING CONTEST

Maria	
Melissa	
Ming	
Marta	

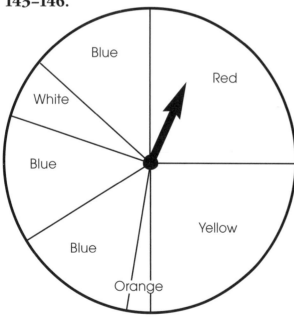
= 10 scorpions

140. Who handled 55 scorpions?

_____

141. How many more scorpions did Ming handle than Melissa handled?

_____

142. Which two handled 100 together?

_____

Use the spinner to answer questions 143–146.

Blue

Red

White

Blue

Blue

Yellow

Orange

_____ 143. How many possible outcomes?

_____ 144. Which is most likely?

_____ 145. Which is least likely?

_____ 146. Which are equally likely?

Write the probability for each event. Use 0 or 1 or any fractional number in between.

_____ 147. a flipped coin will land on heads

_____ 148. 2 odd numbers will have an even sum

_____ 149. a toss of a die will yield a 4

_____ 150. you live in Alaska

_____ 151. a month begins with the letter M

Write the number of possible outcomes for each of the following:

_____ 152. flip of a coin

_____ 153. toss of one die

_____ 154. pick a day of the week

_____ 155. flip a coin twice

Hal wants to break the world record for the number of miles hitch-hiked. He is looking for some good shoes to wear. His closet contains:

4 black shoes (B)
7 red shoes (R)
9 gray shoes (G)

He reaches into the dark closet and grabs a shoe. Tell the probabilities:

156. P (B) = _____

157. P (R) = _____

158. P (G) = _____

159. P (not G) = _____

Hal chooses some socks for his long trip. His drawer contains these:

5 red socks (R) 4 orange socks (O)
3 blue socks (B) 10 white socks (W)
2 purple socks (P)

Tell the probability for these:

160. P (P or O) = _____

161. P (W) = _____

162. P (not W) = _____

163. P (R, P, or B) = _____

164. P (P) = _____

Name _____

SKILLS TEST ANSWER KEY

Language Arts Skills Test

1–5. Student titles will vary. See that student has given an appropriate, accurate title to each: Something such as:
1. The Biggest Painting
2. So Much Music!
3. The Most Sunken Treasure
4. A Productive Painter
5. The Largest Cake Ever
6. Answers will vary some. Most have to do with large numbers or records.
7. largest hula dance
8. limbo stick
9. largest twist dance
10. most exhausting dance
11. 2010
12. New York
13. Answers will vary.
14. Answers will vary.
15. hearing
16. You usually do not think of "hearing" sun.
17. dog's toenails, heels on dance floor
18. lightning, seashells
19. 3 of these: crashing, cracking, click, snapping, buzzing, boom, scraping, pitter, cracks, whispers, rumble, roaring, chopping
20. Answers will vary.
21. mad
22. asteroids, boot nails on Matterhorn, Paul Bunyan chopping
23. terrible, awful, boring
24. person was awakened from a peaceful slumber
25. He doesn't like it.
26. P, S, M
27. A
28. I
29. M, P
30. P
31. S, P
32. E
33. 4, 5, 2, 3, 1
34. Answers will vary. See that student follows the pattern accurately.
35. yes
36. 3
37. Knighthood Revisited
38. The Adventure Store or Decked Out Company
39. Decked Out Company
40. The Adventure Store
41. yes
42. $120
43. The Adventure Store, Little Egypt
44. yes
45. natron
46. Any 2 of these 3: You'll have to be tied . . . Your dinner will float . . . Someone will have to tell you . . .
47. a
48. b
49. Answers will vary.
50. 1
51. 4
52. 3
53. 2
54. c
55. outside a dwelling on and below a balcony
56. Answers will vary.
57. Answers will vary. Check for accuracy.
58. j
59. k
60. g
61. n
62. p
63. c
64. h
65. o
66. m
67. l
68. d
69. e
70. borscht
71. a vicar
72. flotsam
73. a mariner
74. no
75. savory
76. crude
77. terrified
78. absence
79. snatched
80. Answer will vary.
81. She can write with both hands.
82. g
83. h
84. d
85. k
86. t
87. s
88. p
89. o
90. m
91. b
92. e
93. f
94. b
95. c
96. e
97. d
98. g
99. l
100. b
101. e
102. j
103. k
104. i
105. g
106. a
107. d
108. a
109. b
110. g
111. i
112. c
113. buried
114. heard
115. threw
116. towed
117. straight
118–121. Answers will vary. See that student makes real words.
122. b
123. b
124. shipwreck
125. sunburn
126. insurance
127. anchor
128. anemometer
129. annual
130. meteorite
131. transparent
132. accept
133–135. Answers will vary. See that student writes 2 correct meanings for each word chosen.
136. j
137. g (or b)
138. a
139. h
140. m
141. k
142. l
143. f
144. n
145. c
146. crocodile (others are sea animals)
147. camera (others are compound words)
148. artichoke (others are plurals)
149. tentacles
150. goose
151. freeze
152. snow
153. argument
154. surfer
155. ie
156. ei
157. ie
158. ei
159. ei
160. ie
161. ous
162. ant
163. ible
164. ius
165. ete
166. el
167. ance
168. tion
169. al
170. ate
171. erupt, envy
172–177. energy, coughed, surprise, scuba, cider, babysitter
178. no
179. yes
180. no
181. no
182. yes
183. no
184. yes
185. radios
186. monkeys
187. loaves
188. messes
189. butterflies
190. geese
191. Atlantic
192. Jupiter
193. Michigan
194. Wednesday
195. Thanksgiving
196. pianoes
197. wierd
198. notbook
199. magecal
200. subbmarine
201. terrifick
202. arithmatic
203. elegent
204. astronot
205. vegetables, sugar, lettuce, tomatoes, noodles
206. pilot
207. people
208. caught
209. molecule
210. llama
211. laughter
212. again
213. appear
214. enough
215. tongue
216. mosquito
217. odor
218. opposite
219. loneliness
220. length
221. please
222. almost
223. necessary
224. Circle: wreath, expel, seize, apologize, oxygen, serious, excellent, quartet, strength, gravity, zero
225. Adopt
226. accept
227. angles
228. thorough
229. diary
230. cereal
231. overdue
232. pried
233. horse
234. break
235. Freak Accidents Reported On Public Beaches
236. Doctor Does Surprise Operation
237. Ski Season Canceled Due To Dangerous Ice Storm
238. Two Hundred Homes Lost in Tornado
239. Elephant Receives Gold Medal
240. F
241. C
242. R
243. F
244. S
245. Sam
246. bears
247. chipmunk
248. crashed
249. could catch

250. watched, blew
251. ADJ
252. ADJ
253. N
254. V
255. N
256. ADV
257. spiders, beds, pepper, soup
258. Friday, Billy
259. fox's teeth
260. foxes' teeth
261. campers' shirts
262. skunk's tail
263. They
264. She
265. him
266. them
267. rowed
268. swam
269. fell or is falling
270. will fly
271. wore
272. wrote or will write or are writing
273. fainted
274. voted
275. is
276. should
277. is
278. have
279. V
280. ADV
281. ADJ
282. N
283. V
284. ADJ
285. ADV
286. faster
287. farthest
288. slimiest
289. best
290. less
291. worst
292. earlier
293. more often
294. most quickly
295. would
296. any
297. anyone
298. ever
299. under
300. into
301. across
302. behind you
303. around the flowers
304. beneath your bed
305. will not
306. they are
307. I have

308. we would or we had
309. our, always, creates, delicious, meals, favorite, once, week, marshmallows, dessert
310. Camp, Sunday, Friday, July
311. Counselor, Joe, Lisa
312. July 15 Dear Mom and Dad, I am having the best time at this camp! You won't believe how well I'm doing. We have terrible food, lots of mosquitoes, and grumpy counselors. Doesn't it sound great? I think I saw an alien, and I fell out of the canoe three times.(!) How much longer can I stay? Your loving son, Manuel
313. d
314. c
315. b
316. b
317. b
318. a
319. a, b, c
320. c
321. d
322. a
323. b
324. a
325. b
326. c

Writing Tasks
Answers will vary on most of the writing tasks. There are no right or wrong answers for Tasks 2, 3, 6, 8, 9, 10, and 12. Answers may vary some on Tasks 4,

5, and 11. Award points to students based on:
- how thoroughly they completed the task
- if they followed directions
- the mechanical correctness of their writing

Task 1: order—7, 4, 1, 5, 6, 3, 2

Task 4: Answers may vary.
1. I found an old sandwich sitting on top of the shelf in the closet.
2. On the radio, we heard about the robber who was caught.

Task 5: These words may be crossed out.
1. totally, whole
2. three-sided
3. In my opinion, I think, not at all, even a bit

Task 7: Figurative language includes bad apple, burned up, out on a limb, let the cat out of the bag, spill the beans, goose is cooked, get your foot out of your mouth, mad-as-a-hatter

Task 11: Words that students eliminate may vary. Statements or words in ( ) are not necessary and should be deleted. Corrected paragraph should read:
Dear Editor:
(In my

opinion,) I believe that the new miniature golf course (which the city has built) owned by the city should change its rules. It does not make sense to refuse kids under 18 to come unless they are with adults. I thought the city built this course to attract kids and give them something good to do in the evenings. This is a wonderful activity for kids, but you are keeping them away. Most teenagers want to go out (for an activity) with their friends, not their parents! Whose bad idea was this? (I protest!) I hope this rule will be changed soon. Sincerely, Adam

Social Studies Skills Test

1. Ohio
2. Louisiana
3. Tennessee
4. Oklahoma
5. California
6. New Jersey
7. Kansas
8. South Carolina
9. New York
10. Montana
11. Atlantic Ocean
12. Pacific Ocean
13. Minnesota

14. Lake Superior
15. Gulf of Mexico
16. K
17. H
18. A
19. C
20. G
21. L
22. E
23. J
24. F
25. B
26. Alaska, Oregon, California
27. Montana, Utah, Colorado
28. Iowa, Nebraska, North Dakota
29. New Mexico, Arizona, Texas
30. Pennsylvania, New York, New Jersey
31. Mississippi, Arkansas, Louisiana, South Carolina, Virginia
32. Maine, Massachusetts, New Hampshire, Connecticut
33. Minnesota, Ohio, Indiana, Michigan
34. Baton Rouge, Cheyenne, Denver, Juneau, Boise
35. Los Angeles, Chicago, Detroit, Miami
36. E
37. B
38. F
39. A
40. G
41. C
42. H
43. I
44. D
45. J
46. B
47. H
48. D
49. F
50. A

51. E
52. G
53. C
54. E
55. G
56. A
57. C
58. D
59. I
60. B
61. F
62. J
63. H
64. C
65. D
66. G
67. A
68. F
69. B
70. E
71. C
72. D
73. G
74. E
75. A
76. H
77. B
78. F
79. I
80. J
81. The National Archives
82. Northern, Western
83. Asia, Europe, South America, North America, Africa
84. all
85. Smithsonian Institute
86. The Antarctic Circle
87. 40°N
88. equator
89. prime meridian
90. North Pole
91. Toronto, Montreal, Vancouver
92. Alberta, Quebec, Manitoba, Saskatchewan
93. Yucatan, Baja California
94. bananas, silver, beans, coffee, cacao
95. Tropic of Cancer, Rio Grande,

Central Plateau, mountains
96. Argentina
97. Argentina, Chile, Peru, Ecuador, Colombia
98. 2:00 P.M. Mountain Time
99. Eastern Time
100. Midnight
101. I
102. H
103. C
104. A
105. B
106. F
107. J
108. D
109. G
110. E
111. a
112. i
113. k
114. d
115. m
116. c
117. h
118. e
119. f
120. g
121. c
122. d
123. b & d
124. a
125. a & d
126. a, c, d, e (Asia is optional)
127. b & c
128. d
129. b & d (Alaska)
130. E
131. H
132. A
133. J
134. B
135. D
136. I
137. G
138. C
139. F
140. a & d
141. a, b, c
142. a, c, d
143. d
144. b, c, d
145. a, c, e
146. Market
147. NE

148. about 2000 feet
149. about 125 feet
150. NW
151. about 1500 feet
152. 4
153. pigs
154. SE
155. Rapunzel Drive to Nature Trail to Market Street to Granny's
156. g
157. h
158. d
159. e
160. i
161. c
162. a
163. f
164. b
165. 1:00 P.M.
166. 9:00 A.M.
167. 2:00 A.M.
168. 5:30 A.M.
169. W
170. S
171. NW
172. SE
173. NW
174. E

Science Skills Test

1. A
2. G
3. F
4. C
5. B
6. photosynthesis
7. respiration
8. carbon dioxide
9. oxygen
10. chlorophyll
11. pine tree, daisy, lily, apple tree
12. E & F
13. A & C
14. B, D, E, F
15. H
16. F
17. A
18. E
19. D
20. B
21. c
22. a
23. c

24. B & C
25. H
26. C
27. F
28. I
29. A
30. K
31. M
32. L
33. B
34. J
35. E
36. aerobic
37. muscle strength
38. muscles
39. b
40. a
41. d
42. b
43. c
44. $NaCl$
45. NO_2
46. H_2O_2
47. $AgCl$
48. C
49. C
50. P
51. P
52. C
53. friction
54. inertia
55. repel
56. volume
57. inclined plane
58. lever
59. pulley
60. c
61. a
62. c
63. a
64. c
65. c
66. a
67. a
68. a
69. a
70. H
71. I
72. C
73. F
74. M
75. K
76. E
77. B
78. O
79. P
80. J
81. D

Math Skills Test

1. 10,500
2. 3,000,000,000
3. 55,920
4. 600,600
5. 8,030
6. 4, 3, 1, 2
7. 5,980
8. 24,000
9. 280,000
10. 600
11. 1, 2, 3, 4, 6, 8, 12, 24
12. 1, 7, 49
13. 1, 2, 4
14. 5
15. 88 R5
16. 6,249
17. 685,612
18. 5,022
19. 324
20. 55
21. 6,500
22. 900,000
23. 240
24. 20
25. 5
26. 55.5
27. 0.344
28. $\frac{7}{8}$
29. $\frac{3}{9}$
30. $\frac{7}{12}$; $\frac{2}{3}$; $\frac{6}{8}$; $\frac{14}{16}$
31. $\frac{12}{16}$; $\frac{9}{12}$; $\frac{6}{8}$
32. $\frac{7}{9}$; $\frac{2}{3}$
33. $\frac{3}{4}$
34. $\frac{3}{4}$
35. $2\frac{10}{20}$ or $2\frac{1}{2}$
36. $7\frac{2}{5}$
37. $4\frac{4}{10}$ or $4\frac{2}{5}$
38. $\frac{57}{8}$
39. $\frac{215}{7}$
40. E
41. D
42. A
43. B
44. C
45. F
46. 0.481
47. 1.8654
48. 1.63
49. 5.9
50. 0.03; 0.3; 3.003; 3.3; 33.33
51. 0.555
52. $\frac{4}{7}$
53. $\frac{3}{8}$
54. $\frac{14}{12}$ or $1\frac{2}{12}$ or $1\frac{1}{6}$
55. $\frac{3}{10}$

56. $\frac{18}{45}$ or $\frac{2}{5}$
57. $\frac{15}{8}$ or $1\frac{7}{8}$
58. $\frac{1}{2}$
59. 8
60. $\frac{21}{6}$ or $3\frac{3}{6}$ or $3\frac{1}{2}$
61. $\frac{16}{15}$ or $1\frac{1}{15}$
62. 14.4
63. 12.5
64. $184.60
65. $2,344.85
66. $206.50
67. $25.00
68. 0.75
69. 0.723
70. 4,736%
71. 53 %
72. $\frac{6}{10}$ or $\frac{3}{5}$
73. 40 %
74. $\frac{80}{100}$ or $\frac{4}{5}$
75. -8, -5, -2, 0, 1, 3, 5, 8
76. -45
77. 2
78. 12
79. $1,113.00
80. 28
81. 2,200
82. 3 gal
83. 2,252
84. a line
85. $\overline{AB}$, $\overline{BF}$, $\overline{EA}$, $\overline{CG}$
86. a ray
87. a point
88. $\overline{AB}$ & $\overline{CD}$, $\overline{AD}$ & $\overline{BC}$, $\overline{BC}$ & $\overline{FG}$, $\overline{EF}$ & $\overline{AB}$
89. an angle
90. a plane
91. A
92. B
93. C, D, E
94. 2
95. A
96. D, F
97. E
98. C
99. G, H
100. 1, 3
101. 2, 4, 5
102. 4
103. 2, 4
104. CD
105. CD, EF, GH
106. AB, AC, AD
107. no
108. true
109. false
110. true
111. A or C
112. A

113. A, C, D
114. E
115. B
116. C
117. D
118. 1,000 cm³
119. 480 in³
120. 13 cm
121. 9 cm²
122. b
123. c
124. c
125. false
126. true
127. false
128. true
129. true
130. compact cars
131. sport-utility vehicles
132. minivans
133. trucks
134. compact cars
135. Leslie
136. Monday
137. Leo
138. Leslie
139. Friday
140. Marta
141. 25
142. Maria and Ming
143. 5
144. blue
145. orange
146. yellow and red
147. $\frac{1}{2}$
148. 1
149. $\frac{1}{6}$
150. 0 (unless you live in Alaska— then it is 1)
151. $\frac{2}{12}$ or $\frac{1}{6}$
152. 2
153. 6
154. 7
155. 4
156. $\frac{4}{20}$ or $\frac{1}{5}$
157. $\frac{7}{20}$
158. $\frac{9}{20}$
159. $\frac{11}{20}$
160. $\frac{6}{24}$ or $\frac{1}{4}$
161. $\frac{10}{24}$ or $\frac{5}{12}$
162. $\frac{14}{24}$ or $\frac{7}{12}$
163. $\frac{10}{24}$ or $\frac{5}{12}$
164. $\frac{2}{24}$ or $\frac{1}{12}$

SKILLS EXERCISES ANSWER KEY

page 22-23

1. B	7. J
2. F	8. K
3. D	9. H
4. A	10. I
5. C	11. G
6. E	12. L

page 24

1. Jamie	4. Jess
2. Jo	5. Jeri
3. Jeri	

page 25

Answers will vary.

page 26

1. the fairies
2. rainbows
3. boas & black panthers
4. dig to the pit of Earth
5. a bunny
6. the stars
7. a time machine
8. the prehistoric air
9. anything
10. winged unicorns' backs
11. in your heart
12. c
13. Answers will vary.
14. Answers will vary.

page 27

1. 4 lbs
2. no
3. carabiners
4. tent, carabiners
5. Climber's Shop
6. $59
7. 3910 Abby Lane
8. Climb of Denali
9. Mountain Supply
10. Camping, Ltd.
11. 2
12. 552-9900
13. Mountain Store
14. $75
15. –60°

page 28

Answers will vary somewhat. This is the general idea of the meaning of the proverbs.

1. Things and time get wasted when you hurry too much.
2. If you don't act, you may lose your opportunity.
3. Take advantage of an opportunity.
4. If you take care of something right away, it will save work later.
5. There's something good about everything that seems bad.
6. Someone who keeps busy doesn't get stuck.
7. If you don't try something, you'll never gain anything.
8. Fish rot in three days, and people get tired of visitors.
9. Fools don't think before they rush into something; smart people do.
10. If you tell a secret, it won't be kept.
11. Pay attention to what you have, not what you might have.
12. Don't count on something until you have it.
13. Don't change your plan while you're in the middle of it.
14. You can't make someone do what you want them to do.

page 29

Answers will vary somewhat. This is the general idea of the meaning of the proverbs.

1. Are you fooling me?
2. She is acting crazy.
3. We're in trouble.
4. You're not saying anything.
5. Leave me alone.
6. He's boring.
7. Be quiet.
8. I'm going to have to give in to you.
9. I am mad at you about something.
10. Don't tattle on your friends.
11. I slept really soundly.
12. I took a chance.
13. She told a secret.
14. She said something embarrassing.
15. Time goes quickly.
16. I thought the test was easy.
17. The accident was the last thing I could handle.
18. The kids are annoying me.
19. I barely passed.
20. I was shocked.

page 30

Answers will vary for 1, 2, 6, and 7.
3. slipped a cut, stabbed
4. one last drop of water
5. could not take another step, could not say a word

page 31

Answers will vary some. Main ideas should be generally close to these:
Thursday, May 18: I am going to hunt for mermaids and I'm excited.
Saturday, May 20: Legend says that mermaids were women of Ireland who were banished from the earth to the sea.
Tuesday, May 23: Many people believe in the existence of sea serpents.
Friday, May 26: I think I saw a mermaid today.

page 32–33

Character descriptions: Answers will vary. Exact wording of story elements will vary.
Theme: mystery
Characters: Madeline, Countess, Porter, Doctor, Mystery Man, Burglar, Mrs. Matisse, Sleeping Man
Setting: Train—Orient Express Plot: A little girl notices many mysterious things on a train. After the lights go out, a dog and a porter are missing and some other things are changed.
Point of View: third person (narrator who is not a character)

page 34

1. no
2. Zurich, Basil, Bern
3. Drop 2 or Drop 3
4. no
5. Tues and Fri
6. no
7. Drop 2
8. no
9. 2
10. 4

page 35

1. 1
2. 2, 3
3. poor visibility, cold, control in the wind
4. visibility, dampness, control in the wind
5. probably good
6. possibly cancel or postpone the race, take shelter

page 36

Answers will vary.

page 37

1. R,P	10. I
2. E,M	11. E,M
3. I, M	12. A, P
4. S	13. A, P
5. I	14. M
6. E	15. P
7. I	16. A
8. A, S	17. PN
9. A	

page 38

Order of numbers for line placement:
1. 4, 1, 5, 2, 3
2. 2, 1, 5, 3, 4 or 5, 1, 2, 3, 4
3. 2, 5, 4, 3, 1
4. 1, 3, 5, 2, 4 or 1, 4, 5, 2, 3
5. 1, 5, 4, 3, 2

page 39

1. a   5. b
2. c   6. c
3. c   7. c
4. b   8. b

page 40

1. F   7. F
2. T   8. T
3. T   9. F
4. T   10. Answers will vary.
5. F
6. F

page 41

Purposes will vary somewhat.
1. c—Purpose: tell readers how Talula deserves to be a star
2. c—Purpose: discourage would-be stars from going to Nashville
3. b—Purpose: inform readers of some news
4. b—Purpose: instruct reader about neon lights

page 42

1. 40 days
2. dries it out
3. 20 or more
4. organs
5. brain
6. putting it into 3 coffins
7. Answers will vary.

page 43

Answers will vary.

page 44

1. 3   6. guitar
2. 5   7. car
3. 1   8. $132,000
4. $341,000   9. 6
5. $370,260   10. $722,260

page 45

1. Shanghai Tower
2. Burj Khalifa
3. Willis Tower
4. Petronas Tower, Zifeng Center
5. Makkah Royal Clock Tower Hotel
6. Burj Khalifa
7. Willis Tower
8. China
9. U.A.E
10. Shanghai World Financial Center

page 46

1. H   8. F
2. B   9. G
3. D   10. G
4. B   11. E
5. C   12. E
6. D, A   13. G
7. A   14. H

page 47

1. d   9. o
2. i   10. e
3. g   11. k
4. h   12. b
5. m   13. f
6. n   14. j
7. l   15. c
8. a

page 48

1. Georgio's
2. drawings of flying machines
3. Charlie, Alicia
4. The Last Supper
5. Charlie
6. Florence
7. Georgio
8. Answers will vary.

page 49

Answers will vary.

page 50

1. fry it for lunch
2. feed it to a fish
3. take it swimming
4. put it in a jewelry box
5. avoid it
6. explore it
7. find an answer to it
8. dance it
9. bake it
10. show it off
11. slide on it
12. make music on it
13. make friends with it
14. send it to school
15. pour water through it
16. hire it

page 51

Answers may vary somewhat.
1. intended
2. washed; huge
3. bridge
4. tornado
5. tossed; storm
6. dragged; hid
7. ocean; earthquake
8. tail; ship
9. crashed; sank
10. mystery

page 52

Answers will vary somewhat. See that student has the general idea of the meaning of each figurative language expression.

It's raining cats and dogs.—It's raining hard.

You drive me up a wall.—You're really bothering me.

Go out on a limb.—Take a chance.

I have a bone to pick with you.—I'm mad at you about something.

You've spilled the beans.—You've told something you should not have.

Don't jump the gun.—Don't be in such a hurry.

She's lost her head!—She's acting out of control.

My car's a real lemon!—My car has lots of problems; it was a bad deal.

page 53

Answers will vary somewhat. See that student has the general idea of the meaning of each figurative language expression.

Jay likes to ham it up.—Jay likes to show off.

What a back-seat driver!—Someone else in the car tells the driver how to drive.

She's got her nose in a book.—She's reading and ignoring everything else.

Don't lose your cool.—Don't lose your temper.

This will cook your goose!—This will really make you mad.

It's the last straw!—It's the last of many things to go wrong.

Keep a lid on it!—Keep from getting mad or being too noisy or wild.

You've put your foot in your mouth again.—You've said something stupid or embarrassing.

page 54

1. minority   6. copyright
2. diagnosis   7. circumference
3. simmer   8. hurricane
4. annuals   9. translucent
5. principal   10. accept

page 55

Answers may vary somewhat.
1. feet
2. sunscreen
3. pocket
4. breathe
5. eat
6. lake, pool, or ocean
7. cupboard, cabinet, or china cabinet
8. break
9. trees

10. temperature
11. water
12. book
13. feet, paws, or legs
14. broom

page 56

Answers may vary some, depending on student's opinions.

1. no
2. yes
3. Answers will vary.
4. no
5. yes
6. no
7. yes
8. Answers will vary.
9. Answers will vary.
10. yes
11. yes
12. throw out
13. no
14. Answers will vary.
15. no

page 57

Answers may vary some, depending on student's opinions.

1. yes
2. no
3. no
4. no
5. no
6. no
7. yes
8. no
9. no
10. yes
11. Answers will vary
12. no
13. no
14. no
15. no

page 58

1. b
2. c
3. b
4. b
5. b
6. c
7. b
8. a
9. a
10. a
11. c
12. a
13. b

page 59

1. a
2. b
3. a
4. c
5. c
6. a
7. b
8. a
9. b
10. a
11. b
12. b
13. a

page 60

Answers will vary. Check to see that student has formed real words.

page 61

Down
1. abalone
2. ecology
3. habitat
4. grotto
7. tsunami
8. mariner
10. weed

Across
5. trough
6. ichthyologist
9. flotsam
11. archipelago
12. fjord
13. sea

page 62

Answers will vary, depending on which word student chooses to change. Most likely possibilities are:

Tom's Nightmare
Eat at Bob's Diner— Great (or good, or wonderful) Food
S.S. Sunset
Danger, Deep Water!
Please Do Not Throw Trash On The Beach
No Sleeping On The Beach
Beach Open 9 A.M. – 9 P.M.
Mystery at Crooked River
The Biggest Dragon
Burglar Steals Jewelry
Earthquake Hits at Noon

page 63

1. destroy
2. meek
3. receive
4. cheerful
5. calm
6. defend
7. divide
8. mischief
9. express
10. timid
11. tender
12. proceed

page 64

Check to see that student has drawn the correct items.

page 65

excitement—act of being excited or exciting
perilous—full of peril
rocky—full of rocks
stormy—like a storm
frighten—to make afraid
nervous—full of nerves
horrific—pertaining to horror
seaward—toward the sea
hardship—state of being hard
fearful—full of fear
courageous—full of courage
survivor—one who survives
hopeless—without hope
dangerous—full of danger
sailor—one who sails
droplets—small drops
terrify—to cause terror
lostness—state of being lost
troublesome—full of trouble
heroism—act of being a hero

page 66

Top answer: The Hole in the Pail

1. bury
2. straight
3. threw
4. caught
5. seas
6. foul
7. pail; break
8. pier; hour
9. beat
10. taught
11. buy; some
12. cents
13. feet
14. flew
15. flee

page 67

Top answer: a wail

1. see; sea
2. son; sun
3. heard; herd
4. steal; steel
5. Would; wood
6. groan; grown
7. weak; week
8. not; knot
9. ate; eight
10. close; clothes
11. toe; tow
12. sore; soar

page 68

Definitions may vary slightly.

1. small sea creature; to grouch
2. down
3. track
4. a fruit; an outing with another person; a particular day
5. spring
6. fire
7. a flying insect; to soar up in the air
8. spot
9. rain; a place to wash; a party for a bride or expectant mother
10. pen
11. container; sport where people hit each other with gloves
12. tick

page 69

"Fragile" is the word that does not fit. Description of classification categories may vary.

1. lizard; mammals or animals in the sea
2. chowder; things floating in the ocean
3. bandit; things on a boat
4. wind; kinds of precipitation
5. lobster; kinds of birds
6. mumble; loud noises or screams
7. ruler; computer parts
8. wrench; kitchen utensils or equipment
9. scorpion; sea animals
10. cactus; things you see on a beach
11. receiver; parts of a book
12. spaghetti; parts of the body
13. redwood; kinds of fish
14. attorney; church leaders
15. stumble; words that mean jump
16. duck; baby animals
17. hazard; kinds of storms
18. frog; reptiles

page 70

Answers will vary, particularly the connotations. Denotations are listed here:
Pirate—someone who robs ships
Sunburn—irritation or blistering of the skin from the sun
Shark—a kind of dangerous fish
Storm—bad weather accompanied by wind and some precipitation such as rain or snow
Island—land surrounded on all sides by water

page 71

Answers will vary depending upon what information students are able to find.

1. Greek word meaning "made from barley"
2. named after a vegetarian named Sylvester Graham; means "made from wheat flour"
3. named after Frankfurt, Germany, where they were first made
4. Latin meaning "round swelling"
5. German word meaning "wafer" (Supposedly first "invented" when a knight in armor sat on a pancake.)
6. Portuguese and Spanish word for a plant in Guinea
7. French word meaning "thin blade of a sword," because the omelettes were thin
8. Spanish word meaning "round cake"
9. named after city of Tangiers
10. French word meaning "moss"
11. Latin word meaning "head," because cabbage is shaped like a head
12. Aztec word meaning "bitter water"
13. Italian word meaning "string"
14. Portuguese and Spanish word meaning "residue or leftover substance"

page 72

Answers may vary.
1. tentacles
2. pasture, barn, stable, or field
3. sail or sailboat
4. hear
5. surfer
6. mice
7. hot
8. lifeguard
9. dull
10. heat
11. feathers
12. snow
13–18. Answers will vary. Check to see that the pairs form accurate analogies.

page 73

Answers will vary on the guesses. Definitions may vary somewhat also. Definitions should be similar to these:

1. to renew or refresh
2. stirred up and muddy
3. changeable
4. twisting, winding
5. not moving
6. gloomy
7. explosive
8. unbelievable
9. rude or crude
10. tiny

page 74

Answers may vary depending upon what resources student has available.
1. Greek
2. Hindu or Indian
3. French
4. Latin
5. French
6. French
7. Persian
8. Latin
9. Latin
10. Latin
11. Latin
12. Greek
13. Persian
14. Latin
15. Spanish or Latin
16. German
17. German
18. Greek
19. Indian, Hindu, or Persian
20. Spanish
21–25. Answers will vary somewhat.
21. "I found it!"
22. a dead-end street
23. appetizer
24. porch with a roof
25. school for young children

page 75

Answers will vary. Check to see that student has formed real compound words.

page 76

1. squid
2. dessert
3. buoy
4. astronomy
5. antonyms
6. biennial
7. insurance
8. anemometer
9. flotsam
10. complaint
11. meteorite

Page 77

These words should be circled:
tommorrow
vollunteer
bennefit
memmory
proffessor
annimal
attenndance
baskettball
catterpillar
bannana
tellescope

Page 78

1. a	6. a	11. a	16. b
2. b	7. a	12. b	17. a
3. b	8. a	13. a	18. b
4. b	9. a	14. a	
5. a	10. b	15. a	

Page 79

Correct words that should be colored:
1. hitchhiker
2. lighthouse
3. nightmare
4. nighttime
5. countryside
6. grandmother
7. wheelchair
8. floodlight
10. sandpaper
12. headache
16. greenhouse
17. heartbreak
18. quicksand
22. seaside

Page 80

Incorrect words to be circled and respelled correctly:
Friday, June 13: circus, laughing, celery, emergency, coughed
Saturday, June 14: phone, phony, judge, citizenship, ridiculous
Sunday, June 15: ghastly, ghosts, celebration, mischief, cider
Monday, June 16: physical, certainly, energized, surprised, photographs
Tuesday, June 17: caught, cyclone, patience, scuba

Page 81

1. children
2. noises
3. messes
4. wishes
5. societies
6. cottages
7. addresses
8. chefs
9. butterflies
10. heroes
11. loaves
12. chiefs
13. geese
14. echoes
15. donkeys
16. women
17. radios
18. keys
19. potatoes
20. athletes
21. lunches
22. foxes
23. counties
24. nests
25. attorneys

Page 82

1. ite
2. ive
3. ise
4. ish
5. ish
6. ize
7. ish
8. ise
9. ive
10. ist
11. ile
12. ize
13. ish
14. age
15. ege or age
16. edge
17. age
18. ist
19. age
20. age

Page 83

1. jealous
2. circus
3. focus
4. tremendous
5. melodious
6. generous
7. marvelous
8. conscious
9. cautious
10. radius
11. outrageous
12. luscious
13. Venus
14. nervous
15. cactus

Page 84

1. distant
2. evident
3. hydrant
4. independent
5. pleasant
6. elegant
7. vacant
8. excitement
9. ignorant
10. importance
11. appliance
12. elephant
13. restaurant
14. science
15. absence
16. insurance
17. attendance
18. evidence

Page 85

1. impossible
2. legal
3. quarrel
4. vacation
5. musician
6. visible
7. adorable
8. cushion
9. carnival
10. fatal
11. magician
12. icicle
13. prevention
14. candle
15. cancel
16. tradition
17. channel
18. travel
19. cancel
20. reversible

Page 86

1. ate
2. ate
3. ate
4. eat
5. ate
6. ate
7. ete
8. ate
9. ite
10. ate
11. ate
12. eat
13. ate
14. ate
15. ete
16. ate
17. ate
18. ite

Page 87

Misspelled words are:

1. supernatural
5. completely
6. feverish
10. biography
11. magical
12. disappear
13. preschool
16. musical
20. advertise

Page 88

Words with no silent letters are:
envy, burglar, bumpy, quiver, automatic, erupt, coconut

Page 89

Words spelled correctly are:
1. slippery
6. soccer
8. stomach

11. suspect
14. serious
15. stereo
22. seventh
23. strengthen
24. scissors
25. hissing
26. surely
27. successful
29. special
30. seize
31. squirm
32. studio

Page 90

William Weightlifter
Wretched Ray
Worst Woodpecker
Weird Wanda Worm
Wrestler Rachel
Weekend Warrior
1. awful
2. wasteful
3. windowsill
4. weight
5. wonderful
6. weapons
7. which or witch
8. we're
9. knowledge
10. wreath
11. whisper
12. wrapping
13. whipped or wiped
14. Wednesday
15. wrinkled
16. weakness

Page 91

1. ea
2. ou
3. ai
4. ui or ai
5. ou
6. au
7. ai
8. ou
9. ea
10. oi
11. ue
12. ai
13. eo
14. ie
15. ou
16. au
17. ea
18. ua
19. au
20. au

Page 92

Correct words to be circled:
bizarre
unique
kazoo
scheme
opaque
gnome
karate
bough
enough
karate

vague
amnesia
mustache

Incorrect words (corrected):
Des Moines
Connecticut
llama
tongue
vacuum
bronchitis
pneumonia
zigzag

Page 93

Sentences will vary. Check to see that the words found on this page are spelled correctly in student's writing.

Page 94

Rule # 1
    Circle: pianos, solos
Rule # 2
    Circle: weird, ancient, neither, height, foreign
Rule # 3
    Circle: pastime
Rule # 4
    Circle: wholly, truly
Rule # 5
    Circle: noticeable, manageable

Page 95

1. meteor
2. galaxy
3. Jupiter
4. astronomy
5. rotates
6. shuttle
7. revolve
8. rocket
9. solar
10. comet
11. atmosphere
12. Saturn
13. astronaut
14. orbits
15. planets
16. launch

Page 96

Menus 4 and 7 have all words spelled correctly.
    Menu #1: 2 mistakes—vegetable, molasses
    Menu #2: 3 mistakes—appetizers, coconut, crumb
    Menu #3: 5 mistakes—cranberries, spinach, salad, sugar, broccoli
    Menu #5: 5 mistakes—pasta, lamb, celery, pineapple, bologna
    Menu #6: 1 mistake—radishes
    Menu #8: 6 mistakes—cheese, biscuits, apricot, chocolate, sundae, banana

Page 97

Words spelled wrong:
wiggle
wobble
stumbling
crawl
revolve
slinking

frolic
cartwheel
scramble
bouncing
escape
climbing
flying
leaping wandered twirling
shaking

Page 98

Words spelled wrong:
multiplication
Pennsylvania
hippopotamus
encyclopedia
bumblebee
Student choices and definitions will vary. Check to make sure that students have spelled the big words correctly.

Page 99

Incorrect words to be corrected:

1. about
2. almost
3. already
4. alright or all right
5. awful
6. because
7. busy
8. candle
9. chief
11. color
14. drawer
15. empty
17. fifth
19. forget
20. forty
21. first
24. hoping
25. hurried
27. knives
29. length
30. listen
32. many
33. often
34. open
35. people
36. please
37. really
39. since or sense or cents
40. stopped or stooped
41. toward
42. truly
43. thought
44. through
45. very
46. which or witch
48. would

Page 100

Cans that should be colored:
#1, #2, #3, #4, #6,
1. 3 mistakes
2. 3 mistakes
3. 3 mistakes
4. 5 mistakes
5. 0 mistakes
6. 4 mistakes

Page 101

1. Report All Accidents Immediately
2. No Horses Allowed on Beach
3. Marshmallow Roasting on Wednesdays Only
4. Public Beach No Lifeguard
5. Beach Closed Until Further Notice

6. No Swimming to the Island
7. Beware! Dangerous Sea Animals
8. Life Preservers Required on Boats
9. Water Is Occupied by Sea Monsters

page 102

1. ADJ—wooden; N—boat; V—sailed; ADV—smoothly
2. ADJ—north; N—wind; V—blew; ADV—hard
3. ADJ—colorful; N—sail; V— flapped; ADV—gracefully
4. ADV—Often; ADJ—brown; N—squirrel; V—chews; N—acorns; ADJ—boat; N—dock
5. N—deer; V—were walking; ADV—slowly; N—shore
6. ADV—Sometimes; ADJ— curious; N—raccoon; V—rides; N—sailboat
7. ADJ—goofy; N—camper; V—fell; ADV—awkwardly; N—water
8. ADJ—Two; N—campers; V—swam; ADV—quickly; V—rescue; ADJ—their; N—friend

page 103

1. Proper—Lisa; Common—key, outhouse
2. Proper—Friday, Billy; Common—key, raccoon
3. Proper—Lisa; Common—trail, snake, path
4. Common—coyote
5. Common—chipmunk, stump, key
6. Common—owl, key
7. Common—bear, berries, patch
8. Common—rabbit
9. Proper—Blue River; Common—shore, beaver, tree
10. Proper—Lisa; Common—skunk, way
11. Proper—August; Common—tracks, ones
12. Common—tracks, door

page 104

1. shines
2. sail
3. row
4. fish
5. drink
6. splashes
7. watches
8. build
9. roast
10. falls
11. skips
12. swim

Stories at bottom will vary.

page 105

1. watched
2. sprayed
3. fished
4. chewed
5. hovered
6. shared
7. talked

8. suggested
9. proposed
10. moved
11. floated
12. enjoyed
Stories at bottom will vary.

page 106

1. slimy, gooey
2. crunchy, purple, a
3. old, moldy
4. clumsy, sticky
5. muddy, thick, cold, Maria's
6. tiny, green, his
7. strange, smelly
8. Hungry, weird, sandwiches

Bottom: strange, slimy, moldy
Menu ideas will vary.

page 107

1. Immediately
2. slowly
3. patiently
4. down, carefully
5. firmly
6. quickly
7. loudly, softly
8. closely
9. early
10. Now, cheerfully, clearly

pages 108–109

1. in
2. across
3. inside
4. under
5. between
6. down

Bottom half of page—answers will vary.

page 110

1. wasn't = was not
2. I'll = I will
3. hasn't = has not
4. it's = it is
5. weren't = were not
6. didn't = did not
7. wasn't = was not
8. wouldn't = would not; he'd = he would
9. He'd = he would
10. Don't = do not
Sentences at bottom will vary.

page 111

Words to be capitalized:
Storm, Hits, Camp, Lookout, There, Tuesday, Fourth, July, Around, Camp, Lookout, Luckily, Hailstones, One, Maria, The, We, Several, Nick, Isaac,

Manuel, The, A, Dr., Smith, Camp, Lookout, When, Isaac, I, The

page 112

Words to be capitalized:
Bigfoot, Sighting, On, Friday, July, Bigfoot, Camp, Lookout, Heidi, Hoggatt, Maria, Lopez, They, Heidi, Maria, Outside, The, Camp, Lookout, The, There, Bigfoot, Pacific, Northwest, The, Oregon, Halloween

page 113

Words to be capitalized:
Tornado, Hits, A, Camp, Lookout, Wednesday, June, Tornadoes, United, States, Luckily, However, An, Fortunately, The, Justin, Loftus, From

page 114

Check student papers for proper punctuation.

page 115

Answers will vary.

page 116

Answers will vary.

page 117

Answers will vary.
Note: For most of the activities on pages 118–141, the answers will vary. Check to see that students have completed the tasks with reasonable responses that fit the directions given. Answers are listed below for the pages that have specific answers or answers that may vary only somewhat.

page 118

Answers will vary, but the following words are the least active ones in the sentences and should most likely be replaced:

1. came, went
2. walked
3. came
4. were
5. ate
6. looked
7. were
8. came
9. were
10. used

page 119

There are many possible answers for most items. These are some possibilities:

1. threatening (or deafening)
2. damp
3. perilous
4. plummets
5. foolish (or crazy)
6. jagged
7. sturdy (or moldy)
8. rushing
9. treacherous (or plunging)
10. fearless
11. moldy (or sturdy)
12. nervous
13. cramped
14. awestruck
15. swirling
16. battered

page 120

Answers will vary.

page 121

Answers will vary.

pages 122-129

Answers will vary.

pages 130–131

Errors are underlined and corrected below. Statements in ( ) are not necessary and could be deleted. Students may make other editing decisions.

Dear Editor:

Why are you saying negative things in your magazine about the new city tax on food in all the restaurants? What is your problem? The tax is for a good cause. Just a small amount on each meal adds up to thousands of dollars for our parks. This is really good for kids. It gives us a wonderful swimming pool, too. This is a small price to pay for so much good stuff. (The cost is really pretty small.) And our restaurants have good food. If I buy a $4.00 sandwich, it only costs 20¢ extra for the tax. Even if someone gets a very expensive meal—say $50.00, the 5% tax still only adds $2.50. That's not bad! It gives us nice, clean places to play soccer and softball.

Sincerely,
Whitney

Dear Editor:

No one has asked the kids! Everyone in the town is talking about year-round school. All the adults keep having hearings and meetings to discuss this. Some committee is making a plan for school to go through the summer. I am really mad! (I am on a dance team.) If something is being planned that changes our whole lives, especially taking away our summers, it is unfair to go ahead without talking to the students. We have opinions, too. We should be the ones to decide this, since it is all about our education.

Sincerely,
Madder Than A Wet Hen

pages 132-133

Answers will vary.

pages 134-135

Letter from Robert Lozenge:
making too many bones; a frog in my throat; raining cats and dogs; I'm pretty burned up; off my rocker.
    Reply from Dr. Free: barking up the wrong tree; up a creek; in the pink
Letter from Veronica Lobes:
tongue-tied; stick my neck out; exercising my head off; pulling your leg; down in the dumps
    Reply from Dr. Free: I'll be a monkey's uncle!; takes the cake; blows my mind; I am stumped; driving you up a wall; quick as a wink
Letter from Sam Troubled:
straight from the horse's mouth; fit to be tied; from sunup to sundown; a chip off the old block!
    Reply from Dr. Free: crying your eyes out; pass the buck; you scream your head off; burn rubber

pages 136-140

Answers will vary.

page 141

Answers may vary some, but should be along these lines:

1. While I was riding The Corkscrew for the third time, a stomachache bothered me.
2. When I was a child, my dad took me on roller coasters every weekend.
3. I'll write in the newspaper about the pirates who robbed ships.
4. The wind picked up while we were riding The Plunge.
5. The clown sold cold ice cream bars with sprinkles to the children.
6. The manager banned some teenagers from The Terror Train because they broke the rules.
7. The kids worried that their mother would never recover after fainting on the ride through The Python's Den.
8. After their teacher fell off her seat into The Raging River, the students tried to pull her back into the raft.
9. To save money for a day at the amusement park, Tim and Tom went to work for Mrs. Burton cleaning her garage.
10. Last, I visited the very scary Haunted Mansion, which was located beside the ticket booth.

pages 146–147

1–3. Check map to see that labels are correct.
   4. Locations of landmarks
      Yellowstone: WY
      Statue of Liberty: NY
      Golden Gate Bridge: CA
      Alamo: TX
      Grand Canyon: AZ
      Kentucky Derby: KY
      Gateway Arch: MO
      Sea World: FL
      Mt. Rushmore: SD
      Space Needle: WA
   5. Check map for accurate route.

pages 148–149

The Fairbanks Frequent Fliers are from Alaska.
   1. OK
   2. ID
   3. MD
   4. CO
   5. IL
   6. GA
The hiking club is from Hawaii.
   7. TN
   8. UT
   9. WY
   10. SD
   11. MN
   12. VA
The Folks & Spokes Club is from Oregon.
   13. LA
   14. MI
   15. AZ
   16. KY
   17. NY
The Alvarez family is from California.
   18. RI
   19. TX
   20. OH
   21. FL
   22. VT
The motorbike club is from Washington.
   23. CT
   24. PA
   25. SC
   26. MA
   27. ME

page 150

Check student maps to see that states are correctly labeled and regions are correctly colored.

page 151

1–3. Check student maps to see that states, cities, and physical features are correctly located and labeled.
   4. Juneau—AK
      Mt. St. Helens—WA
      Mt. Rainier—WA
      Denali—AK
      Crater Lake—OR
      timber sales—CA, WA, OR, AK
      coldest state in U.S.—AK
      biggest state in U.S.—AK
      Seattle—WA
      Space Needle—WA
      active volcano—WA, HI
      50th state—HI
      Portland—OR
      Pearl Harbor—HI
      San Francisco—CA
      Disneyland—CA
      oldest trees—CA
      tallest trees—CA

page 152

Check student maps to see that states, cities, and features are correctly located and labeled.

page 153

Check student maps to see that states are accurately labeled.

Answers will vary somewhat. Check to see that students have completed tasks.

   1. some products: wheat, barley, hay, cattle, milk, sugar beets
   5. Gateway Arch—St. Louis
      Mark Twain's home—Hannibal
      Harry S. Truman Site—Independence, MO
      Pony Express Stables—St. Joseph, MO
   6. Answers will vary.

page 154

1–4. Check student maps to see that states, cities, and features are correctly located and labeled.
   4. Answers will vary.
   5. Arizona—Grand Canyon State New Mexico—Land of Enchantment Oklahoma—Sooner State Texas—Lone Star State
   6. Answers will vary.
   7. Possible answers: Apache, Mojave (or Mohave), Pima, Yuma, Navajo, Pueblo, Comanche, Quechan

page 155

Check student maps to see that states, cities, and lakes are correctly located and labeled.
   1. corn
   2. automobiles
   3. cheese
   4. Indianapolis
   5. Minnesota
   6. Ohio
   7. Chicago
   8. coal
   9. Ontario
   10. Minnesota

page 156

Check student maps to see that states and capitals are correctly located and labeled. See that the student has completed the puzzle.

page 157

Check student maps to see that states and cities are correctly located and labeled.

Down
   1. Wilmington
   2. Potomac
   4. Atlantic City
   7. Hudson
   8. Dupont
   10. New York

Across
   3. Chesapeake
   5. Niagara Falls
   6. Pittsburgh
   9. Lincoln
   11. Philadelphia
   12. Hershey

page 158

Check student maps to see that states and cities are correctly labeled. Answers for industries and natural resources will vary somewhat.

Connecticut—capital: Hartford; river: Connecticut

Maine—capital: Augusta; river: Penobscot

Massachusetts—capital: Boston; river: Charles

New Hampshire—capital: Concord; river: Merrimack or Connecticut

Rhode Island—capital: Providence; river: Blackstone

Vermont—capital: Montpelier; river: Connecticut

page 159

   1. Pacific
   2. Great Lakes
   3. Mountain
   4. Middle Atlantic
   5. Southwest
   6. Southeast
   7. Plains
   8. New England

page 160

1. H	7. I
2. K	8. E
3. G	9. B
4. L	10. C
5. D	11. F
6. J	12. A

page 161

1. Alabama
2. New York
3. Montana
4. Illinois
5. Arizona
6. Michigan
7. West Virginia or Kentucky
8. Arizona
9. New York
10. Kansas
11. Arizona, Colorado, Utah, Oklahoma, or Texas
12. Tennessee

pages 162–163

A. 11	P. 4
B. 24	Q. 19
C. 3	R. 15
D. 1	S. 20
E. 23	T. 10
F. 12	U. 25
G. 16	V. 17
H. 13	W. 18
I. 8	X. 28
J. 14	Y. 27
K. 22	Z. 21
L. 6	XX. 5
M. 7	YY. 29
N. 9	ZZ. 2
O. 26	

page 164

1. NE	14. HI
2. CA	15. MI
3. WY	16. CA
4. UT	17. TN, NC
5. UT	18. KY
6. SD	19. AR
7. CO	20. MT
8. WY, MT, ID	21. NM
9. FL	22. NM
10. CA, NV	23. WA
11. CO, UT	24. ID
12. CA	25. AZ
13. AK	

page 165

Cities to find:

Fargo	Tulsa
El Paso	Albuquerque
Houston	Baltimore
Los Angeles	Buffalo
Miami	Burlington
Milwaukee	Charleston
Mobile	Chicago
Newark	Pittsburgh
New Orleans	Philadelphia
Portland	Cincinnati
Reno	Detroit
Savannah	Fairbanks
Seattle	

page 166

Check student maps to see that all continents, bodies of water, borders, and capitals are accurately located and labeled as directed.

page 167

Answers will vary. Check to see that student has drawn a somewhat accurate map.

page 168

1–2. Check student maps for accurate labels.
3. Northern, Western
4. Africa 3
   Antarctica 3
   Asia 4
   Australia 2
   Europe 2
   North America 2
   South America 3
5. Arctic: Northern, Eastern, Western
   Atlantic: All 4
   Indian: Northern, Southern, Eastern
   Pacific: All 4
6. Northern: North America, South America, Europe, Africa, Asia
   Southern: South America, Africa, Australia, Asia, Antarctica
   Eastern: Africa, Europe, Australia, Asia, Antarctica
   Western: North America, South America, Antarctica, a bit of Asia

page 169

Check student maps to see that the following are accurately located and labeled:
North and South Poles
Arctic and Antarctic Circles
Tropics of Cancer and Capricorn
Equator
Prime Meridian

pages 170–171

1. 30°N and 40°N
2. Alaska and Hawaii
3. Texas
4. 6
5. C
6. D
7. A
8. 3
9. Alaska
10. 9
11. Lake Ontario
12. Gulf of Mexico
13–15. Answers will vary.

pages 172–173

1. 6
2. 12:00 P.M. (noon) CT

3. 10:00 A.M. CT
4. 3:00 A.M. ET
5. Answers will vary.
6. 12
7. earlier; later
8. 4:00 P.M. ET
9. Answers will vary somewhat: The flight took one hour, and MS is 1 time zone west of FL, therefore it was an hour earlier in MS when the flight left FL.

pages 174–175

1–4. Check student maps to see that countries, bodies of water, borders, and capitals are accurately located and labeled.
5. south
6. C
7. Baffin Bay
8. Arctic Circle & Tropic of Cancer
9. Greenland
10. Guatemala, Honduras
11. Pacific Ocean and Caribbean Sea
12. Haiti, Dominican Republic

pages 176–177

Across	Down
3. Ontario	1. Mackenzie
4. Yukon	2. Montreal
5. Quebec	7. Vancouver
6. Alberta	8. Hudson
9. Yellowknife	10. Ottawa
11. Toronto	
12. two	
13. Arctic	

page 178

1. T
2. T
3. F (northwest and southeast)
4. T
5. T
6. F (half instead of all)
7. T
8. F (Gulf of Mexico)
9. F (Rio Grande)
10. T

Viviendo en Mexico means "living in Mexico."

page 179

1. corn	9. bananas
2. cotton	10. coffee
3. silver	11. sugarcane
4. gold	12. copper
5. rice	13. potatoes
6. cacao	14. lead
7. zinc	15. wheat
8. oil	16. beans

page 180

1–3. Check student maps to see that countries, bodies of water, and capitals are accurately located and labeled.

4. Ecuador, Colombia, Brazil
5. Venezuela, Guyana, Suriname, French Guiana
6. Peru
7. Venezuela, Colombia, Ecuador, Peru, Bolivia, Chile, Argentina
8. Galapagos
9. Chile or Argentina
10. Paraguay, Bolivia
11. Uruguay
12. Venezuela, Brazil
13. Falkland Islands
14. Brazil

page 181

1. GA	11. OR
2. AK	12. CA
3. FL	13. PA
4. KY	14. CO
5. ID	15. NJ
6. AR	16. TX
7. KS	17. SD
8. NY	18. NE
9. NM	19. SC
10. NV	20. MS

page 182

1. AK	11. NY
2. RI	12. KY
3. FL	13. NM
4. DE	14. KY
5. HI	15. MD
6. CA	16. MN
7. NY	17. OR
8. CO	18. OR & ID
9. CO	19. AZ
10. GA	20. AK

page 183

1. AK	11. MN
2. HI	12. NH
3. ME	13. WY, MT, ID
4. AK	14. TX
5. CA	15. OK
6. HI	16. WY
7. MO	17. AK
8. CA	18. NV
9. NY	19. AK
10. HI	20. CO

pages 184–185

See student maps. Check to see that student has drawn symbols in the correct places in the tunnels. Also check to see that student's key matches the symbols on the map.

pages 186–187

1. harbor
2. butte

3. skis
4. foothills
5. ocean
6. tractor
7. peninsula
8. cape
9. penguin
10. plateau
11. inner tube
12. banana peel
13. frog
14. river, lake
15. hungry alligator
16. Look to see that student has drawn fish in river source.
17. island, Harry

page 188

TOP: 1–4 Check student's map to see that directions are properly followed.
1. Central Kansas to Chile
2. Chile to Antarctica
3. Antarctica to Switzerland
4. Switzerland to Nanchang, China
5. China to Libya
6. Libya to Australia
Ivanna is taking the rug to Australia.

page 189

Check student's map to see that countries 1–16 have been accurately located and numbered.

page 190

Check for an X on answers
1. New York— all others are countries in Central America
2. El Paso—all others are cities in South America
3. Atlanta—all others are Canadian provinces
4. Pacific—all others are Great Lakes
5. Alaska—all others are cities
6. Atlantic—all others are cities
7. Gulf of Mexico—all others are rivers
8. Chicago— all others are countries in North America

page 191

Answers may vary somewhat.
1. 140 meters
2. 10 meters
3. 50 meters
4. 5 meters
5. 10 meters
6. 5 meters
7. 40 meters
8. 15 meters
9. 25 meters
10. 8 meters
11. 10 meters
12. sundae

13. 10 meters
14. 20 meters
15. Sapphire to Topaz

page 192

Check student's drawing to see that it is reasonably accurate.

Measurement answers may vary somewhat.
1. no
2. yes
3. 20 feet or more
4. about 4 feet
5. about 8–10 feet
6. about 3–4 feet
7. Answers will vary.
8. Check drawings for accuracy.

page 193

Student's routes may vary slightly. Check for accuracy.
1. NE
2. N
3. NW
4. S
5. SW
6. S
7. E
8. NE
9. S
10. E

page 194

U.S.S. Starship—5
Mount Tippy—6
Rainfall in Hat County—7
Boot Island—8
Giggle Land—2
Civic Center—1
Western Hemisphere—3
Fruit County Exports—4

page 195

1. yes
2. no
3. umbrella
4. not very
5. 23 inches
6. Acapulco, Mexico City
7. Check student maps for accurate coloring.
8. What is the weather like?

pages 196–197

Answers may vary somewhat on 2–5.
1. River Line
2. 2
3. Northern Loop Line, River Line
4. 1
5. 4
6. no
7. Orange Station

8. 4
9. Northern Loop, River, East–West, South
10. Station 6
11. Station A, River Station, Green Station
12. East–West, River, South
13. yes
14. 5
15. Northern Loop, River
16. 2
17. ⊙
18. East–West, River
19. yes
20. Center City Interchange
21. River Line
22. East–West Line
23. Northern Loop Line
24. South Line

page 198

LIST 1
1. E 3
2. B 1
3. C 2
4. F 2
LIST 2
1. F 1
2. A 1
3. B 2
4. E 2
LIST 3
1. D 2
2. C 1
3. F 3
4. B 3

page 199

1. Go west from T-Rex City and cross Ancestor River at the 10-mile marker.
2. Continue west for 36 more miles on Highway 110.
3. Turn north onto Interstate 18 at Mammoth Tusk Town.
4. Take Interstate Exit 16 and turn east.
5. Cross Ancestor River on Jawbone Road, going east.
6. Travel on Jawbone Road for 30 miles.
7. Turn right onto Raptor Road at the Ranger Station.
8. Take Rib Cage Bridge to Bone Island on Lucky Find Lake.
9. Take the one-way road "B" back to T-Rex Museum.

pages 200–201

The routes students plan will vary. Check to see that they have planned efficient routes and that urgent items are near the beginning, such as . . .

ice sculpture
ice cream
mice
birthday balloons
homework paper
air pump
plunger

page 205

1. Law #2	4. Law #2
2. Law #2	5. Law #3
3. Law #3	6. Law #1

1. motion	7. weight
2. speed	8. mass
3. acceleration	9. energy
4. force	10. work
5. gravity	11. inertia
6. pressure	12. friction

pages 206–207

True statements are:
1, 2, 4, 6, 7, 8, 10, 11, 13, 14, 15, 16, 18, 20, 21, 22, 24, 25, 27, 28, 29, 31 (Colored red)
False statements are: 3, 5, 9, 12, 17, 19, 23, 26, 30, 32 (Colored silver)

The message on the speaker is: Is anyone listening?

pages 208–209

1. c	14. a
2. a	15. a
3. c	16. b
4. b	17. b
5. b	18. b
6. c	19. c
7. b	20. b
8. a	21. a
9. c	22. b
10. a	23. a
11. a	24. b
12. b	25. c
13. c	26. b

page 210

Seed Plants: cactus, pine, bean, daisy, orchid, wheat, oak
Nonseed Plants: fern, liverwort, moss, horsetail

page 211

Check student pictures to see that lines are drawn accurately to plant and flower parts.
Pilfered means *stolen*.

page 212

Labels for top:
1. photosynthesis
2. transpiration
3. respiration

1. Respiration

2. oxygen
3–4. water and carbon dioxide
5. Photosynthesis
6. chlorophyll
7–8. water and carbon dioxide
9. oxygen
10. water
11. roots
12. leaves
13. transpiration
Vital means necessary to the maintenance of life.

page 213

1. snail
2. flatworm
3. jellyfish
4. sea cucumber
5. frog
6. earthworm
7. roundworm
8. sponge
9. ant

page 214

1. O
2. A
3. I, K
4. F
5. M
6. L, G
7. B, C, D, E
8. H, J, N

page 215

1. fish
2. amphibians
3. birds
4. mammals
5. reptiles
See that student has drawn accurate examples of at least one animal from each class in an appropriate spot on the zoo "map."
Liverwort is a mammal.

page 216

1. consumer
2. biome
3. decomposer
4. community
5. predator
6. scavenger
7. ecology
8. habitat
9. chain
10. producer
11. prey
12. web

page 217

A. prey
B. predator
C. habitat

D. community
E. producers, consumers
F. food chain
G. food web
H. parasite
I. scavengers and decomposers
J. compete
K. adaptation
L. fly

page 218

1. Sk-M
2. R
3. C
4. D
5. N
6. C
7. Sk-M
8. R
9. Sk-M or D
10. C
11. Sk-M
12. D
13. N
14. Sk-M
15. D
16. N
17. Sk-M
18. C
19. R
20. Sk-M
21. D
22. R
23. D
24. C
25. N
26. Sk-M
27. Sk-M
28. D
29. N
30. N
31. N
32. Sk-M
33. N

page 219

Check student pages to see that lines are drawn to correct matching bones and muscles. BOTTOM:
1. voluntary
2. involuntary
3. tendons

page 220

Answers may vary some, as students may find simple machines within other items.
inclined plane—ramp
wheel & axle—wheels on cart, wheels on rat
wedge—scissors, screwdriver, cheese
screw—screws, faucet handles
levers—screwdriver, balancing scale, scissors, spray bottle handle
pulley—window shade

page 221

1. ice, water, wind, gravity (instead of arguments, cold hearts, anger, hurt feelings)
2. water (heartbreak)
3. Glaciers (Ex-girlfriends)
4. water (tears)
5. water (sadness)
6. channel (romance)
7. deposited (discouraged)
8. delta (down in the dumps)
9. winds (wishes)
10. soil (sighs)
11. ice (hope)
12. Gravity (Misery)
13. dunes (desperate)
14. ice (valentines); glacier (corsage)
15. rocks (hearts)

pages 222–223

1. igneous, metamorphic, sedimentary
2. igneous
3. pumice
4. geodes
5. nonfoliated
6. pressure
7. igneous
8. fossils
9. ripple marks
10. metamorphic
11. sandstone, limestone, shale, siltstone
12. foliated
13. sedimentary
14. dark
15. metamorphic, sedimentary
16. clastic
17. intrusive
18. slate, marble, quartzite, anthracite
19. sedimentary
20. granite, pumice, feldspar, basalt, felsite
21. nonclastic
22. anthracite
23. extrusive
24. compaction
25. cementation
26. conglomerate
27. breccia
28. shale
29. caves
30. corals

page 224

1. tornado warning
2. windy
3. dew
4. ice storm
5. drought
6. front
7. rain
8. fog
9. sunshine

page 225

1. atmosphere
2. weather
3. 300 miles
4. atmosphere to Earth
5. Earth's surface
6. direction from which they come
7. water vapor
8. lower
9. front
10. drops
11. far above
12. cold air
13. anemometer
14. north
15. weather
16. high

page 226

Information students gather will vary according to reference materials used.

page 227

Magnets 2, 3, 5, 6, 11, 12 have false statements. See that these are colored and that student has drawn a path for the mouse that touches these and no others.

page 232

1. Missing numbers for countries from top to bottom:
101; 27; 26; 50; 9; 15; 35; 5; 8; 9; 11; 7; 7; 10; 17; 17; 15; 3; 15; 8
2. Bulgaria, Brazil, Great Britain, Belarus
3. Poland & Spain
4. China, Italy, Ukraine
5. France
6. Belarus
7. China
8. Germany
9. 17
10. Canada

page 233

1. Missing numbers for countries from top to bottom: 26; 8; 8; 20;
5; 3; 3; 9; 4; 1; 2;
1; 4; 2; 3; 1; 3;
1; 2; 0; 0; 0
2. 183
3. 119
4. 64
5. Russia
6. Canada
7. Germany
8. Canada
9. Italy
10. Netherlands

page 234

Down		Across	
1.	40,973	4.	300,050,008
2.	151,600	5.	2,600,900
3.	900,901	6.	207
7.	71,800,003	10.	12,008,035
8.	610,390	11.	8,351
9.	450,009	12.	909
		13.	300,300

page 235

1. Order of numbers in front of names:
   11; 7; 8; 2; 6; 4; 9; 5; 3; 10; 1; 12
2. Order of numbers in list: 5; 4;
   6; 2; 1; 9; 7; 3; 8

page 236

1.	11,000
2.	270
3.	2,000
4.	360
5.	900
6.	7,490
7.	15,000
8.	5,000
9.	800,400
10.	750,000
11.	1,000,000
12.	101,330
13.	61,000
14.	775,000
15.	10,990
16.	770
17.	98,900
18.	610
19.	600
20.	56,000
21.	900
22.	20,000
23.	600,000
24.	1,510

page 237

1. 7 tens
2. 8 hundreds
3. 8 tens
4. 5 thousands
5. 3 thousands
6. 0 hundreds
7. 5 ten thousands
8. 9 thousands
9. 1 ten
10. 9 ten thousands
11. 6 tens
12. 8 hundreds
13. 8 hundreds
14. 0 tens
15. 5 hundreds

page 238

1. 11,345		4. 11,111	
2. 9,974		5. 1,816	
3. 1,023		6. 10,970	

page 239

1. 271
2. 217
3. 14
4. 42
5. 274
6. 35
7. 407
8. 5,297
9. 3,702
10. 581
11. 5,654
12. 7,275
13. 721,320
14. 12,138

page 240

1.	230 m
2.	2,300 m
3.	930 m
4.	111,000 m
5.	5,050 m
6.	888,800 m
7.	7,170,000 m
8.	80,480 m
9.	2,800 m
10.	250,000 m
11.	440 m
12.	44 m
13.	22 m
14.	100 m
15.	10 m
16.	33 m
17.	880 m
18.	10 m
19.	70 m
20.	6,107 m

page 241

1. Different answer is 201;
   all other answers are 200.
2. Different answer is 795;
   all other answers are 792.
3. Different answer is 96;
   all other answers are 144.
4. Different answer is 588;
   all other answers are 506.
5. Different answer is 630;
   all other answers are 670.

page 242

Across		Down	
1.	293	2.	350
4.	371	3.	419
5.	34	4.	354
7.	93	5.	301
9.	404	6.	369
10.	4,554	8.	369
12.	239	11.	486
15.	926	13.	306
		14.	447

page 243

1. 500
2. 400
3. 855
4. 5
5. 77
6. 22
7. 275
8. 200
9. 13
10. 18
11. 50
12. 25
13. Loretta

page 244

1. K	1. N
2. AT	2. L
3. SPE	3. OW
4. G	4. L
5. DS	5. D
6. I	6. HI
7. E	
8. N	
Speed skating	Downhill

page 245

Correct fractions to color:
3, 4, 5, 6, 10, 11, 13, 16, 19, 20

1. $\frac{3}{4}$
2. $\frac{1}{2}$
7. $\frac{4}{5}$
8. $\frac{1}{2}$
9. $\frac{1}{4}$
12. $\frac{3}{4}$
14. $\frac{1}{2}$
15. $\frac{6}{11}$
17. $\frac{4}{5}$
18. $\frac{2}{5}$

page 246

1. $\frac{19}{10}$ or $1\frac{9}{10}$
2. $\frac{6}{9}$ or $\frac{2}{3}$
3. $\frac{7}{13}$
4. $\frac{4}{6}$ or $\frac{2}{3}$
5. $\frac{15}{20}$ or $\frac{3}{4}$
6. $\frac{6}{11}$
7. $\frac{5}{5}$ or 1
8. $\frac{15}{16}$
9. $\frac{10}{25}$ or $\frac{2}{5}$
10. $\frac{2}{12}$ or $\frac{1}{6}$
11. $\frac{29}{6}$ or $4\frac{5}{6}$
12. $\frac{71}{100}$
13. $\frac{16}{30}$ or $\frac{8}{15}$
14. $\frac{25}{10}$ or $2\frac{5}{10}$ or $2\frac{1}{2}$

page 247

1. $11\frac{6}{8}$ or $11\frac{3}{4}$
2. $26\frac{5}{8}$
3. $17\frac{2}{5}$
4. $10\frac{1}{4}$
5. $11\frac{4}{4}$ or 12
6. $2\frac{4}{5}$
7. $10\frac{7}{6}$ or $11\frac{1}{6}$
8. $10\frac{3}{6}$ or $10\frac{1}{2}$
9. $\frac{4}{5}$
10. $10\frac{1}{11}$
11. $6\frac{4}{9}$
12. $19\frac{4}{5}$
13. $24\frac{4}{5}$
14. $14\frac{2}{3}$ or $14\frac{1}{3}$
15. $5\frac{10}{10}$ or 6

page 248

1. .0183
2. 1.083
3. .115
4. .55
5. 99.7
6. 13.4
7. 500.005
8. 9.78
9. .97
10. 10.83
11. 108.3
12. .234
13. 5.555
14. .978
15. 978.3
16. 11.501

page 249

Trick 1
   7; 8; 4; 2; 5; 3; 1; 6
Trick 2
   3; 6; 8; 7; 2; 5; 1; 4
Trick 3
   3; 5; 6; 8; 2; 1; 4; 7
Trick 4
   4; 1; 6; 5; 3; 8; 2; 7
Trick 5
   7; 6; 8; 1; 3; 5; 2; 4
Trick 6
   4; 5; 6; 2; 3; 1; 7; 8
Trick 7
   7; 5; 1; 3; 8; 4; 2; 6

page 250-251

1. a, c, 50 cups
2. c, d, 64.4 meters
3. a, c, 13°F
4. a, c, 294 spectators
5. b, d, 7 seconds
6. a, b, 22 snowballs
7. a, d, $\frac{25}{30}$ or $\frac{5}{6}$
8. b, c, 38
9. b, c, d, Barry—63 seconds
10. b, c, 112

page 252

1. 225
2. 44
3. 1891
4. 10
5. 15
6. 382
7. 3
8. 3,000

page 253

Blue:
1. 183
2. 74
3. 8
4. 100
5. $\frac{1}{4}$
6. 480
7. 80
8. 144

Red:
9. 12,000
10. 10.08

White:
11. $\frac{7}{20}$
12. 20,000
13. 14
14. 0.1
15. $\frac{3}{5}$

Yellow:
16. 6,000
17. 249

Purple:
18. 120
19. 0.8
20. 6
21. 12
22. 20
23. 11.2

Orange:
24. 1,200
25. 4,800

Green—all others

Colored picture shows parachutes.

page 254

1. 1 team member gets muscles.
2. 1 girl's hair is orange.
3. 1 flower is yellow.
4. 3 hats are green.
5. 7 of the 20 shoes are red.
6. 2 shoes are blue.
7. 4 shirts are blue.
8. Half of the rope is red.
9. 1 shirt has stars.
10. 12 of the 20 socks are purple.
11. 3 shorts are orange.
12. 1 shirt has stripes.
13. 1 pair of long pants is brown.
14. 1 elbow has a bruise.
15. 3 of the 20 knees have bandages.
16. 1 team member gets a new hat.
17. There is mud under 8 of the team members.
18. Bees are stinging 2 team members.
19. Untied shoelaces are on 3 shoes.
20. A dog is pulling on the shirt of 1 team member.

page 255

Answers may vary on 4 and 5.

1. $133.00
2. 630 feet
3. $21.00
4. 11 (plus herself)
5. 4 (plus 1 for Sadie)
6. 80

page 256

Missing numbers in chart: Biff 4; Bob 18; Ben 5; Bud 3; Barb 18; Bonnie 0
Totals read: 29, 31, 17, 32, 109

1. 29
2. Ben
3. Biff, Bob, Barb
4. Bonnie
5. Bonnie
6. Bud
7. Ben
8. Biff and Bonnie
9. Twist
10. Straddle
11. Back
12. Straddle
13. Ben
14. Twist
15. Bonnie
16. 109

page 257

1. pizza
2. coffee
3. ice cream
4. hot pretzels
5. nachos
6. pizzas
7. pennant
8. popcorn
9. hot pretzels
10. drink
11. drinks
12. hot dogs

page 258

1. yes
2. $49.90
3. bridle, blanket, breeches
4. $170.80
5. $23.25
6. 2

7. $255.35
8. curry brush
9. bridle and helmet
10. Answers will vary.

page 259

1. 17 − 4 + 10 = 23
2. 4 x 2 x 2 = 16
3. 56 − 6 ÷ 2 = 25
4. $\frac{1}{2}$ + 1 x 2 = 3
5. 5 − 2 + 3 = 6
6. 1 + 2 x 3 = 9
7. 8 x 3 − 4 = 20 (or 8 − 3 x 4 = 20)
8. 10 ÷ 2 x 3 = 15
9. 20 x 4 − 80 = 0
10. 29 + 10 − 13 = 26
11. 100 x 100 + 1 = 10,001
12. 55 − 50 x 5 = 25
13. 13 + 13 − 13 = 13 (or 13 − 13 + 13 = 13)
14. 81 ÷ 9 x 6 = 54

page 260

1. D
2. C
3. A
4. F
5. B
6. E
7. G

8–10. Check to see that students have accurately drawn the three kinds of line pairs.

page 261

There are several possible answers for this page, particularly for line segments, points, and angles. Check to see that the student has traced or colored at least three of each in the correct color.

page 262

1. F, K, Q
2. B, H, J, L
3. A, G, O, P, E, C

page 263

Answers will vary because different groupings of shapes may create different kinds of triangles. Check student designs to see that triangles are colored correctly.

page 264

Check to see that student has colored design accurately.

1. arrow
2. archery

page 265

Note: In labels for line segments and arcs, the letters may be written as shown below or they may be reversed in each case

(for example, a line segment may be labeled TQ or QT).
1. N
2. TQ, MK
3. NH, NT, NQ, NK, NM
4. Any two of these: RS, MK, TQ, JQ
5. Any four of these:
    HT, HJ, HK, HQ,
    HS, HR, HM
    TJ, TK, TQ, TS,
    TR, TM, TH
    JK, JQ, JS, JR,
    JM, JH, JT
    KQ, KS, KR, KM,
    KH, KT, KJ
    QS, QR, QM, QH,
    QT, QJ, QK
    SR, SM, SH, ST,
    SJ, SK, SQ
    RM, RH, RT, RJ,
    RK, RQ, RS
    MH, MT, MJ, MK,
    MQ, MS, MR

Bottom: Check student circle to see that all 9 elements have been included and properly labeled.

page 266

Spheres (blue):
    baseball, golf ball, ping pong ball, bowling ball, balls at ends of barbell
Cubes (red):
    Step-Up box, energy bar box
Rectangular Prisms (yellow):
    shoe box, stop sign, balance beam
Cylinders (purple):
    chalk, tennis ball can, bar on barbells
Cones (green):
    liniment container, Grizzlies megaphone
Pyramid (orange):
    2000# weight
Triangular Prism (brown):
    tent
See diagram below for correct red path:

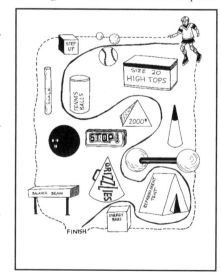

page 267

Top question: neither
1. C
2. C
3. S
4. S
5. C
6. C
7. S
8. S
9. C

page 268

1. E
2. J
3. D
4. B
5. 12
6. A, E, F, G, I, J
7. B, C, D, H, K
8. yes
9. yes
10. C
11. 1
12. G and I

page 269

Students should have the following words circled in the puzzle.

1. years
2. miles
3. minutes
4. ounces
5. feet
6. quart
7. pounds
8. hours
9. tablespoons
10. yards
11. degrees
12. seconds
13. pints
14. cups
15. inches
16. ton
17. teaspoons
18. gallons

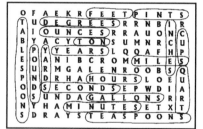

page 270

Circle these item numbers as correct: 2, 3, 4, 6, 7, 10, 12, 13, 16
Corrected answers are:
1. liters (or liters, milliliters, deciliters, and kiloliters)